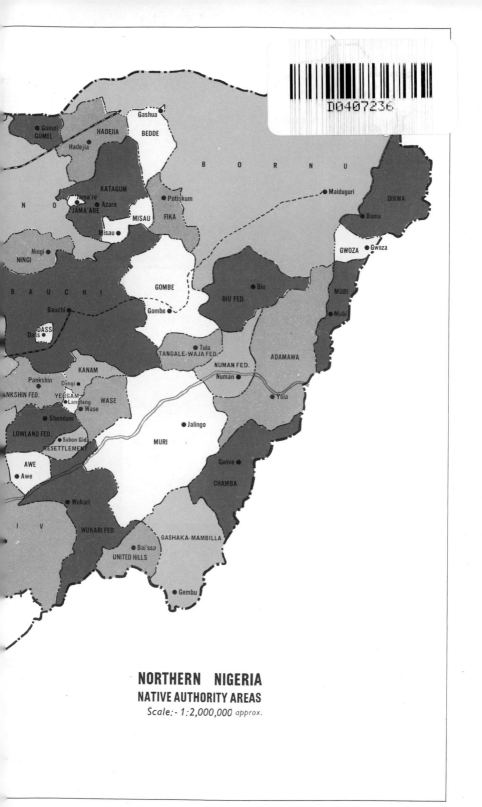

NORTHERN NIGERIA
NATIVE AUTHORITY AREAS
Scale:- 1:2,000,000 approx.

LAW IN AFRICA

Number 5

LAW AND PRACTICE OF LOCAL GOVERNMENT
IN NORTHERN NIGERIA

AUSTRALIA
The Law Book Co. of Australasia Pty. Ltd.
Sydney : Melbourne : Brisbane

CANADA AND U.S.A.
The Carswell Company Ltd.
Toronto

INDIA
N. M. Tripathi Private Ltd.
Bombay

ISRAEL
Steimatzky's Agency Ltd.
Tel Aviv

NEW ZEALAND
Sweet & Maxwell (N.Z.) Ltd.
Wellington

PAKISTAN
Pakistan Law House
Karachi

Law and Practice of
Local Government in Northern Nigeria

by
M. J. CAMPBELL

*Head of the Department of Local Government,
Institute of Administration, Ahmadu Bello University,
Northern Nigeria*

LAGOS: AFRICAN UNIVERSITIES PRESS
LONDON: SWEET & MAXWELL
1963

Published in 1963 by
African Universities Press Limited, Lagos
and
Sweet & Maxwell Limited of
11 New Fetter Lane, London

Printed in Great Britain
by Staples Printers Limited
of London and Rochester

PREFACE

I AM deeply conscious of the honour that the Government of Northern Nigeria has paid to me in asking me to write a book on the present law and the practice of Local Government in the Region. This work would not have been possible but for the experience and guidance of past officers and instructors of the Department of Local Government at the Institute of Administration and of that of officials of the Ministry for Local Government in Kaduna.

This is the first work of its kind dealing solely with local government in Northern Nigeria. Its main purpose is to serve as a textbook for the present law and to form a foundation on which other works and revisions can be built. In a country such as Nigeria, which is developing in all fields so rapidly, it is not possible to produce any work on an aspect of Government activities which will be completely up to date at the time of publication. It is important, however, that such a work is completely up to date and accurate up to a specified date. I have taken as my deadline July 1, 1962, and all statistics and examples have been taken as accurate for that date.

I wish to acknowledge, in particular, the valuable assistance given to me by Mr. D. A. Pott, o.b.e., former Permanent Secretary of the Ministry for Local Government, in reading and criticising my manuscript, and by Mr. H. H. Marshall, c.b.e., former Attorney-General of Northern Nigeria, who spent many hours in painstaking examination of the manuscript to ensure that it was correct in the interpretation of the law. Also the encouragement and guidance accorded to me by my Principal, Mr. S. S. Richardson, o.b.e., who has always found time to give me the benefit of his experience and knowledge. To all these I offer my grateful thanks.

Finally, I wish to acknowledge the help and, most of all, the patience of my own instructional and clerical staff at the Institute of Administration.

MICHAEL CAMPBELL

Institute of Administration, Zaria

NOTE

On July 1, 1962, Residents were still the officers in charge of
the Provinces of Northern Nigeria. The Provincial Administration Law, 1962, however, came into force on September
15, 1962, and Residents were replaced by Provincial Commissioners, assisted by Provincial Secretaries in all thirteen
Provinces. I have therefore changed the title of Resident to
Provincial Commissioner in all except historical contexts in
the main text of this work.

CONTENTS

TABLE OF ENACTMENTS

THE STRUCTURE OF LOCAL GOVERNMENT IN NORTHERN NIGERIA

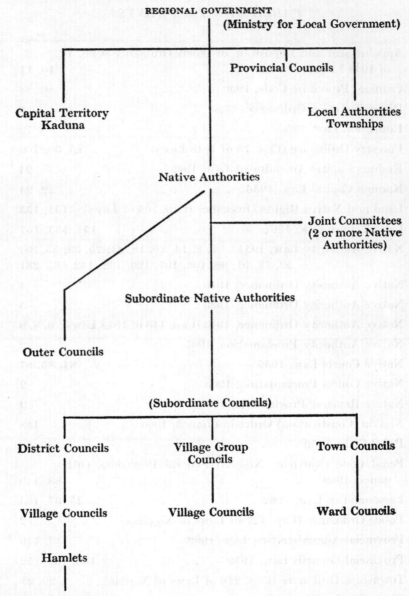

CHAPTER 1

INTRODUCTION

NORTHERN Nigeria has often been cited as the classic example of indirect rule through local authorities. It cannot be denied that it presented the British administrators with a workable system of local government with very few changes to the Emirate system that they found in force at the time of the occupation. Neither can it be denied that there were many areas in which the system of indirect rule was difficult to develop because of ethnic and anthropological differences, for example in the hill districts of the Bauchi Plateau and in the Tiv country; but in the main kingdoms of Northern Nigeria an established and successful form of government was in force which had only to be guided into becoming a highly efficient local government machine. The Muslim kingdoms of Northern Nigeria possessed three great advantages over the indigenous tribal authorities of other parts of Nigeria. They possessed a recognised and accepted taxation system; a judiciary that was separate from the executive, using professional judges who administered an impartial justice; and experienced rulers who were adept at ruling and administering to a large population. The early administrators of Northern Nigeria were impressed with the ability with which the Emirs ruled their peoples and under the able and experienced hands of Lugard they were able to build up a system of local government on the existing foundations in less than a decade that was a model for the whole of Africa.

The occupation of Northern Nigeria was swift and efficient. The normal tenure of life of its peoples was hardly disturbed and the common people accepted the change without rancour because tradition and custom were preserved wherever possible. In setting up the Emirs in the North under the new government, Lugard insisted that certain aspects of rule were to be the prerogative of the central government but that in all else the tradition and control of the natural ruler was to be preserved and supported. The government of the Protectorate reserved the right to control land, to regulate taxation and legislation and to be the sole authority to establish armed forces, and these reservations were included in the letters of appointment given to each Chief. At the time of the

1

installations, however, all sub-chiefs and district and village head-men paid public allegiance to the traditional ruler and he thus ensured their loyalty to his title.

The first years of British occupation were taken up with pacification of the less civilised areas and with the major problems of administering a huge territory with a minimum of staff. Native Courts had been legalised as early as 1900.[1] In 1906 a further Native Courts Proclamation authorised Residents in charge of Provinces to set up courts by warrant either as *Alkali's* courts or as Judicial Councils and these courts were empowered to impose any punishments accepted under native law or custom provided that they did not involve mutilation or cruelty. Capital powers were granted to nine such courts set up in that year.

The first step towards taxation was the Land Revenue Proclama-tion of 1904 which laid down that the Chiefs were to pay one-fourth of their revenue as collected by traditional methods to the Government. At the same time, Residents of Provinces were requested to inquire into the methods used in this traditional collection of tribute and assess the taxability of each area. The traditional methods of taxation in the Muslim emirates were based on the following forms:

(1) *"Zakat"* or alms paid by the Faithful and fixed in relation to the property owned by the payer;

(2) *"Jangali"* or tax paid on livestock;

(3) *"Kharaj"* or tax paid on land; and

(4) *"Jizyah"* (Hausa *"gandu"*), a capitation tax paid to the Chief by conquered tribes.

Of these traditional forms the Government decided to retain two:

(1) *"Jangali"* or cattle tax, and

(2) *"Kharaj"* which was to become a single all-embracing direct tax. This is still known in Hausa as *"Haraji"*.

Both *jangali* and *haraji* might be paid by one person but *jangali* as a general rule was levied only on the pastoral tribes who possessed no property or wealth other than their livestock. The Native Revenue Proclamation of 1906 empowered Residents of Provinces and their staff to assess each area for its taxable wealth and to appoint district and village headmen as tax collectors.

[1] Native Courts Proclamation, 1900.

2

These assessments were based on the wealth of a community. The taxation therefore was based on a percentage of this wealth, not exceeding 10 per cent as a lump sum assessment for the community and not broken down to a flat rate payable by each taxpayer. It was the duty of the district or village headman to break up the community assessment according to individual wealth. As each community, generally a village area, knew the individual wealth of each and all of its members, there was an effective control against oppressive demands by the headman. This community tax was more equitable than a poll or hut tax used in most parts of Africa and was, in effect, a rough and ready form of income tax.

Control of the Chiefs by the central government was at first very slight. The Resident in charge of the Province was a political officer rather than a direct administrator and the Native Authorities were guided by advice rather than by directives. In the non-Muslim areas administration was more direct and, in some of these places, effective control was not obtained until the 1920s. The Native Authority Proclamation of 1907 empowered "recognised" Chiefs to issue legal orders to preserve public order and good government in their areas of jurisdiction. At the end of the first decade of the new century, the Emirs had been pursuaded to become salaried officials and to set up treasuries for the administration of their funds. All traditional tax in the past had been the personal perquisite of the Chief (it was known in Hausa as "*Kurdin Sarki*" or "money of the chief") and it speaks highly of the confidence felt in the Administration that the Emirs allowed the tax and other revenue to be dealt with in a separate treasury subject to modern accounting procedure. The first Native Treasuries were set up in 1911 and in that year it was estimated that the wealth of the Native Administrations in the North was £197,296. A second innovation, accepted by the Chiefs at an early stage, was the policy that the District Heads should live full time in their Districts and work actively for the welfare of the local peoples. Under the Fulani empire District Heads had spent most of their time at the court of the Emir and had left the administration of their lands to slaves or messengers. In Muslim emirates, the chain of command through the District Head to the Village Head and thence to the peasant worked efficiently and well for it was known and recognised. Because it worked so well, however, the administration attempted to impose the same system on non-Muslim areas, in

3

some cases with disastrous results. The important and prosperous Tiv nation in Benue Province, for example, had their own tribal and clan structures which demanded special consideration and it was not until the late 'twenties that the government realised that investigation was needed into the recognised form of local administration. The size and diversity of Northern Nigeria, its many races and cultures, formed a problem in administration and local government that was unique in Africa. Only by trial and error could the smaller units be set up as effective administrations within the broad framework of the law.

The loyalty of the Native Authorities to the new government was put to the test shortly after they were formed. A small and luckily isolated outbreak of Mahdism occurred at Satiru in Sokoto Emirate in 1905. Unfortunately the small British force sent to deal with the insurgents was destroyed and it seemed that the stage was set for widespread revolt against the new rule. The Emirs of Northern Nigeria, however, responded magnificently to the occasion and declarations of loyalty and offers of active support were offered to the Government from all sides. The revolt was put down with ease and a lasting bond of friendship was forged between the British administrators and the Chiefs; one that has always remained. In 1914, the Native Administrations once again showed their loyalty and unity in active assistance in the war against Germany and men from the Native Authorities fought for the British cause in both the Cameroons and in East Africa.

The period between the two World Wars was one of steady if unspectacular development of the Native Authority system and in building up of local government services. The administrators of Northern Nigeria were able to give their full attention to such problems as communications, trade, medical and educational services, knowing full well that the matters of taxation, law and order and the administration of justice could be left safely in the experienced hands of the Native Administrations. The majority of the Native Authorities in the North were still "sole authorities". That is to say, the decision of the Chief was supreme although in most cases he sought the advice of a traditional council. A Native Authority Ordinance was set up in 1916 which has formed the basis on which all subsequent legislation for local government in the North has been built. Its object at the time was to apply to the whole of Nigeria (the Protectorate of Northern Nigeria was amalgamated with the Colony and Protectorate of Southern Nigeria in 1914) the legislation already in operation in the North. No major change in legislation took place until 1933 when a new Ordinance was introduced as a result of the investigations into Native Administration carried out by the then Governor, Sir Donald Cameron. Under this Ordinance, the Native Authorities could be constituted as

(1) Sole Chiefs;
(2) Chiefs associated with Councils;
(3) Councils; and
(4) Groups of persons.

Native Authorities were set up or revoked by the Governor, who could also restrict their powers under the law if he saw fit to do so. The law defined the class of persons who were subject to the rule and authority of the Native Administration as all natives in the area who are ordinarily subject to the jurisdiction of a native court. This, however, could be extended to other classes of persons, *e.g.*, native strangers, if so approved by the Governor. It was the duty of Native Authorities to prevent crime. They were also empowered to make Orders and Rules for the regulation and control of their services and were the regulators of native law or custom. No mention, however, was made of the powers or functions of Native Treasuries in the Ordinance and legislation on taxation was kept as a separate Ordinance.

Sir Donald Cameron was anxious that the Native Authorities should face up to changing conditions in Africa and the world. It was a fault of the Residents of Provinces of the time that they tended to insulate the Chiefs from the outside world and preserve at all costs the status quo of the traditional emirate. Western education did not meet with the whole-hearted approval of most of the Chiefs and the Muslim Emirs preferred encouragement of Islamic education and literacy in Arabic. It is unfortunate in the light of subsequent events that Western education and a great many more schools were not encouraged and established in the Northern emirates during this period. To bring the Chiefs into closer contact with their peoples it was suggested that advisory councils should be encouraged wherever possible at village level. The Chiefs were also urged to travel both in other parts of Nigeria and overseas in order to broaden their outlook and to bring them in contact with other cultures and administrations. The insulation of the North from the outside world and its influence of change came to an end with the Second World War. Shortages of staff and money during the period of conflict prevented any major change in the system of administration, but undoubtedly the Northern emirates found themselves rudely awakened by the influx of stranger elements brought by the war and by the awakening of national politics. A new Ordinance was passed in 1943 which augmented and amended the law of ten years earlier but there were no major changes in policy. In 1940 also, the Direct Taxation Ordinance replaced legislation passed in the 'twenties. The basic rate of taxation in each Native Authority was fixed by the Provinces Resident, who could also impose taxation for higher income groups and for special trades. The lump sum assessment had given way in most areas to a basic rate per adult male worked out on the general wealth of the Native Authority area.

An attempt to keep the traditional councils of the emirates in touch with the needs and wishes of the taxpayer was the establishment of Outer Councils. These were advisory bodies containing a cross section of the population taken from all walks of life which brought suggestions for the consideration of the Native Authority. Having no powers of its own, the Outer Council was only a limited success and did not enjoy the popularity originally hoped for. It did assist the Native Authority, however, by bringing suggestions for future development and by drawing attention to real or imagined grievances.

In 1945, the annual conference of the Residents of Provinces recommended a vigorous growth of District and Village Councils within the Native Authorities. In order to give these Councils, especially those of the District, some interest and encouragement, funds were to be put at their disposal based on a per capita rate per taxpayer in the area. As this rate varied from 9d. to 1s. 6d. only, it meant that the average District Council Funds did not amount to a great deal of money but it was sufficient to permit districts to carry out small development projects and the funds were permitted to be kept on deposit and so could be left to grow if they were not totally expended during any financial year.

M. Abubakar Tafawa Balewa, speaking to the Regional Assembly in 1950, brought a successful motion requesting that an investigation should be made into the existing forms of local government in

Northern Nigeria with a view to improving on the present pattern and developing it to cope with modern conditions. At this time, radical changes in the pattern of local government were taking place in both the Eastern and the Western Regions and it was natural that the North should wish to ensure that its own system would develop and keep abreast with national and regional changes. A thorough investigation of existing conditions was carried out by two experienced administrative officers, K. P. Maddocks and D. A. Pott, and their report was published in 1952. This was considered by a joint committee made up of members of the House of Assembly and the House of Chiefs and as a result of their recommendations, a new law was drafted for local government in Northern Nigeria. This became the Native Authority Law, 1954, which, apart from minor amendments, is the law which is operative today.

Northern Nigeria, unlike the East and West of Nigeria which have built up new systems of local government based on the English model, has retained the Native Authority as its main unit of local authority. It has been said that if the wheels of the Native Authorities of the North ceased to turn, the Regional Government would find itself in a very difficult position. This may or may not be true, but certainly the tradition and authority of the Native Authorities form an integral part in the government of the North and one which the common people would not be willing to change.

A Native Authority, in addition to preserving law and order and regulating native law and custom, undertakes a very wide range of services. In addition to these services of its own, it undertakes a further variety of services on behalf of the Regional Government as the latter's agent, even though, until recently, these agency services were a crippling drain on its working capital through the operation of advance accounts. It is the government's tax collector and it is the government's odd job man. There is no standard Native Authority which one can point out as a model. Each one is different. Each one has its own special problems and conditions; many by international standards are not economically viable units. Northern Nigeria in 1962, however, can still be proud of its system of local government whose traditional roots, though criticised as reactionary, have given it stability and popular confidence and one which has managed to keep abreast of modern conditions and to adjust itself, with surprising ease, to new ideas and techniques.

7

Chapter 2

THE CONSTITUTION AND POWERS OF NATIVE AND LOCAL AUTHORITIES

1. Native Authorities

The local government authority of Northern Nigeria is the Native Authority. Its constitution, powers and duties are laid down in the Native Authority Law of 1954. Since this Law was passed it has remained largely in its original form, although amendment laws were passed in 1955, 1957, 1958, 1960 and 1961,[1] conferring relatively minor changes. The Law incorporates much of the former Native Authority Ordinance[2] although this has been modified and adapted to bring it in line with present government policy. This Law is far less concise than the local government Laws of Eastern and Western Nigeria. To some extent this has been deliberate to allow for a degree of flexibility. The Native Authorities of the North vary tremendously in size, population and wealth and the Law has to retain a measure of flexibility to allow for this diversity. At the extremes are:

	Taxpayers	Annual Revenue	Size (sq. miles)
1. Kano Native Authority	757,000	£2 million (plus)	12,933
2. Jama'are Native Authority	5,000	£16,000	149

Both of these are Native Authorities with the same powers and duties under the Law. The Office of Native Authority for any specified area is set up by the Governor of Northern Nigeria.[3] It should be mentioned at this stage that the Governor in exercising his powers under the Native Authority Law does so only on the advice of the Executive Council; this is composed of the Ministers of the Government of Northern Nigeria presided over by the Premier.

The Law provides for the recognition of Native Authorities

[1] No. 3 of 1955; No. 4 of 1957; No. 5 of 1958; No. 37 of 1960; No. 23 of 1961.
[2] Cap. 140 of the Laws of Nigeria, 1948.
[3] S. 3 of the Native Authority Law, 1954.

already in existence at the time of its commencement and deems them to have been constituted under it.[4]

Native Authorities are bodies corporate (section 5 of the Law), that is to say, each is a legal entity separate and apart from its members and may acquire, own or dispose of both movable and immovable property. It has perpetual succession, which means that it exists as a person in law as long as it remains constituted, although individual members of the Native Authority change. As an artificial person also it may sue persons or corporations and it may also be sued in a court of law.

The symbol of the act of a Native Authority is its Common Seal. It is the equivalent of a private person's signature or approval on any written document and expresses the wishes of the Native Authority as a corporate body. As almost all the Native Authorities operate and exercise their powers and functions through the medium of some form of Council it is important to define carefully the use and custody of the Common Seal. The Native Authority Law states that the Common Seal of the Native Authority need not be used on contracts or instruments which have no legislative effect, if these documents would not require to be under seal when entered into or executed by a private person. In this case such documents can be executed or entered into by any person that the Native Authority cares to delegate for this purpose.

On the subject of what documents do in fact require the impression of the Common Seal the Law remains silent. The following documents, however, it is suggested, should receive the Common Seal of a Native Authority to attest to their validity:

(1) Legislative Instruments;
(2) Any Instrument or document which is to be approved by the Governor or a Minister;
(3) Contracts exceeding a value specified by the Native Authority Council's Standing Orders;
(4) Any Instrument vesting or delegating a power to a Subordinate Native Authority or a Council;
(5) Application for loans;
(6) Any form of taxation;
(7) Rights of occupancy;
(8) Petitions to Ministers;

[4] S. 26 of the Law.

9

(9) Delegation of powers to sign documents on behalf of the Native Authority Council;
(10) Deeds;
(11) Licences for which no other method of issue is provided;
(12) All Instruments or other documents that require the approval of the Governor or a Minister of State should bear the Common Seal of the Native Authority whether the particular instrument or document is of legislative effect or not.

The Common Seal should be affixed to documents in the presence of the Council (in accordance with its standing orders) and a record should be kept of the occasions on which it is used.

The Law provides further that the Governor may grant to any Native Authority, either at the time that it is constituted under section 3 (1) of the Law or at any subsequent time, a suitable symbol of office. This we may take to mean as being a mace or similar ornament. It does not mean the staff of office of a Chief presented to him on the occasion of his installation even although the Chief may be the head of the Native Authority. The staff of office is a personal symbol of the Chief's authority as the traditional ruler of his people, it should not be connected with the authority of a constituted Native Authority administering a specified area.

1. *The Constitution of Native Authorities.* Almost all the Native Authorities of Northern Nigeria, of which there are seventy, have Chiefs as their heads. In most cases they are the holders of those traditional posts recognised by the British Government when indirect rule was first established through the traditional rulers sixty years ago.

The Chiefs themselves are appointed in accordance with custom and approved, graded[5] or deposed by the Governor under the Appointment and Deposition of Chiefs Ordinance and, in accordance with the Constitution of Northern Nigeria, on the advice of a Council of Chiefs composed of:

(1) The Premier as Chairman;
(2) Those Ministers of the Government appointed as such from among the Members of the House of Chiefs;

[5] Chiefs are graded as First Class (silver-headed staff of office), Second Class (large brass staff of office), Third Class (small brass staff of office), and unclassified (small brass staves of various designs).

(3) Up to four members co-opted by the Premier from among the Members of the House of Chiefs to discuss the particular matter in hand.

This Council supersedes the former procedure laid down under the Appointment and Deposition of Chiefs Ordinance,[6] whereby the appointment of the Chief was approved and he was graded or deposed by the Governor himself without advice. The recognition of a Chief, however, is still subject to the Governor's formal approval.

2. *Types of Native Authorities.* The Native Authority Law[7] provides for five different types of Native Authorities. They are:

(1) A Chief or other person in Council;

(2) A Chief or other person and Council;

(3) A Council;

(4) A Group of Persons;

(5) A sole Chief or other person.

The appointment of types (1), (2) and (5) is vested in the Premier. The appointment of types (3) and (4) is vested in the Minister for Local Government. In practice the appointment of a new Native Authority is decided by the Executive Council; a memorandum setting out the facts and recommendations being submitted by the Minister for Local Government. If it is decided that the Native Authority should be constituted as types (1), or (2), or (5) then the authority to do so will be issued by the Premier. If, however, the Native Authority is to be constituted as either type (2) or type (4) then the Minister for Local Government will issue the authority.

The composition of the Council in types (1), (2) and (3) is laid down by the Minister for Local Government either:

A. Specifically—that is to say of all or any of the following classes of persons:

(a) Persons named or approved by the Minister for Local Government;[8]

---

[6] Cap. 12 of the Laws of Nigeria, 1948.
[7] S. 6 of the Law.
[8] Normally on the recommendations of the Provincial Commissioner of the Province concerned after consultation with local leaders and the Chief of the area concerned.

11

(*b*) Holders of Offices named by the Minister.

These may be holders of traditional offices in the hierarchy of the Chief concerned; they may be known as Chiefs although not approved as such under the Appointment and Deposition of Chiefs Ordinance. Such holders of traditional offices are often Administrative or Executive Councillors holding executive posts and as such are salaried staff of the Native Authority.

Examples of such posts are "*Waziri*", generally chief executive officer for the Chief; "*Wali*", the legal adviser; *Sarkin Tsabta*, the Councillor for Health; "*Ma'aji*", the Native Treasurer as Councillor for Finance. It should be noted that the appointment in this case is by office and not by name and that these Councillors are *ex officio*.

(*c*) Persons nominated in such manner and for such a term as the Minister may prescribe.

Nominated members are appointed either:

(i) Where there are no elected members and certain groups of the native community merit representation, *i.e.*, smaller ethnic groups within the main ethnic group of the area or subordinate councils; *OR*

(ii) Where there is elected representation on the Council but where it is necessary to cover those groups who have obtained no representation, or inadequate representation on the Council. An example of this is in the case of the nomadic Fulani of the area who do not exercise the right to vote, but who, by virtue of the cattle tax that they pay, contribute to the wealth of the Native Authority.

Nominated members may be appointed for a specified period of time; usually if the period of tenure is not specified it is the same period of tenure as that of an elected member.

(*d*) Persons elected in such manner and for such a term as the Minister may prescribe. These are members elected to the Council by the electorate of the area. Electoral Regulations to Native Authority Councils are made by the Governor-in-Council. The electoral areas may be laid down either by the Minister or by the

Governor-in-Council in the Regulations. Normally they are contained in the Electoral Regulations in the form of a Schedule. For detailed explanation of such Regulations please see Chapter 8.[9] Native Authority Council members are normally elected for a period of three years. They do not normally hold executive posts on the Councils.

(e) Persons selected to be members in accordance with the native law and custom of the community concerned. This provides for those leaders of the community, either religious or traditional, not covered by either (a) or (b) above, whose standing in the community warrants their presence on the Native Authority Council;

OR

B. By the general directive that the composition of the Council shall be regulated by the native law and custom of the community concerned. This form, however, is dying out and Native Authority Councils are now almost always specified as in paragraph A.

As a corollary to the above, if the Native Authority is constituted as a Group of Persons, the Minister for Local Government may specify the composition of that group either in detail as in paragraph A above, or the general directive that it should be set up in accordance with the native law and customs of the community.

THE CHIEF-IN-COUNCIL. There are thirty-nine Native Authorities constituted as Chiefs-in-Council.[10] They include:

The Sultan of Sokoto-in-Council,
The Shehu of Bornu-in-Council,
The Emir of Kano-in-Council,

three of the largest Native Authorities of the North. The Law sets out in some detail the relations of the Chief with his Council. The Chief normally presides at all meetings of the Council[11] and he must normally consult with his Council in the exercise of the powers and functions of the Native Authority. There are, however, provisos to both these requirements.

If the Chief is absent from his area, temporarily incapacitated by illness or unable to attend the Council for any other reason,

[9] *Post*, p. 132.
[10] As at July 1, 1962.
[11] S. 7 of the Law.

another person, specified in the standing orders of the Council, may preside in his place.[12]

The Chief may dispense with consultation with his full Council:

(1) In matters which, in the judgment of the Chief, are too unimportant to require the advice of the Council. The assessment of the importance of business is left to the judgment of the Chief and "unimportant matters" are taken to mean minor policy decisions which occur in the day-to-day affairs of the Native Authority.

(2) In matters which again, in the judgment of the Chief, are so urgent that it would be detrimental to await the summoning of a full Council to discuss them. In these cases the Chief takes action on his own initiative to deal with the problems but he must then report his actions to the Council at the first available opportunity with the reasons for so doing.

In both exceptions, however, the Chief may not take action entirely on his own but he must consult with at least two members of his Council.[13]

The Law specifies further that the Chief shall act in accordance with the wishes of his Council and in the case of a difference of opinion the majority vote of the members present and voting must be considered to be the decision of the Council. If a motion is put to the vote the Chief does not have an original vote but in the event of the votes on both sides being equal he has a casting vote to ensure a decision. The Law, however, in stating that the Chief shall act in accordance with the wishes of his Council allows a proviso. The Chief may disregard and act in variance to the wishes of the Council on any matter of policy if he considers it expedient to do so in the interest of order and good government of the area.[14] If, however, the Chief decides to disregard the wishes of his Council he must inform the Governor immediately of his decision together with his reasons. He may do so through the Divisional Officer and the Provincial Commissioner of the Province. At the same time, any member of the Council may request that his own

---

[12] It should be noted that if a Chief dies or is deposed, provision is made under s. 11 (3) of the Native Authority Law for the Council to act as the Native Authority until such time as the successor is appointed.

[13] S. 7 (3) of the Law.

[14] S. 7 (5) (b) and (7) of the Law.

opinions are included in the minutes of the Council so that his position, in any subsequent inquiry, is clear.

It is the duty of the Governor in consultation with the Executive Council to consider the decision of the Chief *vis-à-vis* the decisions of the Native Authority Council. In doing so he must assess both aspects of the case and bear in mind the results that his action may have upon the relationship of the Chief with his Councillors. The Governor may decide:

(1) Not to interfere with the decision of the Chief. In this case he supports the Chief in his decision; or

(2) To refer the matter back to the Chief for a further discussion with his Council in the hopes of a compromise being reached acceptable both to the Chief and to the Council.

Should the question be re-discussed, but, after a second meeting remain a stalemate, the Governor must decide finally either to support the decision of the Chief by not interfering further, or he must take what other action he considers expedient in the circumstances. If he gives any such directions the Native Authority must by law comply with them.

THE CHIEF-AND-COUNCIL. The provisions of the Law affecting Native Authorities constituted as Chiefs-and-Council give less power to the Chief to act on his own initiative. He must at all times consult with his Council and he must at all times take their advice. Unlike the Chief-in-Council he cannot act contrary to their wishes for any reason whatsoever. The Law emphasises the fact that his powers in Council are no greater than any other Chairman.

It is with this object in view that the Law specifies that the Chief has an original vote, in the same way as any other Councillor, as well as a casting vote. The casting vote is to be used only in the event of an equal number of votes being cast for and against a motion. Provision is made for the Council to continue to act as the Native Authority under another Chairman during the temporary absence of the Chief on business (*e.g.*, sittings of the House of Chiefs) or due to sickness. For such an event provision is made under the Standing Orders of the Native Authority Council for a Chairman to act in the absence of the Chief.

There are eleven Native Authorities constituted as Chiefs-and-Council. They are in areas where, previous to the arrival of the

British, no single traditional Chief controlled the area and in consequence the position of the Chief *vis-à-vis* the community is less stable.

This must not be taken to infer, however, that a paramount Chief has been appointed by the Government against the wishes of the people. In all such cases, *e.g.*, Jos, and Tiv, the Chief selected has been appointed with the approval of the sub-chiefs and the people and has welded together in a single loyalty an area which in the past was split into a series of tribal or clan groups with no loyalty to any beyond the immediate confines of their own small areas.

COUNCILS. The Native Authority Law makes no particular mention of Native Authorities constituted as Councils, of which there are eighteen in the Region. It is accepted practice, however, that Native Authorities so constituted are in fact federations of small native authorities who have sought federation in order to remain economically viable units of local government. In such cases the original Native Authorities lose their status as such and become Subordinate Native Authorities[15] to the new Federated Native Authority. Thus, for example, the former Native Authorities of Biu, Shani and Askira are now Subordinate Native Authorities to the Biu Federation Council.

The Chairmanship of the Federation Council may be resolved in a variety of ways. If the original Native Authorities all had Chiefs of equal status the decision is difficult and one which must be decided amicably at the beginning of the Council's life if it is to hold the confidence of the community. The Chairman or President may be appointed:

(1) By name or title: this has been done where one Chief is senior in status or tradition or is fully acceptable to the others, *e.g.*, the Chief of Koton Karfe in Kwara Native Authority;

(2) In rotation of Chiefs, each Chief holding office in turn for a stipulated length of time, *e.g.*, Wukari Federation, term of service—one year; Gwari Native Authority term of service—six months; Tangale Waja, term of service—one month;

---

[15] For details of the constitution and powers of Subordinate Native authorities see *post*, pp. 18, 19.

(3) By election by the Council members or by elected members of the Council only, *e.g.*, Akwanga Native Authority election of one of three Chiefs for a period of three years by the elected members only; Lowland Federation, election of any person other than a Chief by the members (with at least a two-thirds majority) for a period of three years.

GROUPS OF PERSONS. There are no Native Authorities at present constituted as Groups of Persons. The Law gives us no exact definition of the meaning of the term and how it differs from a "Council". It may be assumed, however, that "Groups of Persons" will no longer play any part in the local government pattern of Northern Nigeria. The difference between a Group of Persons and a Council seems to be that of continuity; a Group of Persons elects a Chairman at every meeting from amongst its members: a Council conversely has a fixed Chairman who by law[16] is named in the Standing Orders. "Groups of Persons" Native Authorities in the past were set up in hill pagan areas where small ethnic groups wished to preserve their independence over neighbouring groups as much as possible.

SOLE NATIVE AUTHORITIES. This is a Chief or any other person acting as sole authority. Originally most of the Native Authorities now constituted as Chiefs associated with Councils were sole Chiefs. There is provision for setting up an Advisory Council[17] to assist the sole authority. The appointment of its members is in the hands of the authority himself with the approval of the Premier in the case of a Chief, and of the Minister for Local Government in the case of any other person acting as the authority. Once approved the Advisory Council may not be changed except with government permission. The Council's duties as its name suggests are mainly advisory, but the authority may require the Council to perform certain duties provided that the limits of these duties are clearly defined in the Standing Orders of the Council. In the absence or temporary incapacity of the authority the Advisory Council may act as the Native Authority[18] and must make interim Standing Orders for the conduct of its business. On the return of the Chief

[16] S. 52 of the N.A. Law.
[17] S. 63 of the Law.
[18] S. 11 of the Law.

or the person who is the statutory authority these interim standing Orders will, of course, lapse.

The Premier may by notice in the *Gazette*[19] appoint an Administrative Officer to act as a sole Native Authority, for example, when the office is vacant.[20] This occurs when a Native Authority has been dissolved and before a new authority has been appointed. It is not intended that such an appointment should be permanent. There are two such "caretaker" Native Authorities at the present; in Tiv where the new constitution of the Native Authority has been complicated by parochialism and unrest, and in Ningi where no decision has yet been reached on the appointment of a Council. Administrative Officers so appointed are not limited, as are Chiefs, to taking decisions only when within the limits of the Native Authority area. This is necessary as the headquarters of the Division may be outside the area of the Native Authority to which a Divisional Officer has been appointed.

Details of the numbers of Native Authorities and their types year by year over the past five-year period are:

COMPOSITION OF NATIVE AUTHORITIES	1958	1959	1960	1961	1962
(1) Chief-in-Council . . .	43	42	43	39	39
(2) Chief-and-Council . .	9	8	7	11	11
(3) Council	12	12	17	18	18
(4) Group of Persons .	—	—	—	—	—
(5) Sole Chief or Other Person .	—	—	—	—	—
Administrative Officers (Caretaker)	—	2	1	2	2
TOTAL NUMBER OF NATIVE AUTHORITIES . . .	64	64	68	70	70

Subordinate Native Authorities

There are forty-nine Subordinate Native Authorities in the Region. To all intents and purposes they are exactly the same in constitution and powers as Native Authorities themselves, except that they are controlled by a superior Native Authority. The definition of a Native Authority in the Law of 1954 includes a Subordinate Native Authority.

[19] Notice in the Northern Nigeria *Gazette*.
[20] S. 12 of the Law.

A Subordinate Native Authority is constituted by the Governor and notice of it published in the *Gazette*.[21] The notice will state to which Native Authority the new authority shall be subordinated. Up to 1960[22] it was possible for Native Authorities themselves to set up Subordinate Native Authorities within their areas but there are no instances of this having taken place.

The powers of a Subordinate Native Authority unless restricted specifically by a Restriction of Powers[23] Order issued by the Governor under section 4 of the Law, or by the Superior Native Authority under section 22 of the Law, may be deemed to be all those powers conferred upon Native Authorities by the Law. These Orders, which require publication in the Regional *Gazette*, may be either:

(1) A Restrictive Order stating that the Subordinate Native Authority shall not exercise the powers conferred upon Native Authorities by certain named sections of the Law, and may only exercise its powers under other named sections with the written approval of its Superior Native Authority; *OR*

(2) An Order vesting certain powers in the Subordinate Native Authority and permitting other powers with the written approval of the Superior Native Authority. Such Orders commence with the premiss: "The Subordinate Native Authority shall not exercise the powers of a native authority under the Native Authority Law except. . . ." This has the effect of limiting the Subordinate Native Authority's powers to those named only.

In both types of Order the powers enumerated may either be specified in the body of the Order or attached in the form of a Schedule.[24]

Subordinate Native Authorities are constituted in exactly the same way as Native Authorities; the following table shows details

21 S. 20 of the Law.
22 Amendment Law No. 37 of 1960.
23 Called also a Vesting of Powers Order.
24 The powers restricted by such orders are those contained in the following sections: Ss. 31, 36, 68, 78, 81, 82, 115 (1), 118 (1), 120, 126, 129 [37 (10), (12), (17), (20), (22), (49), (50), (55), (56), (57), 41 (1) (i), 45, 86, 87, 32, 41, 43, 48, 69, 70, 71, 72, 73, 74, 75, 80] of the Native Authority Law, 1954. Those sections included in square brackets are quoted in some orders. Those not included in these brackets are included in all orders issued to date.

of the numbers of Subordinate Native Authorities in existence in the past five years according to their constitutions:

	1958	1959	1960	1961	1962
Chief-in-Council . . .	19	19	19	19	20
Chief-and-Council . . .	27	27	37	23	23
Council	28	28	14	1	6
Group of Persons . .	2	2	—	—	—
Sole Chief or Other Person .	—	—	—	2	—
TOTAL	76	76	70	45	49

2. LOCAL AUTHORITIES

Local Authorities may be set up under the Townships Ordinance.[25]

Under the provisions of this Law the Governor-in-Council may by Order declare any area to be a Township and define[26] its class and limits together with or without urban Districts attached thereto.

First Class Townships are to be run by a Town Council and the Ordinance sets out in detail its powers and duties. There are, however, no First Class Townships constituted for Northern Nigeria.

Second and Third Class Townships are administered by Local Authorities (L.A.s) who are Administrative Officers appointed by the Minister for Local Government and who are assisted as sole authorities by an Advisory Board. Northern Nigeria contains three Second Class Townships—Kano, Jos and Zaria. Until 1956 Kaduna was also classified as a Second Class Township but in April of that year it was set up as a separate territory under the Kaduna Capital Law, 1956. Details of its subsequent progress are given below. Kano, Jos and Zaria remain as Second Class Townships. The Township areas of these three towns are limited to the commercial areas of foreign traders and the government reservations. The Sabon Gari[27] areas of these towns are not part of the Township but come under the control of the local Native Authority.

The Local Authority is constituted as a "Corporation sole" by

[25] Cap. 216 of the Laws of Nigeria, 1948.
[26] First, Second or Third Class Townships, s. 3 of the Townships Ordinance.
[27] The "new town" (Hausa) area for Southern (*i.e.*, East/West Nigeria) Stranger Communities.

title in order that it may have perpetual succession and the right to acquire property, execute deeds and impose rates and fees.[28]

The members of the Advisory Board are appointed by the Minister for Local Government to hold their seats at his pleasure. *Ex officio* members of the Board are:

(1) The magistrate (until recently the duties of a magistrate were carried out by the Local Authority himself);

(2) The Local Authority; and

(3) The Health Officer.

Other members may be appointed by the Minister as he thinks fit.

The Advisory Boards of the Northern Townships are as follows:

KANO Local Authority, Medical Officer of Health, as *ex officio* members, the Provincial Engineer, Provincial Surveyor, Principal Commercial Officer, Assistant Superintendent of Police, one representative from Chamber of Commerce, and seven influencial citizens (two of whom are members of the Regional Legislature, and the remainder representative of home and overseas trading interest).

JOS Local Authority, Medical Officer of Health, Provincial Engineer, Assistant Superintendent of Police, Legal Advisor to the Township, one representative of the women's community, one representative of commercial interests, five representatives of the Township Community.

ZARIA Local Authority, the Medical Officer of Health, Provincial Engineer, representative of Nigerian Railway Corporation, representative of Lebanese Community, Manager of Electricity Corporation of Nigeria, commercial representatives, Manager of Barclays Bank, Manager of Bank of West Africa.

The duties of the Advisory Board are to discuss and recommend on any matters affecting the health, order and good government of the Township. Minutes of the Board are sent to the Provincial Commissioner of the Province for information. Each year the Local Authority prepares estimates through the Board for approval by the Minister for Local Government. The Local Authority raises revenue by rates, fees and charges payable into a Township Fund and may raise loans securable on the property of the authority.

[28] S. 35 (2) of the Townships Ordinance.

21

He is responsible for conservancy, lighting, public health and the provision of public amenities. Rules affecting these services may be made by the Ministry for Local Government. By-Laws may also be made by the Local Authority himself and approved by the Governor-in-Council.[29]

The Kaduna Capital Territory

Kaduna until 1956 was a Second Class Township. Outside the small area of the Township the remainder of the town and the surrounding villages were run as a District of Zaria Native Authority under the control of the District Head, known by title as the "*Magajin Gari*".

The Kaduna Capital Law of 1956[30] combined the areas of the Township, the urban areas of the district and the European and non-European reservations as a Capital Territory to be a separate Territory outside Zaria Province under the control of the Governor-in-Council acting through an Administrator.[31] The new area thus taken over is 45.3 square miles in size.

The Administrator was set up as a corporation sole to ensure perpetual succession, the rights to acquire and alienate property and the right to execute and enter into instruments and contracts. The final authority, however, was vested in the Governor-in-Council.

The Administrator was empowered to exercise over the new area:

(1) All the functions of a Local Authority in a Second Class Township;

(2) The functions of a Native Authority vested in it by native law and customs in respect of the prevention of crime; of powers to trade and provide services; to establish markets and of the power to control strangers who have no means of support; and

(3) The functions of a Native Authority under section 48 of the Native Authority Law, 1954; that is a declaration or modification of native law and custom; provided that this may be exercised only after consultation with and at the request of the Advisory Board.

[29] S. 47 of the Townships Ordinance.
[30] No. 8 of 1956.
[31] A Senior Administrative Officer.

To carry out his functions the Administrator was empowered to make by-laws:

(1) For any of the matters under which a Local Authority of a Township might make by-laws, and

(2) For any of the matters which a Native Authority is entitled to make or issue Rules or Orders under sections 37 and 41 of the Native Authority Law, 1954.[32]

He might also issue Orders as under section 43 of the Native Authority Law, 1954, to be obeyed by all persons to whom they apply, provided that any Orders issued concerned with local law and custom were first of all requested and considered by the Advisory Board.

The Advisory Board set up to assist the Administrator and his officers[33] and of which he was the Chairman, consisted of:

(1) An Assistant Administrator (nominated by the Minister);

(2) One member to represent each Local Council (of which there were four) set up under the Kaduna Capital Law;

(3) Five members appointed by the Governor-in-Council to represent Nigerian commerce; non-Nigerian commerce; Nigerian industry; non-Nigerian industry and education by voluntary (mission) agencies;

(4) Two *ex officio* members, the Divisional Engineer and the Medical Officer of Health;

(5) Any members co-opted by the Governor-in-Council.

Four Local Councils were set up later in 1957 called the Kaduna, North, South, East and West Local Councils. These were set up by Instrument and had elected majorities. Elections for these Councils were held under the authority of by-laws made by the Administrator. The Administrator with the approval of the Premier was empowered to delegate such of his powers as was deemed necessary to the Local Councils. Such powers were, however, revocable at will.

The finances of the Capital Territory over the past five years have been as follows:

---

[32] With the exception of paras. (50) and (58) of s. 37 of the Law.
[33] Assistant Administrators appointed by the Governor-in-Council.

	1957–58	1958–59	1959–60	1960–61	1961–62
	£	£	£	£	£
Ordinary Revenue .	95,497	103,822	136,389	170,033	212,576
Grants—Capital Works . . .	54,500	45,500	69,470	71,699	99,728
Ordinary Expenditure	80,818	88,467	124,952	159,024	181,445
Works Extraordinary	57,050	49,745	71,620	73,949	110,728
SURPLUS . .	£14,679	£15,355	£11,437	£11,009	£31,131

In April 1962 a Kaduna Capital Amendment Law was passed amending the 1956 Law so as to appoint a Native Authority for Kaduna. Most of the powers of the Administrator under the Law were abolished and a Native Authority was constituted for the Capital Territory. This will exercise the powers of a Native Authority under the Native Authority Law, 1954, subject to the conditions enforced by the Kaduna Capital Law. The Advisory Board remains but the Local Councils are replaced by two Administrative sub-areas (districts) of the Kaduna Native Authority. All property formerly vested in the Administrator is now handed over to the Native Authority with the exception of:

(1) The Administrator's own office;

(2) The Motor Licensing Office; and

(3) The Office of Superintendent of Parks and Gardens.

The Administrator is appointed as the Native Authority initially and acts as a caretaker pending a decision on the best form of permanent Native Authority to be set up and on the constitution of its Council.

The Powers and Duties of Native Authorities

Native Authorities are bodies corporate and as such have the powers and obligations given to such bodies.

These powers of a Native Authority[34] extend over all persons who reside or who are for the time being within the limits of the area throughout which its jurisdiction extends and include:

(1) The powers conferred on it by the Native Authority Law, 1954; and

[34] S. 29 (1) of the Law.

24

(2) The powers which it may be given under any other Law or Ordinance, *e.g.*, the Forestry Ordinance, the Personal Tax Law, etc.

A Native Authority may have also powers vested in it by native law and custom. Here, however, the power cannot be exercised indiscriminately over all persons within the area of its jurisdiction, but only over those persons to whom the particular native law and custom applies and who are bound by it, *i.e.*, powers under Muslim Law are not exerciseable over persons who are members of the native community but who are Christians or Animists.

A Native Authority has no powers over persons outside its own area. The obligations and duties of a Native Authority are set out in the Law[35] in a similar form. They are:

(1) Duties imposed upon it by the Native Authority Law, 1954;

(2) Duties imposed upon it by any other Law or Ordinance; and

(3) Duties imposed upon it by any native law or custom.

There is, however, also the general provision that it shall be the duty of a Native Authority to ensure that it maintains order and good government over the area of its jurisdiction.

Native Authorities may sue persons or other statutory bodies in court and conversely they may themselves be sued, *e.g.*, Bornu Native Authority was sued by a person in 1956 for unlawful arrest. There are instances of a Native Authority resorting to court action to enforce its rights especially in the matter of breach of contract.

The Native Authority's main *raison d'être* and obligation to the Regional Government and to the community it serves, is the maintenance of good order and government. The Law states in addition to this general obligation certain specific duties which the Native Authority must carry out to prevent crime.[36] It must interpose to prevent the commission of any offence within the area of its authority. Further, if it has reason to suppose that any person or persons intend to commit any offence, it may order the arrest of such person or persons if there is no other way of prevent-

[35] S. 29 (2) of the Law.
[36] S. 30 of the Law.

25

ing the commission of this crime. Any such person arrested under this authority, however, must be taken before a competent court within twenty-four hours.

The Native Authority may arrest a person from outside its area, then residing or passing through its territory, if it has reason to believe that he has committed a crime of any magnitude, that is to say, any of the offences stated in Appendix A of the Criminal Procedure Code, or any other Law or Ordinance for which the accused may be arrested either by a police officer or by a private person without a warrant of arrest. It may effect the arrest of any person also for any offence for which it is necessary to obtain a warrant if such a warrant has been issued elsewhere. The person so arrested must, however, be brought before a competent court as soon as possible to answer the charges made against him.

Suspected stolen property may also be seized[37] by the Native Authority whether or not the property was supposedly stolen inside or beyond the confines of its territory. Such property is held pending the order of a court having jurisdiction on the matter. The seizure and detention of property must be reported immediately to such a court.

Native Authorities normally delegate these powers to prevent crime to their sub-area administrative heads and to the members, severally or collectively, of their police forces (see Chapter 5).[38] Where this is done, there should be a directive to this effect in writing to the police force and a copy of the directive is sent to the Ministry of Internal Affairs who is responsible for police affairs.

It is the duty of all persons within its area to assist the Native Authority or its agents to whom the duty to prevent crime may be delegated[39] in these or any other lawful duties upon which it is engaged. In the case of natives of the Native Authority area there is a further obligation to assist in carrying out duties imposed by native law and custom. The Law provides a penalty for those who, so obligated, fail or refuse to give such assistance.[40] This penalty is severe and those convicted may be liable for a fine of £100 and/or imprisonment for six months.[41]

[37] S. 30 (4) of the Law.
[38] S. 118 (1) and (2) of the Law.
[39] Under s. 66 of the Law this delegation must be with approval of the Minister for Local Government to whom the Premier has delegated his power under this section.
[40] S. 103 of the Law.
[41] S. 105 (1).

Such a duty of general assistance is capable of wide interpretation and might easily be misused by a Native Authority. In fact it is rarely used; and the rights of the individual are protected by the constitution of the Federation of Nigeria.[42]

The Law provides further that a Native Authority may summon any person within its area to appear before it or before a Native Court. This request may be enforced by arrest under warrant if necessary, and the power to require attendance in addition is vested in Administrative or other Government Officers.[43]

Legislative Powers of Native Authorities

Native Authorities have the power under the Native Authority Law to introduce subsidiary legislation of the following types:

(1) Rules.
(2) Orders.
(3) Instruments.

Rules. The subjects upon which Rules may be introduced are set out in detail in section 37 of the Native Authority Law, 1954, to which section there are sixty-three paragraphs. The subjects enumerated include:

agriculture, animal health, control of hunting and fishing, building standards, control of advertisements, education, election, land usage, public health, public order, prevention of fire, roads and streets, native liquor, trade and industry and rural development.

Rules require the approval of the Governor-in-Council. The maximum penalty allowed for the infringement of a Rule under section 37 of the Law is a fine of £100 or imprisonment up to six months or both.

Under section 41 of the Law, power is also given to Native Authorities to make Rules for the setting up and organisation of markets and for fixing prices for the sale of food therein. These are subject to approval by the Minister of Trade and Industry[44] and

---

[42] More particularly by ss. 19 and 27 thereof.
[43] S. 104 of the Law. A warrant for the arrest may be issued under s. 108 of the Law, but in cases of urgency this may be dispensed with and the arrest carried out by a member of the N.A. or a sub-area head or the N.A. Police.
[44] Delegated to that Minister by the Minister for Local Government in whom the power is vested.

carry a maximum penalty in cases of infringement of £5 or one month's imprisonment. Under section 122, with the approval of the Minister, Rules may be made for the administration and discipline of Native Authority Police Forces and under section 141 for that of prisons and prison staff. Native Authorities have the right to make Rules under certain other Laws. The most common is power vested in Native Authorities under the Forestry Ordinance (section 37) to make Rules[45] for the use and administration of Communal Forest Reserves. Any new Rules under the Native Authority Law for which there is no published precedent are submitted by the Native Authority to the Ministry concerned[46] in non-legal language stating what is required. The request is then passed to the Chambers of the Hon. Attorney-General for drafting and confirmation that the intended Rules are *intra vires*. The draft Rules are returned to the Native Authority where they are discussed and approved by the Native Authority Council;[47] have the Common Seal affixed to them and are signified by the Clerk to the Council. The power of approval is with the Governor-in-Council, but this power may be exercised by the Minister responsible for the subject matter of the Rules if Rules similar in form have already been approved by the Governor.[48] Finally, after approval the Rules are published in the Northern Nigerian *Gazette*.

Where a precedent for the Rules exists it has been the practice to standardise the form of the Rules. Model Rules on many subjects are sent to Native Authorities to provide for their assistance an exact statement of legal requirements. Model type Rules can be prepared and passed by the Native Authorities without the necessity for passing through the hands of the legal draughtsman. Local details for such Rules can be included in schedules attached to them, the body of the Rules remaining the same for every authority setting them up.

An extension of this method of model type Rules is the "blanket" type. Here the Rules are the same for any authority and they are published once only with a schedule attached showing the names of the authorities which have adopted them together with the

[45] Approved by Provincial Commissioners.
[46] *i.e.*, Native Authority Public Health Rules are submitted to the Ministry of Health.
[47] In the event of disagreement on the detail of the draft the Rules would be returned to the Ministry concerned for re-drafting or further investigation.
[48] S. 146A of the Law.

dates of making, approval and of commencement for each Native
Authority. If any new Native Authority wishes to introduce the
same Rules it is accomplished by the publication of a simple
addition to the schedule. The Native Authority itself will, of course,
keep a full signed and approved copy of the Rules as proof of their
validity.

The Governor, after consultation with the Executive Council,
may request any Native Authority to make Rules under sections 37
or 41 of the Native Authority Law, if he considers it should do so
in the interests of the good government of the area. If subsequently
the Native Authority concerned neglects to make such Rules the
Law empowers the Governor himself to make them on its behalf.
Such Rules would then possess the same validity as if made by the
Native Authority itself.[49]

Orders. Orders may be issued[50] by a Native Authority in its own
right in respect of the subjects enumerated under section 43 of the
Law. These include:

> control of gambling, begging, carrying of weapons, bush
> burning, noise in public places, *i.e.*, singing, druming, sounding
> of horns, etc., carrying of lamps at night, subsistence farming.

The Law provides a maximum penalty for any such Order so
issued. This is a fine of £100 or six months' imprisonment or
both.

There is no authority required to issue Orders other than that of
the Native Authority itself, unlike Rules. The Governor-in-Council,
however, may order the Native Authority to issue an Order in the
interest of good government and if it fails to do so he may issue it
himself, as binding on that Native Authority. Conversely, the
Governor may decree that an Order be revoked or may himself revoke any Order already issued by a Native Authority. If he does
the latter he may release from prison any one undergoing sentence
for an infringement of that Order and to direct the repayment
of any fine imposed by a court under authority of that Order.

As mentioned in the section dealing with Subordinate Native
Authorities above, a Native Authority has the power under
section 22 of the Law to restrict the powers of any Native
Authority which is subordinate to it. The Order is published in the

---

[49] S. 42 of the Law.
[50] Under the Law, Rules are "made" but Orders are "issued".

same way as any other Order and requires no other authority other than that of the Native Authority concerned.

A Native Authority is empowered, in addition under the Water-Works Law, 1961, if it is the "prescribed authority", to issue Orders with the approval of the Government for the operation and control of the water supply for which it is responsible.[51]

Under the Forestry Ordinance[52] a Native Authority may issue Orders to set up Forestry Reserves or Communal Forestry areas.[53] Such Orders are approved by the Provincial Commissioner of the Province concerned, after consultation with the Chief Conservator of Forests.

ORDERS TO INDIVIDUALS. The Native Authority Law, 1954, enables Native Authorities to issue an Order to any native[54] in its area who is not a member of the native community and who cannot produce reasonable proof of means and legitimate labour for the support of himself and his dependants. The person concerned must leave the area of the jurisdiction of the Native Authority within fourteen days of the service of the Order. The person so ordered, however, has the right of appeal against his eviction to a Magistrate's Court, but must prove to the court that his means and legitimate labour are adequate to support himself and his dependants before the Order of the Native Authority can be set aside. Failure to observe the provision of such an Order may make the offender liable to a fine of £25 or to imprisonment for six months or to both such penalties.[55] This type of Order has been used in the past by Native Authorities to rid their towns of the unmarried women who practice prostitution.

PUBLICATION OF RULES AND ORDERS. Rules and Orders are signified in accordance with the Standing Orders of the Council after the impression of the Common Seal of the Native Authority.

In the event of the Standing Orders of a Native Authority not having been made and approved by the Minister for Local Government, the Minister may issue special instructions as to the signification of Rules and Orders. The following is the most common form of signification in practice:

[51] S. 9 of Water-Works Law of 1961.
[52] Cap. 75 of the Laws of Nigeria.
[53] An explanation of these is given in Chap. IV of this work.
[54] Native in this context means a native of Nigeria ordinarily subject to the jurisdiction of a native court. It would be *ultra vires* for a Native Authority to apply this power to any person not a native of Nigeria.
[55] S. 47 of the Law.

Made by the "X" Native Authority this
15th day of DECEMBER 1962.

The Common Seal of the
"X" Native Authority was
hereto affixed in the
presence of .... } L.S.

....

....

Signified in accordance with the "X" Native Authority
Standing Rules, 1954, and dated the 25th of NOVEMBER 1954.

....
Clerk to the Council.

The approval of the Rules is by the Minister concerned in person
except where these are approved by the Governor-in-Council where
the approval is given in the following form:

Approved this 29th day of DECEMBER 1961
By His Excellency's Command.

....
Clerk to the Executive Council.

Both Rules and Orders (other than Orders to individuals) have
to be published in the Regional *Gazette* and made known to the
community in the customary manner.[56] This means normally that
an announcement is made in the Subordinate Councils of the
Native Authority; the District and Village Heads are informed,
and in some cases the local town crier makes an announcement to
the people on market days. The date of commencement of a Rule
or Order is most often taken as the date of publication in the
Gazette. It is never retrospective, *i.e.*, a date before publication; but
it may state in the body of the Orders or Rules that they will
commence on a specific date *after* publication, *e.g.*, Rules affecting
payment of fees may begin on the 1st of April following as the
beginning of a new financial year.

[56] S. 146 of the Law.

31

Copies of all Rules and any Orders under section 43 made by Native Authorities, or by the Governor on their behalf, must be deposited as follows:

(1) One copy in the Office of the Minister for Local Government;
(2) One copy in the Provincial Office concerned;
(3) One copy in the Divisional Office;
(4) One copy in the main office of the Native Authority;
(5) One copy with the Scribe of every Native Court having jurisdiction to enforce the Orders or Rules.[57]

The Law provides a saving for Rules and Orders issued under the former Native Authority Ordinance before the 1954 Law was published. The Native Authority in such cases may either:

(1) Amend, vary or repeal the previous subsidiary legislation, or
(2) Declare that the former subsidiary legislation is to continue to be binding as if made under the authority of the 1954 enactment.

If a Native Authority takes over the area of a Local Authority[58] it will take over the by-laws of that authority and administer and retain or amend them as if they had been made by itself.

Where two or more Native Authorities decide to federate to form a Federated Native Authority Council the individual Rules and Orders of the new Subordinate Native Authorities will continue to apply to their own areas only. The new Federated Native Authority may, of its own right, make Rules or Orders which will apply in addition to the whole area of the Federation.

Conversely, if a Native Authority is broken up by Law into two or more Native Authorities[59] the Rules and Orders of the former Native Authority will apply to all the new authorities as if made by them. These Rules and Orders can, of course, be amended or repealed by the new authorities as they think fit thereafter.

Rules for the administration of Native Authority Police Forces made under section 122 of the Law and Rules made under section

---

[57] S. 147 of the Law.
[58] *i.e.*, Kaduna Native Authority when it is formed.
[59] *e.g.*, Dikwa Emirate in 1960 was split to form Dikwa N.A. and Gwoza N.A. The former Dikwa N.A. Subsidiary legislation was then binding upon both the new Native Authorities. S. 50 of the N.A. Law refers.

141 in respect of prison staff and prisoners are, in both cases, made as "model" Rules and are accepted as such by all Native Authorities. Separate copies of the Rules are, of course, made formally by each Native Authority and deposited in the same way as any other Rules.

Rules and Orders made under the provision of the Native Authority Law, 1954, form section "C" of the annual publication of the Laws of Northern Nigeria.

From time to time the Ministry for Local Government issues a Check List of all local government subsidiary legislation for the benefit of Provincial Commissioners and Native Authorities. It should be noted, however, that such Check Lists never remain up to date for long as new subsidiary legislation for Native Authorities is published almost every week.

Rules and Orders made under the provision of the Native Authority Law, 1954, may be summarised as follows:

	Rules	*Approval*	
Must be published in the Regional *Gazette* and copies deposited in accordance with section 147	Under section 37	Governor or Ministry concerned	Affect Government policy
	Under section 41 (Markets)	Minister for Trade and Industry (del.)	
	Under section 122 (Police)	Minister for Internal Affairs	
	Under section 141 (Prisons)	Minister for Internal Affairs	
	Orders		
	Under section 43	Nil	Only affects the Native Authority concerned
	Under section 22	Nil	
	Individual Orders		
	Under section 45	Nil	
	Under section 47	Nil	

Details of subsidiary legislation made under other Laws and Ordinances are contained in the legislation concerned.

Instruments. Under section 55 of the Law a Native Authority may and if directed by the Minister for Local Government shall set up Subordinate Councils by Instrument. These Councils are defined as those established for districts; towns; village areas;

wards or other administrative sub-areas.[60] All Instruments are subject to the approval of the Minister and they are published in the Regional *Gazette*. Such Instruments must provide for:

(1) The name of the Council;

(2) The functions and powers of the Council;

(3) The composition for the Council, *i.e.*, membership; this must include elected members who will form a majority in the Council;

(4) The Chairmanship (including Vice-Chairmanship) of the Council; and

(5) The summoning and frequency of meetings of the Council.

Instruments invariably, by custom, also include details of:

(1) The revenue and finance of the Council, and

(2) The Standing Orders of the Council which are made by the Council but are approved by the Native Authority.[61]

Councils are dissolved by the same method as they are established. New Instruments will revoke previous ones. Some Native Authorities of recent years have issued a model Instrument to cover all their Subordinate Councils. Blanks are left to cover the title, membership and Chairmanship of each Council, but the functions and powers and other details are the same throughout. Details of the name, composition and Chairmanship of each Council is given in a schedule attached to the model Instrument.

Instruments are also required in the same form as those of Subordinate Councils to set up Outer Councils for Native Authorities.[62]

Details of Councils set up by Instrument by Native Authorities as at July 1, 1962, were as follows:

Outer Councils	.	.	.	24
District Councils	.	.	.	465
Town Councils	.	.	.	45
Village Councils	.	.	.	250
Village Group Councils	.	.	77

[60] It is not necessary for an administrative sub-area head to be appointed before a Council is set up.
[61] S. 60 of the Law.
[62] Details of the functions of Subordinate Councils and Outer Councils is given in detail in Chap. 3.

Powers of a Native Authority with regard to Native Law and Custom[63]

The Native Authority is the custodian of native law and custom.[64] As this is largely unwritten law it is continually, if imperceptibly, changing and its details are known best by elders and traditional Councillors and by Court Members. It does not apply to any criminal matters which are now covered by the Penal Code. Its most important functions are marriage and inheritance. Section 29 of the Law states that the Native Authority may exercise over all persons to whom the local law and custom applies all such powers as may be given or vested in it by such custom. It is, moreover, the duty of the Native Authority to perform and not to neglect the obligations imposed upon it by the native law and custom.

Native law and custom is further mentioned in the Native Authority Law in section 48 which empowers the Native Authority to record in writing a declaration of what it considers to be the native law or custom on any matter for the whole or for any part of the territory under its jurisdiction. This declaration may be made by the Native Authority on the orders of the Provincial Commissioner concerned (to whom the Governor has delegated this power). Every such declaration requires the approval of the Governor who must verify its accuracy before publication. As a corollary to this, a Native Authority may submit to the Governor a written modification of existing native law and custom if it is expedient for the good government and welfare of its area. The Governor should satisfy himself:

(1) That the modified custom is not repugnant to natural justice, equity or good conscience;
(2) That it does not contravene any written Law or Ordinance; and
(3) That it is expedient.

The modification is then published by the Native Authority and, although not stipulated in the Law, is printed in the Regional *Gazette*.

The declaration must be made known to the native community in the customary manner and thereafter it comes into force.

[63] It must be noted that native law and custom includes Muslim personal law.
[64] The Traditional ruler may, of course, hold special powers under native law and custom which he alone may exercise. The same applies to "King makers" or custodians of a *juju* (*Tsafi*).

There are seven examples of Native Authorities making use of this section;[65] all of them affect the Riverain areas of the Region.

A Native Authority may also publish Rules or Orders forbidding or restricting dangerous or repugnant customs, e.g., the Prohibited "*Kutis*" Rules of Igbirra Native Authority[66]: the Control of Juveniles accompanying Koranic Mallam Rules published by twenty-nine Native Authorities; and the Beggar Minstrel Orders issued also by twenty-nine Native Authorities.

In reference to the powers of Native Authorities with regard to native law and custom, great care must be taken to ensure that they are applied only to the native community which accepts them as part of its tradition.

The Relationship between Native Authorities and the Central Government

Native Authorities are set up by the Regional Government. They are also dissolved by it. In theory, therefore, there is strict control of the local administrations by the central legislature. It must be remembered, however, that the vast Northern Emirates of Northern Nigeria controlling large populations and holding the power and prestige accorded to them by history and tradition are far more autonomous in character than is at first realised by reference to the Law alone.

In constituting the office of Native Authority for any area the Governor may limit the powers to be vested in it as the Government[67] thinks fit. There are cases of Native Authorities having their powers under the Native Authority Law restricted. Section 16 of the Law gives power to the Governor, Premier or Minister as necessary to revoke, suspend or vary any of the constitution and appointments made by them in setting up Native Authorities. This may be done at any time. The sweeping effect of this provision, however, is modified by section 19A of the Law which stipulates that the Governor has the power:

(1) To direct any Chief or member of the Council of a Native Authority should cease to act in the capacity of a member of a Native Authority; and

---

[65] e.g., Tiv N.A. Declaration of Marriage Rules NRLN 149 of 1955.
[66] No. 15 of 1956.
[67] S. 4 of the Law.

(2) To appoint others in their place; provided that an impartial inquiry is held first into the maladministration of the Native Authority or individuals thereof.[68]

Section 19 of the Law gives the power of dismissal of any Chief or member of the Native Authority from the Native Authority to the Governor at any time. There is a proviso, however, that should the person to be dismissed be an elected member, *i.e.*, elected by adult male suffrage, he should be given the period of one calendar month in which to make representation against his dismissal for the Governor's consideration.

The Central Government takes care in the Law to control the appointment of certain senior staff by a Native Authority.[69] Failure to observe impartiality and fairness in the selection and appointment of all other staff may be the subject of an impartial inquiry[70] set up by the Governor. If the inquiry reveals that there is partiality or unfairness in the selection or promotion of Native Authority staff,[71] then the Governor-in-Council may order any member of the Native Authority staff who feels aggrieved to appeal to the Governor against the decision of the Native Authority concerning his appointment or terms of service, and that the Governor may restrict or take over completely the powers of that Native Authority in respect of the appointment, dismissal and control of all its staff.

Perhaps the most effective control of Native Authorities by the Central Government is through their revenue and finance. The controls may be summarised as:

(1) Control of tax through the Personal Tax Law, 1962;[72]
(2) Control of rates by approval of Rules introducing them (section 77 (1) and 37 (50) of the Law);
(3) Control of annual estimates of revenue and expenditure by approval through the Ministry for Local Government which lays down certain necessary standards for financial soundness (section 86 (1) of the Law);
(4) General control of the system of Native Authority treasury accounting through the accounting rules known as Financial Memoranda (section 88 of the Law);

[68] *e.g.*, Ilorin N.A. in 1958; Zaria N.A. in 1961.
[69] See Chap. 7 for details.   [70] S. 36A of the Law.
[71] *e.g.*, Igbirra N.A. in 1958.
[72] Part III Community and Cattle Tax.

(5) Control of additional expenditure above that approved in the Estimates in all but Grade A (i) Treasuries;

(6) Control by audit of all Native Treasury accounts (sections 89–99 of the Law); and

(7) Control by the Minister for Local Government of the powers of the Native Authority to borrow and lend funds.

The Native Authority Law provides many controls over the powers of Native Authorities and their Subordinate Councils. Indeed, the Native Authorities have few powers which are not qualified to some extent by Government control. A Native Authority is liable to be fined £50 on conviction of wilful neglect in respect of:

(1) Its duty to prevent crime in its area;

(2) Its duty to follow the directions of an Administrative Officer of the Government towards any person under section 104 of the Law;

(3) Its duty to issue, enforce or revoke Orders if so directed by the Governor;

(4) Its duty to enforce any Rules made by it under the Law, or made by the Governor under the provisions of section 42 and abuse of any authority conferred on it by the Native Authority Law by any other Law or by any native law and custom.[73]

The Regional Government has on more than one occasion declared its policy towards the Native Authorities. The Premier made the following explanation to the House of Assembly in 1956:

"... In every country where there are democratic institutions the relationship between the Government in power and local government bodies is bound to present certain problems. Nigeria is no exception to this rule. The Regional Government therefore believes that a clear statement of its policy on this subject will be of value in allaying any doubts which may exist among Native Authorities and political parties of the opposition.

---

[73] S. 102 of the Law. Court proceedings against a Native Authority for wilful neglect of its duties would not be taken without the prior consent of the Governor-in-Council.

"The Government of the Northern Region recognises that, just as the constitution provides different spheres of activity for the Federal Government on one hand and the Regional Government on the other, so the law defines separate fields for the Regional Government on one hand and the Native Authorities on the other. Within the field of Local Government, the Regional Government is ready to grant Native Authorities complete freedom of action provided always that certain essential conditions are observed. These conditions are that Native Authorities should retain the confidence of the great mass of their people, that they should discharge adequately the duties and responsibilities assigned to them, that they should conduct their financial affairs in a prudent and responsible fashion, and that they should maintain the standards of honesty and impartiality required in a country approaching independence.[74]

"The Regional Government, which is ultimately responsible for law, order and sound administration, must however, reserve to itself the right to intervene in local government matters if these conditions are not met. This right is recognised by the law which has provided certain over-riding powers. These are financial, executive and legal, and they vary in range from the ability to withhold a small grant to the power of the Governor-in-Council to annul the appointment of a Native Authority.

"Wide as these powers are, however, they cannot be arbitrarily exercised. They are subject to two great sanctions of democratic representative government, namely, the rule of law and freedom of discussion. Native Authorities are constituted under and safeguarded by legal processes and any Government which sought to suppress them or encroach upon their statutory rights would have to proceed according to law. Such a move, whether justified or not, would be reported in the press and could be made the subject of a debate in the Regional legislature. Consequently, any Government which took action against a Native Authority from improper motives would risk exposure at the bar of public opinion.

"These are the safeguards which democracy provides to preserve the weak against the strong and they are just as

[74] Regional independence was attained in March 1959.

important in constitutional as in human relationships. The Regional Government affirms its faith in these safeguards and pledges itself to observe them in the spirit as well as the letter. In particular, it is resolved to treat all Native Authorities irrespective of their political sympathies, with strict impartiality and scrupulously to refrain from any action which could be attributed to political bias. Native Authorities may, therefore, rest assured that, provided that they for their part discharge their statutory and moral obligations, they will not be subject to unjustifiable interference or undue influence by the Regional Government."

The following year the Regional Government was obliged to define the functions of members of the House of Assembly *vis-à-vis* the Native Authorities to prevent interference by the former in the latters' affairs. It was made quite clear that elected representatives had no right to interfere with local government Councils unless they were members also of the Council concerned.

In March 1962 the Premier of Northern Nigeria in speaking to the House of Chiefs felt that the control of Native Authorities by the Central Government should be emphasised once more. In the last two years there have been inquiries into the activities of certain Native Authorities and the Ministry for Local Government had been obliged in 1961 to impose stricter controls on Native Treasuries. The Premier of Northern Nigeria in speaking to the Chiefs affirmed the policy as follows:

"The Government is aware of some concern among a considerable number of the members of the House over the relationships between the Government and certain Native Authorities. Fears have been expressed that some Native Authorities have become too powerful and that they tend to ignore the instructions of Government. These fears have not only been expressed in this House but also outside it among the general public especially from letters I personally received daily, requesting for a commission of inquiry into certain Native Authorities.

"If a Native Authority co-operates with this Government, carries out promptly and efficiently its lawful directives and maintains an efficient administration which has the confidence of the people of the area, then this Government will give that Native Authority every help and assistance.

"If, however, a Native Authority, whether it be big or small, fails to carry out the lawful instructions and directives of the Government or administers its area inefficiently, then the Government will take forceful and direct action to remedy the situation.

"The action which the Government can, and will if necessary, take against Native Authorities who try to defy it, will vary according to the circumstances. In the most serious circumstances the Government can, and if necessary, will dissolve a Native Authority. Small Native Authorities can be merged together into a large unit if circumstances demand such action. Large Native Authorities can, if necessary, be divided up into smaller units.

"Let there be no misunderstanding. This Government fears no local organisation but is only tolerant. It will carry out its duty and deal with any unit or individual who may try and oppose its policies and lawful directives. These policies and directives are all based on our desire and duty to bring efficiency, justice and a higher standard of living to all our people and to stamp out the evils of nepotism, misrule, corruption and poverty wherever they may remain. We are determined to carry out this responsibility and duty which history and circumstances have imposed upon us. Anyone who tries to prevent us, does so at his own peril.

"Let me, however, end by emphasising my unshaken confidence in the Native Authority system by which the Native Authorities administer their own local affairs and my belief in the complete loyalty to the policies of the Government of the vast majority of Native Authorities."

Administrative Controls over Native Authorities

These may be achieved either by directives from the Central Ministries or by payment of grants by the Ministries to local authorities for the carrying out of public services to their special requirements. Of these two methods the second has proved to be the more effective. Local control of Native Authorities is given by departmental officers of Ministries at a Provincial level. This year the Government of Northern Nigeria decided that there should be more influence by Government technical officers over recruitment, promotions and disciplinary action concerning Native Authority technical staff than formerly, as unqualified or incompetent staff in technical posts in Native Authorities would prejudice the economy of the country. Technical officers of Ministries should be consulted over major policy issues affecting technical skills and when estimates of expenditure for the coming financial year are being prepared. Minimum qualifications for all technical posts are now laid down by the Ministries concerned and Native Authorities may employ only those who possess these qualifications. Promotion to key posts also will be approved only after the agreement of the local Ministry representatives have been given to them. These departmental officers also act as the recommenders of the Native Authority grants and where grants are involved their advice is normally followed by the Native Authorities. Whilst the Native Authorities are always ready to welcome technical assistance from departmental officers, however, they are perhaps not so eager to accept advice on their administrative arrangements. The complications of administrative control of Native Authorities by the Central Government are enhanced by the diversity of both size and wealth of the various local authorities in the Region. Many of the smaller ones cannot be acceptable as economic units of their own and only the use of joint services allows them to continue as viable units. Finally, the training of technical and clerical staff of the local authorities by the Regional Government has done much to standardise procedures and ensure adequate standards throughout the whole Region.[75]

[75] See Appendix 1 for details of training facilities offered to Native Authorities by the Regional Government.

LOCAL AUTHORITIES

DETAILS OF NATIVE AUTHORITIES OF NORTHERN NIGERIA
AS AT JULY 1, 1962

PROVINCE	NATIVE AUTHORITY	SIZE IN SQ. MILES	TAX-PAYING POPULATION	CONSTITU-TION	ORDINARY REVENUE 1962–63 *
DAMAWA	Adamawa	18,558	68,983	C. in C.	246,840
	Muri	10,884	57,481	C. in C.	136,535
	Numan Fed.	2,214	25,391	Council	89,260
AUCHI	Bauchi } Dass }	14,516	110,732	{ C. in C. } { C. and C. }	359,076
	Gombe	6,481	83,737	C. in C.	277,240
	Jama'are	149	5,424	C. in C.	17,960
	Katagum	7,000	88,305	C. in C.	276,720
	Misau	890	27,051	C. in C.	86,340
	Ningi		15,180	Caretaker	44,730
	Tangale-Waja Federation	24,924	27,393	Council	78,215
ENUE	Awe (See Nassarawa)			C. in C.	
	Idoma	3,722	82,097	C. in C.	185,870
	Keffi } Lafia }	3,949	{ 19,715 { 34,010	C. in C. C. in C.	61,975 108,970
	Nassarawa	5,563	26,780	C. in C.	77,850
	Tiv	9,861	202,833	Caretaker	490,095
	Wukari Fed.	6,223	30,734	Council	90,400
ORNU	Bedde	2,000	17,153	C. in C.	52,775
	Biu Federation	2,920	35,443	Council	107,040
	Bornu	32,005	302,392	C. in C.	1,043,735
	Fika	1,669	31,594	C. in C.	95,865
ORIN	Borgu	10,908	16,372	C. in C.	68,640
	Ilorin	2,647	110,805	C. in C.	374,915
	Lafiagi } Pategi }	4,164	{ 9,309 { 5,931	Council C. in C.	27,590 20,151
ABBA	Bunu (B)	928	See Kabba	C. in C.	
	East Yagba		See W. Yagba	C. in C.	
	Igala	4,982	100,485	C. in C.	299,232
	Igbirra	1,141	32,179	C. and C.	115,280
	Ijumu (I)	320	See Kabba	C. and C.	
	Kabba (K)	96	BIK, 11,324	C. and C.	44,660
	Kwara Fed.	1,629	15,103	Council	64,280
	West Yagba (See E. Yagba)		11,347	C. in C.	41,895

* By Treasuries.

DETAILS OF NATIVE AUTHORITIES OF NORTHERN NIGERIA—*continued*

PROVINCE	NATIVE AUTHORITY	SIZE IN SQ. MILES	TAX-PAYING POPULATION	CONSTITU- TION	ORDINAI REVENU 1962-6
KANO	Gumol	1,205	32,886	C. in C.	91,24
	Hadejia	2,493	72,369	C. in C.	176,98
	Kano }	12,933	{ 776,690	C. in C.	1,966,54
	Kazaure		27,608	C. in C.	65,88
KATSINA	Daura }	9,466	{ 40,519	C. in C.	105,21
	Katsina		388,854		963,29
NIGER	Abuja	2,237	19,025	C. in C.	66,83
	Agaie	874	7,254	C. in C.	26,07
	Bida	4,867	53,174	C. in C.	192,43
	Gwari	4,119	31,192	Council	114,47
	Kamuku	1,637	5,314	Council	22,33
	Kontagora (Wushishi)	9,132	36,048	C. in C.	102,81
	Lapai	1,713	7,851	C. in C.	26,74
	Wushishi	599		C. in C.	
	Zuru	16,488	29,902	Council	79,47
PLATEAU	Akwanga Fed.	1,315	20,730	Council	60,34
	Jos	1,435	62,260	C. in C.	265,95
	Kanam (See Pankshin)		11,668	C. in C.	30,84
	Lowland Fed.	4,800	29,816	Council	73,11
	Pankshin Fed.	3,679	44,660	Council	130,46
	Resettlement		See Yargam	Council	
	Wase	2,227	8,323	C. in C.	26,91
	Yergam		8,838	C. in C.	21,39
SARDAUNA	Chamba	3,500	22,858	Council	71,13
	Dikwa	4,220	50,750	C. in C.	151,57
	Gashaka/ Mambilla	5,300	15,570	Council	87,31
	Gwoza	1,000	16,642	C. in C.	31,74
	Mubi	1,600	40,498	Council	95,56
	United Hills	1,300	3,451	Council	9,96
SOKOTO	Argungu	3,356	39,199	C. in C.	109,27
	Gwandu	6,207	98,333	C. in C.	270,4
	Sokoto	25,608	478,394	C. in C.	1,004,3
	Yauri	1,306	19,907	C. in C.	66,6
ZARIA	Birnin Gwari	See Zaria		C. in C.	11,7
	Jama'a Fed.	1,597	26,471	Council	95,0
	Zaria	16,488	173,118	C. in C.	554,5

* By Treasuries.

LOCAL AUTHORITIES

SUBORDINATE NATIVE AUTHORITIES OF NORTHERN NIGERIA
AS AT JULY 1, 1962

PROVINCE	NATIVE AUTHORITY	SUBORDINATE NATIVE AUTHORITY	CONSTITUTION
ADAMAWA	Adamawa	Yungur	C. in C.
	Muri	Zinna	C. and C.
	Numan Fed.	Bachama	C. and C.
		Batta	C. and C.
		Longuda	C. and C.
		Mbula	C. and C.
		Shellen	C. and C.
BAUCHI	T/Waji Fed.	Cham	Council
		Dadiya	C. and C.
		Kaltungo	C. in C.
		Waja	C. in C.
		West Tangale	C. in C.
BENUE	Tiv	Abinsi	C. and C.
		Katsina Ala	C. and C.
		Makurdi	Council
	Wukari Fed.	Donga	C. in C.
		Takum	C. in C.
		Wukari	C. in C.
ILORIN	Borgu	Western Borgu	Council
KABBA	Igala	Bassa Komo	C. and C.
	Kwara Fed.	Aworo	C. in C.
		Eggan	C. in C.
		Kakanda	C. in C.
		Koton-Karfe	C. in C.
		Kupa	C. in C.
		Lokoja	C. and C.
NIGER	Zuru	Dabai	C. and C.
		Donko	C. and C.
		Fakai	C. and C.
		Sakaba	C. and C.
		Wasagu	C. and C.
PLATEAU	Jos	Jos Town	U/Council
	Lowland Fed.	Gerkawa	C. and C.
		Kofyer	Council
		Montol	C. and C.
		Shendam	C. in C.
	Pankshin Fed.	Angas	C. and C.
		Ron-Kulere	C. and C.
		Sura-pyem	Council

SUBORDINATE NATIVE AUTHORITIES OF NORTHERN NIGERIA—*continued*

PROVINCE	NATIVE AUTHORITY	SUBORDINATE NATIVE AUTHORITY	CONSTITU-TION
PLATEAU	Akwanga Fed.	Mada	C. and C.
		Nasserawa-Eggon	C. and C.
		Wamba	C. in C.
ZARIA	Jema'a Fed.	Jaba	C. in C.
		Jema'a	C. in C.
		Kagoro	C. in C.
		Moroa	C. in C.
BORNU	Biu Fed.	Biu	C. in C.
		Askira	C. in C.
		Shani	C. in C.

CHAPTER 3

THE INTERNAL ORGANISATION OF THE
NATIVE AUTHORITY

1. NATIVE AUTHORITY COUNCILS

THE composition of the Native Authority Council is laid down by the Minister for Local Government. The Law admits of five types of membership to a Native Authority Council:[1]

(1) Persons named by the Minister. That is to say persons appointed by name or title.

(2) Holders of offices named by the Minister. These may be posts in the Native Authority or traditional posts which carry executive responsibilities.

(3) Persons nominated in such manner and for such term as the Minister may prescribe. This refers to persons nominated to represent a specific interest or persons to be nominated by a Subordinate Native Authority or Council.

(4) Persons elected by the electorate under Electoral Regulations made by the Governor-in-Council;[2] and

(5) Persons selected to be members in accordance with native law or custom, e.g., a traditional "kingmaker" or the custodian of an important local shrine.

There is a further provision in the Law that the Minister may direct that the composition of the Council may be regulated according to the native law or custom in the community.

These types of membership in Native Authority Councils may perhaps be more easily defined under the following three headings:

(a) Elected members that is type (4).

(b) Nominated members that are types (1) and (3).

(c) Traditional members that are types (2) and (5).

---

[1] S. 6 (3) of the Law.
[2] See s. 6 (4) of the Law and Chap. 9 *post.*

47

Elected Members

These are elected under provision of Electoral Regulations made by the Governor-in-Council under section 6 (4) of the Law. The Regulations may provide for the electoral areas for a direct election, or if the Subordinate Councils have already been set up with elected majorities then by means of an indirect election using the Subordinate Councils as electoral colleges. Elected members on Native Authority Councils do not usually hold executive posts or portfolios unless the entire Council is elected, e.g., Igbirra Native Authority, and an Executive Committee is formed.[3] Elected members may be dismissed for misconduct by the Governor but the Law specifies that any member of a Native Authority appointed in a representative capacity shall be given notice of his intended dismissal of one calendar month so that he may submit representations to the Governor on the reasons for his dismissal if he so desires.[4] Members of Native Authority Councils are normally elected for a period of three years and in the event of a vacancy occurring in the first two years of the Council's life a by-election is held. Members are always eligible for re-election.

Nominated Members

These are either persons named in the constitutional direction or persons appointed to represent a special interest. In the event of there being no elected members on the Council, they may serve to represent certain elements of the native community which would be otherwise inadequately represented. This may also be the case in a Council with elected members, i.e., it may be necessary to nominate a person to represent the interests of the semi-nomadic Fulani tribe or, in the north-east of the Region the Shuwa Arabs; peoples whose cattle and cattle tax bring wealth to the Native Authority but who are unlikely to contest an election or to have any representative included amongst the traditional Councillors. Small stranger groups or commercial interests are other examples of the value of nominated members on the Council.

Members so nominated may serve on the Council either for a specified or for an unspecified length of time. They are nominated by the Minister for Local Government.

[3] Now known commonly as the General Purposes Committee.
[4] S. 19 of the Law.

Traditional Members

These are also appointed by the Minister for Local Government. They are either:

(1) *Ex officio* holding traditional executive posts in the hierarchy of the Chief, *e.g.*, *Waziri, Ma'aji, Wali*, etc., or

(2) Selected in accordance with native law or custom.

It is the traditional Councillor who gives continuity and stability to the Native Authority Council and it is almost always the traditional Councillor who holds the portfolios in a Council which works on the "Ministerial" system. In some Native Authorities the important posts are all held by and passed on to members of the "royal" house. In others, there is a recognised chain of promotion through sub-area headships; in a few the higher posts are open to all on merit alone. In all cases the approval of the Chief is necessary before any person is appointed.

Of the present seventy Native Authorities in Northern Nigeria 72 per cent have elected members and 51 per cent have elected majorities. It is the policy of the Regional Government that in course of time all Native Authorities will have elected majorities. A time limit, moreover, has been set for this desirable objective, as the end of the 1962 calendar year. The individual types of Council for each of the present Native Authorities are given in the appendix to this chapter. They may be summarised as follows:

(1) Traditional and nominated members only .   .   5

(2) Traditional; nominated and an elected minority .   7

(3) Traditional; nominated and an elected majority .   36

(4) Caretaker Native Authority (sole authorities) .   2*

(* Previously Chief with elected minority—Ningi; and Chief with elected majority—Tiv.)

The size of the Native Authority Councils varies according to the area. As a general rule it may be said that the peoples of the Riverain area[5] demand a higher representation than their counterparts farther north. The limits of size are Agaie Native Authority with sixty-nine members as the largest Council in the Region and Gumel and Kazaure Native Authorities with six members each as the smallest. The following table gives a summary of relative sizes of Councils.

[5] Ilorin, Kabba and Benue Provinces.

49

MEMBERSHIP	NUMBER OF NATIVE AUTHORITIES
(1) Less than 12 members. .	15
(2) 12–19 members . . .	13
(3) 20–30 members . . .	21
(4) 30 or more members . .	19
(5) Caretaker (sole authorities) .	2

Native Authority Councils work in one of the three ways: (1) by the portfolio or Ministerial form, or (2) by the Committee system, or (3) by the Administrative Councillor system.

The Portfolio System

This means that the main services of the Native Authority are divided up and each traditional Councillor is given a portfolio for responsibility of one or more of these services and the departments dealing with them. The following are the main departments of a Native Authority:

(1) Judicial.
(2) Police.
(8) Prisons.
(4) Local Government (Subordinate Councils).
(5) Finance.
(6) Natural Resources (Forestry, Agriculture and Animal Health).
(7) Medical.
(8) Education (including public enlightenment).
(9) Works.

There are normally not enough traditional Councillors to admit of one Councillor per department. Portfolios therefore are often combined and some of the common combinations are:

Police and Prisons; Medical and Education; Police, Prisons and Judicial; Local Government and Finance; Medical and Education.

There are examples of each department being linked with every other one with the exceptions that Judicial has never yet been linked with Works or with Natural Resources.

It is the duty of the Councillor charged with the responsibility of a department to bring up matters of policy affecting that department for discussion in the Native Authority Council and to see that the Council's decisions are carried out. He does *not* deal directly with the staff of the departments concerned but through a Head of Department.[6] These are normally as follows:

For (1)	Judicial	Court Registrar (or the Alkalai or Native Court Presidents concerned).
(2)	Police	The Chief of Police.
(3)	Prison	The Head Warder or Superintendent of Prisons.
(4)	Local Government	The Local Government or Development Secretary.
(5)	Finance	The Native Treasurer.
(6)	Medical	The Health Superintendent.
(7)	Education	The Schools Manager, Education Secretary or Senior Visiting Teacher.
(8)	Natural Resources	Agriculture—Supervisor of Agriculture.
		Forestry—Supervisor of Forests or Senior Forester.
		Veterinary—Head Veterinary Assistant or Supervisor of Animal Health.
(9)	Works	The Supervisor of Works.[7]

For this system to be successful there must be close co-operation between the Head of Department and the Councillor, both in initiating policy and in carrying out policy approved by the Native Authority. There is a danger always of the Councillor, who is untrained, interfering with the work of the staff of the department and this in some cases had led to a conflict of loyalties amongst the departmental staff.

Wherever possible the Councillor concerned should put up memoranda on motions of policy after discussions with his Head of Department concerned. The Head of Department will not normally attend the Native Authority Council meeting as he is not a member but he may be called in "in attendance" if there are

---

[6] He is, however, responsible for keeping a watching brief on the votes of charge controlled by each Head of Department.

[7] There are variants in those titles in some N.A.s. These, however, are the most common titles for Heads of Departments.

technical matters to be discussed. When a decision has been reached the minute concerned will be sent to the Councillor for action and he will then discuss with the Head of Department the most effective way of carrying out the Council's decisions.

An example of a Native Authority Council using the "portfolio" system is given at the end of the chapter.

The Committee System

The Native Authority Law permits Native Authorities to set up committees for any purpose, provided that the permission of the Minister for Local Government is obtained.[8] A copy of the resolution of the Native Authority Council appointing a committee is sent to the Minister who approves by normal letter. The resolution will contain:

(1) The composition of the committee;
(2) The tenure of office of its members;
(3) The functions of the committee.

There is no publication of the approval. In addition to the general provision in the Law to appoint committees there are the following specific provisions concerning committees:

(1) Under section 36 (6) the Premier may direct a Native Authority to establish a committee to deal with the appointment and dismissal of its staff; and
(2) Under section 83 (2) the Minister for Local Government may direct a Native Authority to set up a Finance Committee to manage its financial affairs. A directive from the Minister in January 1962 has directed all Native Authorities to set up Finance Committees if they did not already possess them and stipulated certain action to be taken monthly by the committee.[9]

The success of the committee system depends upon the influence of the committee Chairman. Working in a more informal atmosphere than that of a Council the Chairman must become an active participant in the discussion and work of the committee and stimulate a corresponding activity in the members. The Chairman will also be the only active liaison between the committee and the

[8] S. 65 of the Law.
[9] See Chap. 6, *post*, for greater detail.

work of the departments under its control and it will be his duty to supervise the departments by working with the Head of Department in much the same way as the Executive Councillor. It is extremely important therefore, that this official is chosen with some care by the Native Authority and that he is much more than a figurehead or merely an interpreter of Standing Orders at the committee meetings. Committees may be either Advisory or Executive.

The Executive Committees may be delegated any of the powers and functions of the Native Authority itself with the following exceptions:

(1) The power to enact subsidiary legislation;
(2) The power to raise money either by rates or by loans;
(3) The power to make Standing Orders for the Native Authority; and
(4) The power to appoint committees themselves.

The size of the committee will depend on the wishes of the Native Authority Council. It is generally considered that a committee should not have more than ten members and not have less than four. If the Native Authority Council has two or more political factions then representation in the same proportion should be observed in the quorum of any committee with executive powers; the Law lays down that at least one-third of the members of any Native Authority committee must be members of the Native Authority;[10] up to two-thirds may, however, be recruited outside the Native Authority Council from staff or from persons not connected in any way with the Native Authority, *e.g.*, a parent may be included on the Education Committee. In addition a committee may invite any person to attend a committee for a particular purpose. The visitor in such a case may join in the debate and have all the rights of an appointed member except that he may have no vote.

There are two types of committee which require additional explanation.

An Executive Committee of a Native Authority.[11] This is set up in an entirely elected Native Authority Council or in an area where it is difficult to get a quorum of the Native Authority Council to sit regularly to deal with the day-to-day affairs of the Native

[10] S. 65 (2) of the Law.
[11] Now known more commonly as the General Purposes Committee.

53

Authority and to ensure that the approved policy is carried out. It is a particular feature of the "Federal Council" type of Native Authority. The persons on this committee, unlike the rest of the Council, are full-time Councillors and they are paid a salary or an allowance. They may not hold any other post in the Native Authority whilst they are so employed.

The Executive Committee is normally given all the powers of Native Authority to exercise in respect of the routine administration other than:

(1) To approve the annual estimates;
(2) To make recommendations other than to the Native Authority regarding the incidence of taxation;
(3) To approve amendments to Native Authority Five-year Development Plan;
(4) To delegate the control of expenditure under Financial Memoranda;
(5) To appoint or dismiss any Native Authority employee on a salary of Grade F or above, or to dismiss any Village Head.

The Tenders Board. Any contract the value of which exceeds £50 must be put out to tender by advertisement and be awarded from amongst the tenders received by a Tenders Board. There is no limit to the size of the Native Authority contracts that may be so awarded. Financial Memoranda which lays down the procedure to be followed in all matters concerning Native Treasury finance stipulates that the membership of the Native Authority Tenders Board should be:

(1) The Head of the Native Authority or his representative;
(2) The Head of the Native Authority Department concerned, *e.g.*, in all public works this would be the Supervisor of Works, for Education the Schools Manager, etc.;
(3) The Divisional Officer or his representative; and
(4) The appropriate Local Government Departmental Officer, *e.g.*, for buildings a Government Works Superintendent, for an Educational contract the Provincial Education Officer, etc.

Committee Procedure. All committee meetings are held *in camera* and the public and the Press not permitted to attend. The procedure in committee is less formal than that of a Council. The

Secretary to the committees is normally the Clerk to the Native Authority Council.[12] Minutes from the committees are submitted to the Native Authority Council for approval except in those matters over which executive control has been delegated to the committee itself.

Standing Orders for the conduct of business in committees are made under requirement of the Law by the Native Authority.

The committee system is used in those Native Authorities which have large elected Councils and a considerable volume of business.

An example of a Native Authority working on the committee system is given at the end of the chapter.

The Administrative Councillor System

The Administrative Councillor system need be mentioned only briefly as it is on its way out, and very few Native Authorities operate it. This is a system whereby certain Councillors act as executives of the Native Authority, that is to say that in addition to being members of the policy-making body of the authority, they also operate and supervise departments. It was a device used in the past in areas where the paucity of educated officials has forced a combination of legislature and executive to ensure administrative efficiency.

2. NATIVE AUTHORITY COUNCIL PROCEDURE

Native Authority Councils must make Standing Orders[13] in respect of the following matters.

(1) The minimum number of members necessary to constitute a meeting of a Native Authority. That is to say, to define a quorum.

(It should be noted here, however, that a Chief-in-Council may under certain circumstances work without a quorum but with two or more members only. This has been explained under the description of such a Native Authority's constitution.[14]) Without the presence of the necessary quorum no valid decisions can be taken by the Council.

(2) The number of persons in the Native Authority Council whose presence is sufficient to validate any resolution or other act

[12] He may on occasion be a Head of Department.
[13] S. 52 (1) of the Law.
[14] p. 14 in Chap. 2.

of the Native Authority. This is known as the minimum voting majority and is a device to ensure that action is only taken on resolutions which are carried by a reasonable majority. In those Councils which boast an elected majority it is necessary to ensure a majority of elected members in favour of passing any motion.

(3) The manner in which the assent of the Native Authority is to be given to documents. In normal correspondence this is usually the signature of either the Chief or the Chief Scribe to the Native Authority.

(4) The design and custody of the Common Seal. The design of the Common Seal is decided by the Native Authority and an imprint of the Seal is put on the Standing Orders as evidence. Its custody is the responsibility of either the Chairman (the Chief) or the Clerk to the Council.

(5) Procedure at meetings of the Native Authority. Under this heading is included details of the Rules of debate; the duties of the Clerk to the Council and the method of voting.

(6) The manner in which notices are sent, giving notification of meetings and the subjects to be discussed. This deals with the preparation and publication to members of the agenda of meetings.

(7) The times of meetings and the necessary notification for them. Meetings may be divided into three categories:

(a) *Ordinary meetings* held at specified intervals, *e.g.*, weekly on Thursdays at 9.0 a.m., monthly on the first Monday of the month, etc.

(b) *Special meetings.* Called by the Chairman on an urgent matter which cannot await the next normal meeting. Only the urgent matter is discussed on such occasions and nothing else is included on the agenda.

(c) *Extraordinary meetings* called by the Chairman on behalf of the Councillors themselves after at least one-third of the latter have requested him in writing to do so. Notice for meetings will vary from place to place dependent on the ease with which members may attend and the distances from the meeting place of their homes.

Provision should be made for calling special meetings as soon as possible when they are required.

(8) Control of the public at meetings. Most Native Authorities, especially those of the large Muslim Emirates, prefer to conduct

their meetings in private. Members are more likely to speak their minds without reservation when there is no danger of their remarks becoming made public. Native Authorities also prefer to issue press releases to newspapers and radio reporters rather than allow representatives of the Press into Council meetings. Most Native Authorities have information officers whose duty it is to inform the Press and the public of the Native Authority's decisions. Should the public be admitted to Council meetings there is a further device for excluding them from any particular debate. This is achieved by converting the Council into a committee by resolution whereupon all strangers must leave as committee proceedings are held in secret.

(9) For the due, proper and orderly conduct of business. Under this heading may be provision for collective responsibility and the power of the Chairman to deal with disturbances and unruly members.

The Law also permits other Standing Orders dealing with procedure to enable decisions to be put into effect as quickly and as efficiently as possible. Normally it is the Clerk to the Council who initiates action once the minutes of the meeting have been completed and copies are sent either:

(a) In the "portfolio" type of Native Authority to the Councillor concerned for action; or

(b) In the "committee" type of Native Authority to the committee concerned through its Chairman.

All Standing Orders made by Native Authorities require the approval and countersignature of the Minister for Local Government who keeps a copy of them. In the case of Subordinate Native Authorities the approval of the Superior Native Authority is required prior to that of the Minister.

In the event of a Native Authority failing to make Standing Orders or making unsatisfactory ones, the Minister may make Orders on its behalf.[15] Caretaker or sole Native Authorities must have Standing Orders both in respect of themselves and for any Advisory Council that may be set up to assist them.

The form in which agenda are prepared varies from place to place. The following form, however, is recommended by the Ministry for Local Government:

[15] S. 52 (6) of the Law.

(1) Prayers—If these are held it is important to ensure that they are said for all religions present, and not just for the religion of the majority.

(2) Announcements—Made by the Chairman.

(3) Confirmation of the Minutes—Read out by the Secretary.

(4) Matters arising from the Minutes—Confirmation that action has been or is being taken on past decisions.

(5) Reports by Committees or Councillors—Dependent on type of Council. Committees will submit their minutes for approval.

(6) Sealing of Council Documents—Affixing Common Seal and recording details where necessary.

(7) Questions—Written or oral Questions asked by members.

(8) New Business—Motions must be proposed and seconded before debate can be opened on them.

(9) Any Other Business—These include items received after preparation of the agenda which the Chairman may allow at his discretion.

8. Subordinate Councils of a Native Authority

A Native Authority may divide up its area with the approval of the Minister for Local Government into administrative sub-areas. These areas may be controlled by sub-area heads who are paid officials of the Native Authority. The following chart shows the most common divisions:

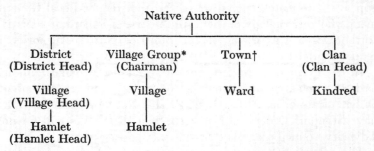

* In those areas where there is no traditional authority higher than the Village Head.
† The Chairman of a Town Council is normally the District Head of the District in which the town is situated. It may be the town headman, if such a person exists.

Councils may be established for any administrative sub-area or combination of sub-areas and if they are to be given any powers then they should be set up by Instrument. The Minister for Local Government reserves the right to dissolve any such Councils or to extend their statutory lives if he thinks fit. The form of Instrument setting up a local Subordinate Council has become formalised by Law;[16] it must provide for:

(1) The name of the Council;
(2) The functions of the Council;
(3) The composition of the Council;
(4) The Chairmanship of the Council; and
(5) The summoning and frequency of meetings of the Council.

It also contains, by custom, details of:

(1) The finance of the Council; and
(2) The provision for Standing Orders for the Council.

The Powers and Functions of a Subordinate Council

With the approval of the Minister for Local Government a Native Authority may delegate to a Subordinate Council:

(1) Any of its powers under the Native Authority Law, 1954, with the following exceptions:[17]
   (a) Its powers to limit the powers of a Subordinate Native Authority;
   (b) Its powers to make Rules under section 37 of the Law except in respect of the rates for and the general administration of the services the Subordinate Council may provide;
   (c) Its power to create administrative sub-areas;
   (d) Power to invest money;
   (e) Powers to surcharge persons if so recommended by the Auditor and to take civil action for payment;
   (f) Any powers connected with the establishment and administration of a police force.
(2) Any functions under any other legislation as may be prescribed by the Minister.[18]

---

[16] S. 58 of the Law.
[17] S. 64 of the Law.
[18] These must be published in the Regional *Gazette*.

The powers and functions of a Subordinate Council have now been formalised in model Instruments and are set out and divided into:

(1) Vested powers given to it by the Native Authority in respect of all or any of the following services:[19]

    (i) Adult literacy;

    (ii) Animal pounds;

    (iii) Baboon control;

    (iv) Buildings and structures which are declared by the Native Authority to be the responsibility of the Council;

    (v) Cattle tracks, other than trade cattle routes;

    (vi) Cemeteries;

    (vii) Commercial motor vehicle stations;

    (viii) Communal forest areas;

    (ix) Communal plantations;

    (x) Community centres;

    (xi) Control of communal labour;

    (xii) Fire services;

    (xiii) Forestry seedling nurseries;

    (xiv) Fruit-tree nurseries;

    (xv) Grazing grounds;

    (xvi) Lodging houses;

    (xvii) Markets and slaughter places;

    (xviii) Maternity welfare clinics;

    (xix) Parks, gardens, recreation centres and open spaces;

    (xx) Reading rooms and libraries;

    (xxi) Recreational facilities;

    (xxii) Roads and drains which are declared by the Native Authority to be the responsibility of the Council;

    (xxiii) Sanitary services;

    (xxiv) Settlement areas;

    (xxv) Street lighting;

    (xxvi) Village planning and improvements;

    (xxvii) Water supplies.

There are, however, the following provisos:

    (a) There must be no powers to make Rules under section 37 of the Native Authority Law other than to impose rates or to regulate these services.

---

[19] These appear in a schedule to the Instrument.

(b) These services must be administered in accordance with the general policy of the Native Authority and under the supervision of the salaried staff of the Native Authority.

(c) The services will be subject to inspection by Native Authority Councillors and Heads of Departments.

(2) Delegated powers[20] from the Native Authority.

(a) To engage temporary or daily paid staff in respect of the services it operates.

(b) To impose local rates for its services if necessary.[21]

(c) Powers of a Native Authority under sections 41 (making of Rules for markets), 47 (control of strangers) and 48 (declaration and modification of local law or custom), in the area of its jurisdiction.

(3) Advisory powers on the following matters:

(a) Appointment of Village Heads;

(b) Exercise of powers under section 120 of the Labour Code Ordinance in respect of communal labour;

(c) On setting up and closing of markets;

(d) Town and village planning; and

(e) Any other matter referred to it by the Native Authority.

In some cases Native Authorities do not delegate the powers of (2) (b) or (c) above to their Subordinate Councils and the extent of vested powers may also vary from place to place.

The Composition of the Council

It is laid down in the Law that the Council shall be composed of:

(1) Elected members who shall form a majority of the whole Council including the Chairman;

(2) Such ex officio members as the Native Authority may prescribe;

(3) Such nominated members as the Native Authority may prescribe.

[20] Delegated powers may not be further delegated by a Subordinate Council to a committee under the principle of *delegatus non potest delegare*.

[21] It should be noted that Rates may only be imposed as a result of Rules made under s. 37 (50) of the Law and that such Rules require the approval of the Governor-in-Council.

All Instruments setting up local Councils are gazetted.[22] "Model" type notices may be prepared to cover all Subordinate Councils in one Native Authority area but an individual signed copy of its Instrument must be kept by each Council.

The most common type of Subordinate Council is that of the District. The District Head is its Chairman and the *ex officio* members are the village area heads. District Councils normally meet quarterly.[23] There are forty-five Town Councils set up by the Instrument. Their form and functions are identical to those of District Councils. Only in few places, *e.g.*, Ilorin, have Village Councils been set up by Instrument and their powers and functions are in the main advisory. Village Councils exist in many places but they have never formed an effective tier in the local government pyramid although they are in theory the first tier below the District Council. The emphasis has always been placed on the District Council as the first effective tier of local administration.

The finances of Subordinate Councils vary from Native Authority to Native Authority. In most areas these are still based on District Council Funds; a form of grant based on the tax-paying population. In others, however, local revenue is collected and annual estimates are operated with the assistance of the Native Authority Treasury.[24]

Standing Orders of Subordinate Councils are made by the Councils but require the approval of the Native Authority.

4. THE OUTER COUNCIL

This is a device for keeping Native Authorities which have inadequate elected membership abreast of the current opinion and popular requirements in their areas. It is a representative and consultive body which has no executive powers or functions of its own and which does not form part of the Native Authority, although the Native Authority establishes it.[25] The Native Authority is in no way bound to accept its advice. It is set up by

[22] See Chap. 2 *ante.*
[23] Instruments provide for three types of meeting:
Ordinary, i.e., quarterly or monthly.
Extraordinary, summoned by the members themselves providing at least one-third of them apply in writing to the Chairman.
Special, summoned by the Chairman to discuss urgent matters which cannot await the next ordinary meeting.
[24] See Chap. 6 *post,* for greater detail.
[25] S. 57 of the Law.

Instrument in the same way as that of a Subordinate Council and its functions are set out as follows:

(1) (a) To examine existing or proposed Native Authority subsidiary legislation and to make recommendations regarding it;

(b) To initiate proposals for new Native Authority subsidiary legislation which the Council considers necessary or desirable;

(c) To initiate, examine and advise on plans and schemes for economic development and social welfare;

(d) To draw the attention of the Native Authority to any abuse, injustice hardship or legitimate cause of complaint within the field of local government and to make suggestions for its removal or relief;

(e) To review all aspects of local government and to make to the Native Authority such recommendation for the better conduct of affairs as shall seem necessary or desirable.

(2) The Native Authority shall not in any case be obliged to act in accordance with the advice, recommendations or such proposals of the Council and may reject or modify such of these as it may see fit.

The majority of the members of the Outer Council are elected under special electoral rules made by the Native Authority under section 37 (20) of the Law. The Emir (or Chief) and all the members of the Native Authority Council are normally *ex officio* members and there may be also certain Heads of Departments. Nominated members will cover those sections of the community not adequately represented by the elected members.

Outer Councils meet normally twice per year. The non-official members receive allowances for attending the meetings.

The Internal Organisation of the Native Authority

EXAMPLE OF A SMALL NATIVE AUTHORITY COUNCIL
ORGANISED ON THE "PORTFOLIO" SYSTEM

DIVISIONS	COUNCILLORS	DEPARTMENTS	HEAD OF DEPARTMENTS
Administration and Judicial	Emir	Central Administration	Chief Scribe
		District Administration	
		Village Administration	
		Native Courts	Chief Alkali
Natural Resources and Co-operatives	Ciroma*	Veterinary	Veterinary Supervisor
		Agriculture	Supervisor of Agriculture
		Forestry	Chief Forestry Assistant
Works Local Government Medical and Health	Wambai*	Works	Works Supervisor
		Survey	
		District Council Funds	Development Secretary
		Medical Health	Superintendent of Health
Police and Prisons	Sarkin Yaki†	Police	Chief of Police
		Prisons	Chief Warder
Education	Dan Iya*	Provincial Secondary School	School, Manager
		Senior and Junior Primary Schools	
		Adult Education	Senior Literacy Organiser
Finance	M. Adamu Kongo	Treasury	Ma'aji (Native Treasur

* Traditional Councillors.

THE INTERNAL ORGANISATION OF THE NATIVE AUTHORITY

EXAMPLE OF THE ORGANISATION OF A LARGE NATIVE AUTHORITY COUNCIL WITH MUCH WORK

COMMITTEE SYSTEM

THE EMIR-IN-COUNCIL

	General Purposes Committee	Finance Committee	Establishment Committee	Education Committee	Local Government Committee	Development Committee	Tax Advisory Committee	Water Management Committee
Council Committees								
Summary of Powers in Instruments	All N.A. Powers *except* section 65 N.A. Law; powers of other committees; Development Plan; appointments; dismissal, remuneration and discipline of those in section 36 N.A. Law, Alkalai District Heads; Estimates	Approval of AISEs and advances, excluding fixing, collecting or waiving fees and charges	Establishments powers over those in Grade E or below, except for those in section 36 N.A. Law and District, Village, Ward and Sub-Ward Heads and Alkalai	Powers in Education Law	Standing Orders; elections; section 4 of Council Instruments; disputes between Councils (other than boundaries); sub-estimates	Priorities of works; Site-boards; policy for departments noted below; co-ordination of Councils' development; Medical and Health	Section 15 (2) of Personal Tax Law, 1900	Approval† of AISEs if savings quoted
Head of Division responsible for action	Local Government Secretary (through Council Secretary and Waziri)	Native Treasurer	Administrative Secretary	Education Officer	Local Government Secretary	Development Secretary	Chief Tax Registrar	Water-works Manager
Departments Working to Committees	Judicial; Police; Prisons	Native Treasury (and all Departments)	(All Departments)	Education, Adult Education	Subordinate Councils	Agriculture; Forestry; Veterinary; Survey; Works; Co-operative; Medical; Health; Social Welfare	Tax Office	Water-works

†See Chapter 6 *post.*

COUNCILS OF NATIVE AUTHORITIES OF NORTHERN NIGERIA
AS AT JULY 1, 1962

PROVINCE	NATIVE AUTHORITY	CHAIRMAN	TRADI-TIONAL	NOMI-NATED	ELEC-TED	TOTAL
ADAMAWA	Adamawa	Lamido (Emir)	4	15	6	25
	Muri	Emir	3	7	5	15
	Numan Fed.	Chiefs of: Batta Bachama Lorguda Mbula Shelle	7	3	11	21
BAUCHI	Bauchi	Emir	4	6	6	16
	Dass	Chief	11	—	7	18
	Gombe	Emir	8	3	—	11
	Jema'are	Emir	1	3	5	9
	Katagum	Emir	2	7	4	13
	Misau	Emir	2	6	6	14
	Ningi	Caretaker	(1	4	5	10)
	Tangale-Waja Fed.	Chiefs of: Cham Dadiya Kaltungo Waja W/Tangale	6	11	10	27
BENUE	Awe	Emir	13	13	12	38
	Idoma	Chief	1	—	33	34
	Keffi	Emir	3	15	14	32
	Lafia	Emir	6	3	18	27
	Nassarawa	Emir	6	14	10	30
	Tiv	Caretaker				
	Wukari Fed.	Aku Uka	6	5	27	38
BORNU	Bedde	Emir	1	5	2	8
	Biu Fed.	Emir	2	9	—	11
	Bornu	Shehu	4	14	—	18
	Fika	Emir	1	10	4	15
ILORIN	Borgu	Emir	3	4	15	22
	Ilorin	Emir	7	9	32	48
	Lafiagi	Emir	3	20	27	50
	Pategi	Emir	7	6	22	35

†Proposed.

PROVINCE	NATIVE AUTHORITY	CHAIRMAN	TRADI-TIONAL	NOMI-NATED	ELEC-TED	TOTAL
KABBA	Bunu	Chief	10	—	12	22
	East Yagba	Chief	1	7	13	21
	Igala	Atta (Chief)	21	7	34	62
	Igbirra	Ohinoyi (Chief)	3	1	20	24
	Ijumu	Chief	4	—	20	24
	Kabba	Chief	3	9	13	25
	Kwara Fed.	Chief	6	23	24	53
	West Yagba	Chief	1	7	—	8
KANO	Gumel	Emir	2	4	—	6
	Hadejia	Emir	3	5	—	8
	Kano	Emir	5	13	5	23
	Kazaure	Emir	2	4	—	6
KATSINA	Daura	Emir	8	2	2	12
	Katsina	Emir	9	12	5	26
NIGER	Abuja	Emir	1	3	5	9
	Agaie	Emir	28	5	36	69
	Bida	Emir	1	7	12	20
	Gwari	Elected	18	4	30	52
	Kamuku	Elected	9	5	15	29
	Kontagora	Emir	1	8	5	14
	Lapai	Emir	18	2	36	56
	Wushishi	Chief	3	2	6	11
	Zuru	Chief	5	4	—	9
PLATEAU	Akwanga Fed.	Chiefs of: Nasarawa Nada Wamba	3	—	21	24
	Jos	Chief	32	1	21	54
	Kanam	Emir	6	2	9	17
	Lowland Fed.	Elected	10	—	20	30
	Pankshin Fed.	Chiefs of: Angas Ron-Kulere Sure Pyem	3	13	24	40
	Resettlement	Elected	—	11	—	11
	Wase	Emir	2	7	7	16
	Yergam	Chief	2	8	10	20

COUNCILS OF NATIVE AUTHORITIES OF NORTHERN NIGERIA—*continued*

PROVINCE	NATIVE AUTHORITY	CHAIRMAN	TRADI-TIONAL	NOMI-NATED	ELEC-TED	TOTAL
SARDAUNA	Chamba	D/Heads of: Sugu Yelwa Mbulo Toungo Jada Lendo	6	2	15	23
	Dikwa	Emir	6	3	8	17
	Gashaka/ Mambilla		2	6	12	20
	Gwoza	Chief	19	—	34	53
	Mubi	Chief	7	—	15	22
	United Hills	D/Heads of: Tigon Ndoro Kentu	3	2	25	28
SOKOTO	Argungu	Emir	3	3	2	8
	Gwandu	Emir	1	7	2	10
	Sokoto	Emir	3	12	5	20
	Yauri	Emir	1	4	2	7
ZARIA	Birnin Gwari	Chief	9	5	17	31
	Jema'a Fed.	Emir	4	8	25	37
	Zaria	Emir	3	7	6	16

INSTRUMENTS SET UP BY NATIVE AUTHORITIES OF NORTHERN NIGERIA
AS AT JULY 1, 1962

PROVINCE	NATIVE AUTHORITY	OUTER COUNCIL	DISTRICT COUNCILS	VILLAGE GROUP COUNCILS	T/COUNCILS	OTHERS
ADAMAWA	Adamawa	1	15	—	2	
	Muri	1	11	—	1	
	Numan Fed.	1	—	18	1	
BAUCHI	Bauchi	1	13	—	1	
	Dass	—	—	—	—	
	Gombe	—	5	—	1	
	Jama'are	—	—	5	—	5 Village area
	Katagum	1	9	—	1	
	Misau	1	5	—	1	
	Ningi	—	3	—	—	
	T/Waja Fed.	—	—	—	—	
BENUE	Awe	—	—	—	—	
	Idoma	—	22	—	1	
	Keffi	—	5	—	1	
	Lafia	—	4	—	1	
	Nassarawa	—	6	—	1	
	Tiv	—	16	—	1	
	Wukari Fed.	—	4	—	2	5 Village area
BORNU	Bedde	—	—	—	1	
	Biu Fed.	—	—	—	1	
	Bornu	1	21	—	3	
	Fika	—	—	6	1	
ILORIN	Borgu	—	9	—	—	
	Ilorin	—	18	—	1	240 Village/ Ward Councils
	Lafiagi	—	3	—	—	
	Pategi	—	3	—	—	
KABBA	Bunu	—	—	—	—	
	East Yagba	—	5	—	—	
	Igala	—	9	—	—	
	Igbirra	—	8	—	—	
	Ijumu	—	—	—	—	
	Kabba	—	—	—	—	
	Kwara Fed.	—	—	—	—	
	West Yagba	—	—	—	—	

INSTRUMENTS SET UP BY NATIVE AUTHORITIES OF NORTHERN NIGERIA—*continued*

PROVINCE	NATIVE AUTHORITY	OUTER COUNCIL	DISTRICT COUNCILS	VILLAGE GROUP COUNCILS	T/COUNCILS	OTHERS
KANO	Gumel	1	5	—	—	
	Hadejia	1	8	—	1	
	Kano	1	25	—	2	
	Kazaure	1	4	—	1	
KATSINA	Daura	1	5	—	1	
	Katsina	1	21	—	—	
NIGER	Abuja	1	3	—	1	
	Agaie	—	—	—	—	
	Bida	1	7	—	1	
	Gwari	—	1	4	—	
	Kamuku	—	—	—	—	
	Kontagora	1	8	—	—	
	Lapai	—	—	—	—	
	Wushishi	1	—	—	1	
	Zuru	1	—	—	1	
PLATEAU	Akwanga Federation	—	—	43	—	
	Jos	—	19	—	2	
	Kanam	—	4	—	1	
	Lowland Fed.	—	17	—	—	
	Pankshin	—	24	—	—	
	Resettlement	—	—	—	—	
	Wase	—	3	—	1	
	Yergam	—	—	—	—	
SARDAUNA	Chamba	—	7	—	—	
	Dikwa	1	7	—	—	
	Gashaka Mambilla	—	2	—	—	
	Gwoza	—	1	—	—	
	Mubi	—	7	—	1	
	United Hills	—	—	—	—	
SOKOTO	Argungu	1	6	—	1	
	Gwandu	1	15	—	2	
	Sokoto	1	47	—	2	
	Yauri	1	5	—	1	
ZARIA	Birnin Gwari	—	—	—	—	
	Jema'a Fed.	—	8	—	1	
	Zaria	1	12	—	2	
	TOTALS	24	465	77	45	250

LIST OF DISTRICTS IN NORTHERN NIGERIA

Adamawa	.	.	32	Niger	.	.	49
Bauchi	.	.	50	Plateau	.	.	68
Benue	.	.	60	Sokoto	.	.	74
Bornu	.	.	38	Sardauna	.	.	25
Ilorin	.	.	28	Zaria	.	.	25
Kabba	.	.	37				—
Kano	.	.	40	TOTAL	.	552
Katsina	.	.	26				—

PROVINCE	NATIVE AUTHORITY	NUMBER OF DISTRICTS	
ADAMAWA	Adamawa	16	
	Muri	11	32
	Numan	5	
BAUCHI	Bauchi/Dass	15	
	Gombe	6	
	Jama'are	5	
	Katagum	11	50
	Misau	5	
	Ningi	3	
	T/Waja	5	
BENUE	Idoma	22	
	Keffi	6	
	Lafia	5	
	Nasarawa	6	60
	Tiv	17	
	Wukari	3	
	Awe	1	
BORNU	Bedde	3	
	Biu	7	
	Bornu	22	38
	Fika	6	
ILORIN	Borgu	9	
	Ilorin	13	
	Lafiagi	3	28
	Pategi	3	
KABBA	Igala	20	
	Igbirra	8	
	Kwara	6	
	Kabba	3	37
	East & West Yagba	—	
	Basa Komo		
	Bunu, Ijumu		

71

LIST OF DISTRICTS IN NORTHERN NIGERIA—*continued*

PROVINCE	NATIVE AUTHORITY	NUMBER OF DISTRICTS	
KANO	Gumel	4	
	Hadejia	7	
	Kano	25	40
	Kazaure	4	
KATSINA	Daura	5	
	Katsina	21	26
NIGER	Abuja	4	
	Agaie	—	
	Bida	8	
	Gwari	18	
	Kamuku	6	49
	Kontagora	8	
	Lapai	—	
	Zuru	5	
	Wushishi		
PLATEAU	Akwanga	3	
	Jos	19	
	Kanam	4	
	Lowland Federation	10	68
	Pankshin	25	
	Wase	3	
	Yergam	4	
SOKOTO	Argungu	7	
	Gwandu	15	
	Sokoto	47	74
	Yauri	5	
SARDAUNA	Chamba	7	
	Dikwa	6	
	Gashaka/Mambilla	2	
	Gwoza	—	25
	Mubi	7	
	United Hills	3	
ZARIA	Jama'a	9	25
	Zaria	16	

CHAPTER 4

JOINT SERVICES BETWEEN NATIVE AUTHORITIES

IN some of the smaller Native Authorities difficulty is experienced in finding funds to cover the recurrent expenditure needed for the more important services such as a police force; a treasury; public works; education; etc. Failure to operate such services would necessitate action by the Central Government either to take over the services itself or to amalgamate smaller Native Authorities to produce an economically viable unit of local government. To avoid such drastic steps being taken against them such Native Authorities may form Joint Committees with their neighbours to run specific services as joint enterprises. This has the advantage of allowing the Native Authorities concerned to remain independant in all other matters. A Joint Committee may also be set up to deal with a problem common to two or more Native Authorities which may be dealt with (more advantageously) under one authority.

The Native Authority Law provides for Joint Committees to be set up with the approval of the Ministry for Local Government by the Native Authorities concerned. A committee is set up by Instrument jointly and severally by the Native Authorities involved and the Instrument is published in the *Gazette*.[1] The persons appointed to the committee and the manner and conditions of their appointment are agreed upon jointly by the participating authorities. Provided that at least one-third of the members of the committee are members of the Native Authorities concerned the remainder of the members need not be members of the authorities. The committee Instrument itself is constant in form and contains provision for:

(1) The membership and term of office of the members of the committee and the number of members appointed by each Native Authority.

(2) Eligibility of members for re-appointment. (The approval of the Provincial Commissioner to these appointments is sometimes required.)

[1] S. 68 of the Law.

(3) The appointment of a Chairman. This is not mentioned in all cases. It may be:

   (a) The Provincial Commissioner or his representative, or

   (b) A person nominated by the Provincial Commissioner, or

   (c) A person appointed by the committee from amongst its members.

(4) Removal of members by Native Authorities from the committee. This is normally with the approval of the Provincial Commissioner.

(5) The remuneration payable to members of the committee recommended jointly by the Native Authorities concerned and approved by the Minister for Local Government.[2]

(6) The functions of and services provided by the committee. Once a service is operated by a Joint Committee the individual Native Authorities have no right to interfere with it in any way or to assume the powers delegated to the committee. The powers of a Joint Committee may include:

   (a) Power to engage and dismiss employees;

   (b) Power to enter into contracts;

   (c) Power to fix, collect or waive fees;

   (d) Power to acquire or depose of property;

   (e) All or any of the functions of Native Authority in connection with the prevention of crime and maintenance of law and order;

   (f) The power to request natives of the area to appear before the committee, a government officer or before a Native Court in connection with the duties imposed upon it (see sections 103 and 104 of the Native Authority Law); and

   (g) Powers of a Native Authority with regard to police forces or prisons if these are the services to be operated.

[2] S. 69 (2) of the Law.

(7) The provision of Standing Orders for the committee. These are subject to the approval of the Native Authorities jointly.[3]

Joint Committees are set up as corporate bodies. As such they enjoy perpetual succession the right to sue (and to be sued) and hold a Common Seal in the same way as a Native Authority itself.

A Native Authority which has delegated any of its powers to a Joint Committee may not revoke its delegation without first of all obtaining the consent of the Minister for Local Government. The Minister may at any time, however, direct that a function held by a Joint Committee is returned to a Native Authority or that a Joint Committee be completely dissolved. Such a change would not normally take place until the end of the financial year.[4]

There are eight Joint Committees in operation at present in Northern Nigeria. The following table gives details:

[3] Prior to 1960 these Standing Orders were subject to the approval of the Provincial Commissioner.
[4] S. 74 (1) of the Law.

PROVINCE	NATIVE AUTHORITIES	SERVICES	MEMBERSHIP	REMARKS
ILORIN	Lafiagi Pategi	Police Force	8 members	1 year term of office Set up under NRLN 250/5
KABBA (1)	Bunu Ijumu Kabba (B.I.K.)	Native Treasury Prison Public Works Medical and Health Veterinary Forestry Agriculture	10 members	3 year term of office Set up under NRLN 97/5
KABBA (2)	East Yagba West Yagba	As for B.I.K.	6 members	3 year term of office Set up under NRLN 509/5 and 17/59
KABBA (3)	Bunu Ijumu Kabba East Yagba West Yagba	Primary Education	6 members	3 year term of office Set up under NRLN 176/5
KABBA (4)	Igala Igbirra Kabba Kwara East Yagba West Yagba Bunu Ijumu	Provincial Secondary School, Junior Secondary School, Dekina	Chairman and 8 members	2 year term of office Set up under 154/61
BAUCHI (1)	Jama'are Katagum Misau	Veterinary Services	6 members	2 year term of office Set up under NRLN 347/5 and 463/57
BAUCHI (2)	Gombe Tangle- Waja	Veterinary Services	5 members	2 year term of office Set up under NRLN 112/6
NIGER	Kontagora Wushishi	Native Treasury Police Force	10 members	3 year term of office Set up under NRLN 197/5

CHAPTER 5

THE SERVICES PROVIDED BY NATIVE AUTHORITIES

THE services provided by the Native Authority to the community that it serves may be divided into three main types—protective services, welfare services and services of convenience. The first group of protective services include police forces, the provision of justice through the Native Courts and fire-fighting units (limited at the moment to the urban areas). The welfare services divide themselves into two main groups, (a) personal welfare services, and (b) services which deal with the environment of the community. Convenience services for the community include such things as the provision of roads, ferries, markets, urban and rural water supplies. It may be argued that the provision of a safe water supply is a protective service or even a personal welfare service. The following diagram shows the various services divided under the headings mentioned above for the sake of convenience and the reader will undoubtedly note several marginal services which might be included under more than one heading as, for example, in the case of water supplies. This duplication has not been shown because duplication might give the impression of more services being supplied than in fact occurs. Even so the diagram shows clearly the many ways in which the Native Authority of Northern Nigeria serves its community and how varied are the services that if offers.

1. EDUCATION AND PUBLIC ENLIGHTENMENT

Native Authorities are responsible for 39 per cent approximately of all primary education in the Region, the remaining 61 per cent being operated by voluntary agencies. To date only a fraction of the child population has been reached in many areas, although Kano Native Authority has begun a scheme for universal primary education in its area.[1] All Native Authorities are anxious, however, to improve existing education facilities and they are encouraged to do so by the Regional Government by:

---

[1] In 1960 it was estimated that 11 per cent of children of the age group 6–13 years were receiving primary education.

THE SERVICES PROVIDED BY NATIVE AUTHORITIES

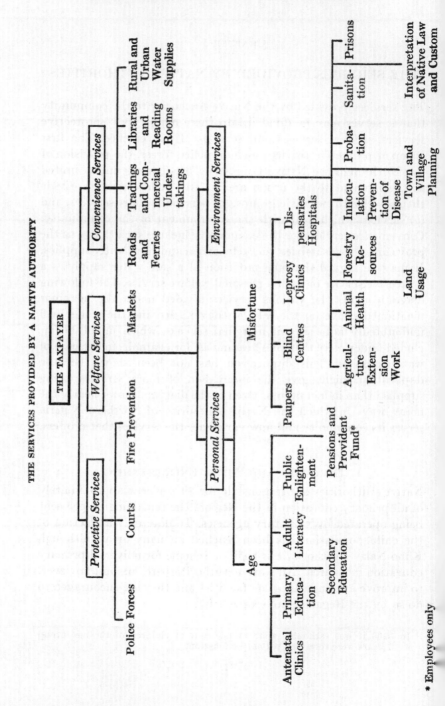

(1) Reimbursement of salaries of trained teaching staff;

(2) Grants per pupil for maintenance of schools; and

(3) Capital grants for the erection of school buildings and non-expendable equipment.

The details of the recurrent grants payable under (1) and (2) above are given in Schedule "A" to the Education Law, 1956.[2]

Capital grants payable are 50 per cent of the total expenditure up to a maximum of £350 per classroom on a new school or an extension to existing schools. The site and buildings must be approved by the Provincial Education Officer who is the local representative of the Ministry of Education.

When a Native Authority wishes to open a new school application must be made to do so through the Divisional Officer and the Local Education Committee to the Provincial Education Officer. Final approval is given by the Chief Inspector of Education[3] who requires assurance that staff and funds are available for the new project. A pilot school may be set up in a temporary building initially, but to attract a capital grant must be built in permanent materials within four years. Primary education over seven teaching years is divided into Junior Primary four years, and for Senior Primary three years. Both sexes are recruited for primary education on the basis of two-thirds boys and one-third girls per class. In many areas it is still necessary to force parents to send and maintain their children at school, and fifty Native Authorities enforce School Attendance Rules under section 37 of the Native Authority Law to enable their local representatives (normally District Heads) to recruit and keep children at school. All Junior Primary schools in the Region[4] are now day schools, children being fed by relatives or parents. In some areas still, however, children live and are fed and housed in the village in which the school is situated by temporary guardians during the term periods. Children are taught in their vernacular for the first year; thereafter the medium of instruction is English;[5] the sexes are segregated in Senior Primary education, in some cases the girls are taught at Provincial level.

[2] No. 17 of 1956. A new Law is, however, being drafted.
[3] S. 16 of the Education Law, 1956.
[4] There are no Junior Primary Schools run by Native Authorities which now have boarding facilities although in the past this was a common practice.
[5] There are in 1962 3,072 Junior Primary Classes under N.A. supervision

There are fifty Secondary schools in the Region[6] of which eighteen are run by the Native Authorities.

Provincial Secondary schools are maintained jointly by the Native Authorities who use them and by the Ministry of Education. The staff is also a joint responsibility.

No fees are payable by parents for Junior Primary education except in these areas where there is a definite desire by parents to send their children to school. Fees payable to Senior Primary and Secondary education vary from one authority to another.[7] The Native Authority controls and inspects its schools through a School's Manager and by visiting teachers.

Public Enlightenment, previously known as Adult Education, is the responsibility of the Ministry of Information. All Native Authorities operate schemes for adult literacy and maintain reading rooms and radios. The more wealthy are able to operate mobile cinemas and even newspapers employing a large staff of information officers and artisans.

Adult Literacy

In most areas the District Council is responsible for the adult literacy schemes in its area, supervision and co-ordination by the Native Authority being exercised by a Senior Literacy Organiser. Each District runs one or more "schemes", each scheme being comprised of twenty to thirty literacy classes and being supervised by an organiser. It is the duty of an organiser to visit each class at least once per month and a report on it is submitted to the Chairman of the District or equivalent Council.

Classes are of six months' duration and meet in the evenings, two or three times per week. There are two classes (sessions) per annum. They consist of up to twenty-five students of ages ranging from 15 to 35 years. Teaching is in the vernacular by part-time instructors who are paid allowances. These vary from 8s. 6d. per month to 25s. as the Native Authority considers fit. The Government assists Native Authorities by a grant of £3 per class per session (*i.e.*, £6 per class per annum) in respect of any class which obtains more than seven literacy certificates in a session. In

[6] As at July 1, 1962.
[7] Figures available in the latest report give the following rates for schools' fees: (*a*) Junior Primary varying from nil to £1 per annum; (*b*) Senior Primary varying from 10s. to £3 per annum; (*c*) Secondary Schools varying from £3 to £36 per annum with a personal maximum of £108.

addition there is an annual grant of £50 per trained organiser, provided the scheme which he is administering is considered efficient by the Ministry's representative.

Women's literacy classes are held with women instructors. In the Muslim Emirates, where the women are in purdah, these have to be conducted in compounds in the privacy of the women's quarters. In addition to literacy the women are taught simple hygiene and child welfare.

An important adjunct to adult literacy is the provision of reading material for literates. Some Native Authorities publish their own news sheets, *e.g.*, *"Sodanji"* by Kano Native Authority, and others subsidise book shops. All, however, erect and maintain reading rooms, where newspapers, periodicals and a small selection of books can be read free of charge. Most reading rooms also have radios where programmes in the vernaculars of the Region can be heard in the evenings.

An important aspect of public enlightenment is the mobile cinema. There is a regional service of mobile cinemas run by the Ministry of Information, but in addition to this the more wealthy Native Authorities operate their own cinemas and in some cases make their own propaganda films.

2. MEDICAL AND HEALTH SERVICES

Native Authorities operate the following medical services:

(1) Hospitals;
(2) Dispensaries;
(3) Antenatal and Child Welfare Clinics;
(4) Ambulance services;
(5) Treatment of endemic diseases.

Only two Native Authorities now operate their own General Hospitals. All junior- and middle-grade employees are employed by them but the doctors, nursing sisters and a nucleus of senior nurses are provided by the Ministry of Health. Recurrent costs for the financial year 1962–63 are as follows:

	Personal Emoluments	Cost of Maintenance
Kano Native Authority	£60,000	£101,000
Sokoto Native Authority	£19,000	£17,000

Twenty-five per cent of the cost of salaries of trained hospital staff is reimbursed by the Regional Government. Other Native Authorities who previously ran their own hospitals, *e.g.*, Katsina, Ilorin Bornu, still show hospital staff under Head XIII A Medical of their estimates. These are staff who have remained as staff of the Native Authority despite the fact that the hospital as a whole is staffed and run by the Ministry of Health.

All Native Authorities maintain dispensaries; the recommended coverage is one dispensary per 15,000 head of population.[8] The Ministry of Health awards a capital grant of 50 per cent of the cost of erecting a dispensary to an approved plan and this may also include erection of a "model" compound for the dispensary attendant. Dispensaries also attract a grant of £100 per year towards maintenance expenses provided that they conform to standards laid down by the Ministry of Health and that they are operated by properly qualified staff.

Dispensary attendants are trained by the Ministry of Health in Kaduna. Treatment in Native Authority dispensaries is free to all.

Midwives are also trained by the Ministry. Deliveries are conducted in the homes of the mothers but difficult labours are sometimes treated at welfare centres if no hospital is nearby. Health centres and welfare clinics attract a grant of 50 per cent of capital cost in some way as do dispensaries. Child health and maternity care is supervised on a Provincial basis by the Senior Health Sister of the Province.

Leprosy clinics are held for non-infectious cases in rural areas, normally on market days. Native Authorities receive assistance from UNICEF to operate these clinics. Infectious cases are segregated in "leper settlements" controlled either by the Native Authorities or by voluntary agencies who provide housing, water supplies and other amenities for those living therein.

Control of other endemic diseases such as yaws, malaria and sleeping sickness is organised partly by the Ministry of Health and partly by Native Authorities. Assistance is given by UNICEF for specific schemes.

---

[8] There may be either fee-paying dispensaries provided by voluntary agencies or non-fee-paying (Government assisted) Native Authority dispensaries.

Health Services

These services include:

(1) Inspection of general sanitation and sanitary measures;
(2) Vaccination;
(3) Prevention of cerebro-spinal meningitis and other epidemic diseases;
(4) Food inspection;
(5) Registration of births and deaths;
(6) Conservancy;
(7) Anti-malaria control.

Health staff are trained by the Ministry of Health at the school of Hygiene, Kano. The salaries of trained health staff are 50 per cent reimbursable by Government.

3. PUBLIC WORKS

Native Authorities provide public works services in varying degrees according to their wealth and responsibilities. Most Native Authorities operate a works yard which provides artisans for the purpose of all or any of the following services:

(1) Operating and maintaining Native Authority transport;
(2) Maintaining Native Authority buildings;
(3) Construction of buildings;
(4) Maintenance of Native Authority roads and bridges;
(5) Maintenance of public utilities, *i.e.*, street lighting, urban water supplies, etc.;
(6) Extension of rural water supplies, *i.e.*, dams, wells, etc.;
(7) Works on behalf of the Central Government.

The equipment and staff available for these services and the standards maintained vary considerably. For example, Kano Native Authority employs some eighty artisans in its works department, whilst Kamuku Native Authority employs only two.

Until 1960 Native Authorities operated services extensively on behalf of the Central Government and operated advance accounts on its behalf. This proved too great a strain on working capital, however, and funds must now be made available prior to work being put in hand on behalf of Government. One of the important services rendered by Native Authorities to the Regional Ministry of Works is that of maintaining trunk roads as a joint responsibility. In addition to Federal and Regional trunk roads the Native Authority is responsible for maintaining all unclassified roads in its area.

The standards of artisans working with Native Authorities are not fixed and are still, generally speaking, low. Supervisors of Works train their own apprentices and all too few of these obtain the technical training they require in a proper institution. Trade testing by the Regional Government is carried out, however, as far as staff permits and the senior artisan grades can only be filled by persons who have passed the necessary requirements set by these tests. Craft schools run by the Ministry of Education help to provide trade-tested carpenters, blacksmiths and bricklayers.

Survey

Not all Native Authorities can afford to maintain a survey section. Those that can do so employ trained survey assistants, chainmen, etc., for such work as laying out of sites, plotting extensions to urban areas, land settlement, demarcating boundaries and in preparing drawings, plans, etc. They are trained by the Ministry of Land and Survey.

4. THE NATIVE COURTS

The law governing the setting up and operation of Native Courts is the Native Courts Law, 1956, as amended. Native Authorities do not set up their own judiciary but maintain and administer Native Courts set up in their areas.

Emirs and Chiefs by tradition have their own courts but the memberships of these courts is not decided by them. They are appointed as Presidents of such courts by the Governor.[9] He does so, however, only after consultation with the Judicial Service Commission. The membership of these courts is approved by the Provincial Commissioner.

Native Courts are established by law, by the Provincial Commissioner of the Province concerned and are subject to confirmation by the Minister of Justice. It is the practice for the Provincial Commissioner to obtain agreement in principle from the Ministry

[9] S. 3 of the Native Courts Law.

before submitting Court Warrants for confirmation. In most Native Authorities there is a Native Court of first instance in each District.

Native Courts may be of two types:

(1) An *Alkali* sitting by himself, or with assessors where necessary; or
(2) A President and members, of which there must be a specified quorum in order to hear cases, and with additional assessors, where necessary.

Every Native Court has a registrar or scribe whose special duties are to:

(1) Prepare all warrants and writs;
(2) Record all the proceedings of the court not recorded either by the President or members;
(3) Register all orders and judgments of the court; and
(4) Account to the Native Treasury for all moneys received or paid out by the Native Court.

In courts administering Muslim law *Mufti's* or assistants may be appointed to assist the *Alkali*.

Native Courts normally also have messengers to execute writs and other processes issued by them.

The appointments of *Alkali*, registrars and scribes are made by the Native Authority but must be approved by the Provincial Commissioner of the Province. In the case of Native Courts other than that of an *Alkali* the Provincial Commissioner himself makes the appointment including that of the President. The appointment of Native Court members and *Alkali* is subject to the confirmation of the Judicial Service Commission. In practice this means that the *Alkali* or member is appointed subject to confirmation by the Commission if he proves satisfactory in his duty up to and for a period of six months. *Alkali* and court members may also be dismissed by the Provincial Commissioner if necessary with the confirmation of the Judicial Service Commission.

The salaries and remunerations of court members are laid down by the Native Authority concerned bearing in mind the advice as to salary scales given by the Ministry for Local Government and by the Ministry of Justice. This is subject to scrutiny by the Provincial Commissioner.[10]

[10] S. 7 of the Native Courts Law.

There are five grades of Native Courts: "A", "A" limited, B, C and D. Their powers are laid down in a schedule to the Native Courts Law reproduced below.

The gradings and powers of courts may be altered by order by the Governor-in-Council. Only courts properly set up by warrant may try any case criminal or civil. The Law to be administered by Native Courts consists of:

(1) In criminal cases (a) the Penal Code, 1959, under the Criminal Procedure Code, 1960, and any subsidiary legislation made thereunder; (b) Any other written law which the court is authorised to enforce by any order made by the Governor-in-Council; (c) All Rules and Orders made under the Native Authority Law or any which the Native Authority is empowered to make under any other Law.

(2) In civil cases (a) the native law and custom prevailing in the area and binding between the parties provided it does not conflict with any written law or is repugnant to natural justice, equity and good conscience; (b) the provisions of any written law which the court is authorised to enforce by an order made by the Governor-in-Council; (c) the provisions of all Rules and Orders made under the Native Authority Law or which the Native Authority is empowered to make under any other law.

There are also specific directions for the hearing of mixed civil cases and for the guardianship of children (sections 21 and 23 of the Native Courts Law).

Proceedings in Native Courts are open to the public except in cases:

(1) Where the administration of justice would be rendered impracticable, in the opinion of the court, by the presence of the public; and

(2) In which persons under the age of 17 years are involved.

Legal practitioners may not appear to act for, or assist any party in a Native Court.

The line of appeal from Native Courts of the first instance is shown in the following diagram:

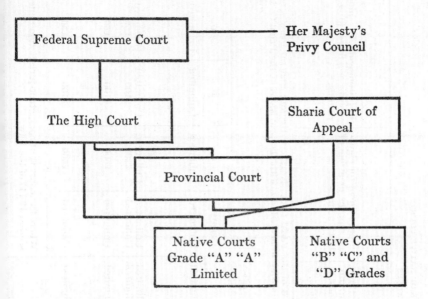

Powers of Transfer and Review

Provincial Commissioners and Divisional Officers have the power to stay the hearing of any case before a Native Court at any stage of the proceedings.[11] They may then:

(1) Transfer the case to another Native Court; or

(2) Transfer the case to a Magistrates Court or District Court;[12] or

(3) Report the case to the High Court for possible transfer thereto.

Grade "A"; "A" Limited or "B" Native Courts have the power to:

(1) Remit cases before them to a lower grade Native Court which has competent jurisdiction in the matter; and

(2) Transfer cases from lower grade courts within the area of their jurisdiction to be heard by themselves if it appears that the matter in hand is beyond the jurisdiction of the lower court.

[11] S. 32 of the Native Courts Law. There are, however, provisos to this statement and it is necessary to read the section in detail.
[12] A District Court is that of a magistrate hearing civil suits.

LIMITS OF JURISDICTION OF GRADES OF NATIVE COURTS

PART 1—CRIMINAL CAUSES

A	A LIMITED	B	C	D
Unlimited, but no sentence of death to be carried out until it has been confirmed by the Governor. (See section 31 of the Law.)	Limited only by absence of jurisdiction in homicide cases; otherwise unlimited.	Imprisonment for three years or a fine of one hundred and fifty pounds.	Imprisonment for eighteen months or a fine of thirty pounds.	Imprisonment for nine months or a fine of fifteen pounds.

Courts of all grades have power subject to the provisions of section 3 of the Penal Code (Northern Region) Federal Provisions Ordinance, 1960, to award a sentence of caning and of symbolic or Haddi lashing in accordance with the provisions of the Penal Code and the Criminal Procedure Code. (Amended by Law No. 10 of 1960.)

PART 2—CIVIL CAUSES

TYPES OF CAUSES	A	A LIMITED	B	C	D
(1) Matrimonial causes and matters between persons married under native law and custom or arising from or connected by native law and custom other than those arising from or connected with a Christian marriage as defined in section 1 of the Criminal Code. (Chapter 42.)	Unlimited	Unlimited	Unlimited	Unlimited	Unlimited
(2) Suits relating to the custody of children under native and custom.	Unlimited	Unlimited	Unlimited	Unlimited	Unlimited
(3) Civil actions in which the debt, demand or damages do not exceed the amounts specified in the respective columns hereof.	Unlimited	Unlimited	£200	£100	£50
(4) Causes and matters relating to the succession to property and the administration of estates under native law and custom where the value of the property does not exceed the amounts specified in the respective columns hereof.	Unlimited	Unlimited	£500	£100	£50
(5) Causes and matters concerning the ownership, possession or occupation of land in which the value of the subject matter does not exceed the amounts specified in the respective columns hereof.	Unlimited	Unlimited	£500	£100	£50

Where the court is of competent jurisdiction under section 19 (4) of the Law.

Native Courts must submit six-monthly reports of all cases heard before them together with details of judgments given to the Commissioner of Native Courts through the Divisional Officer.

The Divisional Officer is also empowered to request copies of Native Court proceedings at any time and he may also examine Native Court records.

A Provincial Commissioner may review any proceedings, either criminal or civil, of *any* Native Court in his Province.

A Divisional Officer may review proceedings of Grade "C" and "D" Courts only on his Division.

A Native Courts Advisor[13] also has access to all Native Courts' records and may review "C" and "D" Grade Courts not already reviewed by either the Provincial Commissioner or the Divisional Officer.

In reviewing a case the reviewing officer may:

(1) In the case of a Grade "C" or "D" Court:

   (a) Reverse, amend or vary the decision of the court; and

   (b) Make such order or pass such sentence as necessary;[14] or

   (c) Transfer the case to another court.

(2) In the case of a Grade "A", "A" Limited or "B" Court the Provincial Commissioner may:

   (a) Order a retrial, or

   (b) Transfer the case at any stage to another court but not set aside or amend the proceedings of the court.

5. THE DEVELOPMENT OF TRADE AND INDUSTRY

Native Authorities are permitted by law to engage in trade or industry provided that they obtain the prior approval of the Minister of Trade and Industry (to whom the Minister for Local Government has delegated his power under the Native Authority Law).[15] They may do so with the provisos that (a) the commercial venture engaged in furthers the development and welfare of the

---

[13] Set up under s. 53 of the Law by the Minister of Justice to check the proceedings of Native Courts and to assist the Commissioner for Native Courts.

[14] Within the powers of the Native Court concerned.

[15] S. 31 of the Law.

area of their jurisdiction and (b) that the venture satisfies a public need which cannot otherwise be met by private enterprise.

A Native Authority is in no way intended to set up in commerce in direct competition with private enterprise.

Examples of such commercial undertakings are:

(1) Public utilities such as piped water supplies and street lighting.
(2) Purchase of scrap metal in bulk for resale to blacksmiths.
(3) Printing presses.
(4) Sale of corn to control inflation.
(5) Motor parks.
(6) Sale of dairy produce.
(7) Mechanical ploughing on payment by small-holding farmers.
(8) Ferry services.
(9) Wood workshops producing furniture, etc., for resale.
(10) Weaving and hand-loom cloth manufacture.
(11) Manufacture of saddlery.

The Native Authority is also conerned with the encouragement of local trade and is empowered by law to control the markets within the area of its jurisdiction.[16] It is given the power to open or close local markets, to provide amenities and staff, and to charge rents and stallages in all those markets within its area. Control of existing markets is often delegated to the Subordinate Councils of the Native Authority. Rules for operating markets may be made by a Native Authority with the covering approval of the Ministry of Trade and Industry to provide for such matters as:

(1) The payment of market fees.
(2) Fixing of days and times on which markets are to be opened. Fridays and Sundays are probably the most popular days by tradition for markets, whilst in Nupe and Yoruba areas night markets opening at sunset and closing before midnight are not uncommon.
(3) Prescribing weights, scales and measures to be used in the sale of any produce.
(4) The examination of produce or articles of food.
(5) Fixing maximum prices for retail sales of any article of food.

[16] Ss. 32–35 of the Law.

90

(6) Controlling the sale of native liquor.

(7) Generally regulating use of the market and its approaches, *e.g.*, preventing the riding of bicycles in the market area.

A market is defined in the Native Authority Law as "a concourse of buyers and sellers having stalls or occupying places exceeding twenty in number". The Law is quite specific on the subject of market control. Only the Native Authority may establish markets unless special permission is obtained from the Minister for Local Government. To set up an illegal market renders the person or persons responsible liable on conviction to a fine of up to £50 or to three months' imprisonment (or both) with an additional £5 fine for every day that the market continues to operate after such a conviction. Persons using such a market, moreover, after it has been ordered to be closed are also liable to a fine of £1.

6. NATIVE AUTHORITY POLICE FORCES

Native Authority police forces, of which there are sixty-one, come under the overall control of the Minister of Internal Affairs. They are set up under section 115 of the Native Authority Law with the approval of the Ministry and their general duties are laid down in the Native Authority Police Rules. The power to limit the number of persons comprising a force is delegated to Provincial Commissioners[17] who may also dismiss or suspend all or any of the members of a force.[18]

There is an Assistant Commissioner of the Nigeria Police whose special function it is to inspect, grade and advise on Native Authority police forces. Forces are graded as A, B, C and Rural Constabulary and the grading of each force is in accordance with its size and efficiency.

The following are the gradings of forces in operation in Northern Nigeria on July 1, 1962:

Grade A	11 forces
Grade B	13 forces
Grade C	24 forces
Rural Constabulary	13 forces

There are two types of grants payable by the Central Government to Native Authorities in respect of their police forces:

[17] S. 116 of the Law; the vested power lies with the Minister.
[18] Not enforced in practice without consultation with the Minister.

(1) *Efficiency Grant.* In respect of every Native Authority policeman who has satisfactorily passed a course at the Kaduna Police College as at April 1 of the financial year concerned. The grant varies with the grading of the force—Grade A=£110–120; Grade B=£90–100; Grade C=£70–80 and Rural Constabulary=£50–60 per man. The grant is claimed from the Commissioner of Police, Kaduna, as soon as possible after the beginning of the new financial year.

(2) *Proficiency Grant.* Claim for the calendar year from the Commissioner of Police, Kaduna, and prepared as soon as possible after December 31. It is 100 per cent reimbursement on Good Conduct Pay, Language Allowances, etc., as laid down in the Native Authority Police Rules.

Inspection of police forces is normally carried out by the Superior Police Officer in charge of the Province. The Law also provides for a Superior Police Officer[19] of the Nigeria Police to be deputed to advise a Native Authority on its force in respect of its composition, discipline, training, efficiency and employment.[20]

This means that the deputed officer is adviser to the force and he reports on its efficiency and value to the Commissioner of Police from time to time. He may be given full operational control of the force if the Native Authority so wishes and approval is given by the Commissioner and the Minister.

Native Authority police are trained and organised in the same way as Nigeria Police except that they do not carry or are trained in the use of arms. They are, however, trained in riot drill and may use tear gas smoke to disperse crowds if necessary. The Chief of Police is appointed by the Native Authority only on the approval of the Premier. Several Native Authority forces are organised to include traffic and criminal investigation sections. To obtain promotion or to qualify for inclusion in a grant, every constable must have passed a six-month course of training at the Nigeria Police College in Kaduna.[21] Almost all Native Authorities now insist on literacy as a qualification in recruitment.

On appointment every recruit of a Native Authority police force must by law[22] make and sign a declaration in the following form:

[19] As defined in the Police Ordinance (Chap. 127 of the Law of Nigeria).
[20] S. 124 of the Law.
[21] A separate Native Authority Police Wing of the Nigeria Police College is to be opened shortly.
[22] S. 117 of the Law.

"I .... do solemnly and sincerely declare that I will obey all lawful orders of the (Chief whom I serve and[23] the) Officers of the force placed over me and subject myself to all Ordinances, Laws and Rules relating to the force now in operation or which may hereafter from time to time be in operation."

The Native Authority may give a general authority to its full force or to certain ranks of that force to operate its powers under section 30 of the Native Authority Law in connection with the prevention of crime. If it does so copies of the authority have to be sent to:

(1) The Provincial Commissioner;
(2) The Minister of Internal Affairs;
(3) The Commissioner of Police, Northern Region.

Native Authority Police Rules

Native Authority Police are recruited by a selection committee of not less than three persons of whom one must be the Chief of Police.

Recruits must be:

(1) Certified as physically fit by a Medical Officer;
(2) Between the ages of 18 and 30 years;
(3) Not less than 5 ft. 6 in. in height and possess an expanded chest measurement of 36 in.;
(4) Be literate in Hausa or some language approved by the Native Authority.

Police are engaged for six years in the first instance, thereafter for three year re-engagements up to eighteen years. After eighteen years service re-engagement is annually.

Police are required once recruited:

(1) Not to take part in any other trade or calling;
(2) To serve and reside wherever they may be directed by the Native Authority;
(3) To carry out their duties without fear or favour and with strict impartiality and courtesy towards the public;
(4) To appear in uniform at all times when on duty unless specially employed on plain clothes duty;

[23] In the case of forces under a first class Chief only.

(5) To refrain from any political association as laid down in the Native Authority Police Forces (Membership of Political Associations) Rules, 1958.

The Native Authority Police Rules list misdemeanours of members of the forces as:

(1) Offences which include such items as failure to attempt to suppress a riot, desertion, striking a superior officer, failing to report mutiny or sedition and giving false information. For any such offence he is liable on conviction to imprisonment up to six months.

(2) Offences against discipline. Forty-one examples of such offences are enumerated in the Rules and include such items as absence from parades, untidiness, drunkenness, insubordination, malingering, etc. The Native Authority may delegate to a committee or the Chief of Police the right to deal with such offences for which the punishments are:

(a) for non-commissioned officers and above (normally dealt with by the Native Authority itself)
  (i) Dismissal;
  (ii) Reduction in rank or grade;
  (iii) Stoppage of an increment;
  (iv) A fine not exceeding thirty shillings;
  (v) Reprimand;

(b) for other police officers
  (i) As in (i) and (ii) above;
  (ii) Imprisonment up to one hundred and sixty-eight hours (seven days);
  (iii) A fine not exceeding ten shillings;
  (iv) Confinement to barracks up to fourteen days;
  (v) A reprimand.

Police officers under the grade of lance-corporal who have (a) served for at least three years, and (b) have not been awarded a major punishment may be awarded a first good conduct badge. Thereafter further good conduct badges may be awarded at three-yearly intervals provided the officer's record remains clean. Each good conduct badge entitles the owner to 2s. 6d. per month per badge. Promotion is on merit and normally three years service in

94

the lower grade must be completed before promotion to a higher one. The Native Authority may also award an officer a certificate of commendation in respect of any outstanding service to the force.

7. NATIVE AUTHORITY PRISONS

A Native Authority with the approval of the Minister of Internal Affairs may declare by Order that any building or collection of buildings is to be:

(1) A prison[24] or
(2) A lock-up.[25]

The law stipulates that a prison may house

(1) Persons awaiting trial before or convicted by a Native Court.
(2) Persons arrested without a warrant and awaiting appearance before a Magistrates Court or a Native Court.
(3) Persons committed into custody by a magistrate, a Provincial Judge or the Supreme Court.[26]

On the other hand a prisoner may not be detained in a lock-up for more than fourteen days either awaiting trial or awaiting removal to a prison to complete sentence or when sentenced to not more than that length of sentence.

Control of Prisons. Advice to Native Authorities in the Region on their prison administration is through the Assistant Director of Prisons, Kaduna, as the Regional representative of the Federal Prisons Service of Nigeria.

The detailed inspection of a Native Authority prison devolves in the Councillor or the committee with the responsibility for prisons within the Native Authority and monthly statistical reports are submitted by the Native Authority to the Assistant Director countersigned by the Divisional Officer. The latter or his representative will normally accompany the Native Authority representatives on a weekly inspection of each prison and its inmates.

The following are *ex officio* Prison Visitors and may inspect a Native Authority prison or lock-up at any time:

(1) The Chief Justice;

[24] S. 129 of the Law.
[25] S. 132 of the Law.
[26] S. 131 of the Law.

(2) Members of the Executive Council;

(3) Judges of the High Court;

(4) The Commissioner of Police;

(5) Any Principal Medical Officer;

(6) The Senior Officer of the Q.O.N.R. in the Region or a field officer nominated by him;

(7) A magistrate within the Magisterial District concerned appointed by the Minister;

(8) Not less than five other persons within the Province selected by the Provincial Commissioner.[27]

The person in charge of the prison and who has legal custody of all prisoners therein is the Prison Superintendent or a Chief Warder. He is appointed by the Native Authority at its discretion. The clerical work of the prison is carried out by a prison scribe who comes directly under the control of the head warder for supervision; the remaining warders and wardresses are in addition subjected to a disciplinary code. These form a uniformed force and their conditions of service and discipline are laid down in Rules made under section 141 of the Native Authority Law by the Native Authority with the approval of the Governor after consultation with the Executive Council.[28] The Prison Superintendent or the Native Authority itself, if it does not delegate the power to the former, may deal with offences against discipline as named in the Rules by the prison staff. Such offences include inciting mutiny amongst the staff, being drunk on duty, allowing prisoners to escape, etc. The punishments for which, in order of severity, are listed as:

(1) Admonition;

(2) Reprimand or severe reprimand;

(3) Fines not exceeding one-half of a month's salary;

(4) Reduction in grade; or

(5) Dismissal.

Prisoners. Prisoners are segregated into the following categories:

(1) Convicted criminal prisoners other than juveniles;

(2) Debtors;

---

[27] S. 135 of the Law. The Power is delegated to Provincial Commissioners by the Minister of Internal Affairs. Prison Visitors may include Social welfare workers or representatives of various religious denominations.

[28] The present Rules are of the model type made in 1960 and approved by all Native Authorities and Joint Committees running prison services.

(3) Prisoners on remand or awaiting trial and appellants;
(4) First offenders;
(5) Convicted juveniles;
(6) Female prisoners.

Categories (3) and (6) are kept separate from all other categories and category (4) is kept apart wherever possible from habitual offenders.

Female prisoners are kept in a separate block of the prison and are under the control of wardresses. They are not expected to undergo hard labour.

A prisoner may be transferred from one prison to another by the order of the Provincial Commissioner[29] by means of transfer order and endorsement of the warrant. A prisoner may be transferred also to a hospital or other suitable place for observation outside the prison on an order signed by the Divisional Officer concerned.[30]

Should a prisoner after examination by a Medical Officer be adjudged of unsound mind and certified as such a Provincial Commissioner, after consultation with the Native Authority, may order his removal from the hospital.

The Prison Rules deal also with the admission, release, diet, labour, clothing, discipline and health of prisoners. Prisoners may earn remission of sentence for good behaviour and industry if they are not convicted of an offence against discipline. This remission may be up to one-third of the sentence in respect of sentences of one calendar month or more. Prisoners may be visited by friends or relatives at specified times or under special circumstances.

In addition to the Prison Rules the Governor may make regulations applying to all or certain Native Authority prisons in respect of:

(1) Regulating the legal custody of persons under sentence of death;
(2) The granting of licences to prisoners to be at large; and
(3) The conditions under which persons awaiting trial or adjudged as judgment debtors are to be kept in custody.

Native Authorities encourage prison industries and the rehabilitation of prisoners. Prison industries include cloth weaving,

---

[29] To whom the Governor and the Minister of Internal Affairs have delegated this power: S. 139 of the Law.
[30] Delegated by Governor and Minister of Internal Affairs: S. 140 of the Law.

making of prisoners' uniforms, mat making, embroidery, market gardening, rope making, quarrying, etc.

Grants by the Central Government. The Northern Nigeria Government, through the Ministry of Internal Affairs, assists Native Authorities who operate prisons by a grant of £30 per annum for every properly trained prison warder. To be classified as "trained" the warder must have passed successfully through a three-months' course at the Warder Training School at Kaduna.

8. THE DEVELOPMENT OF NATURAL RESOURCES

1. Agriculture

All Native Authorities, other than those operating the service through the medium of a Joint Committee, provide agricultural extension services to some degree. The extent and scope of this work depends on the area and on the wealth of the Native Authority.

Liaison with the Ministry of Agriculture is through the Agricultural Officer of the Division and thence through the Provincial Agricultural Officer (P.A.O.) of the Province concerned. Native Authority agricultural staff are given technical training at the School of Agriculture, Samaru, Zaria, and properly qualified staff attract an annual grant to the Native Authority of 50 per cent of the cost of their salaries. Training at Provincial level is carried out at Provincial Farm Centres. At the moment there are seven of these established at Sokoto, Dambatta (Kano), Kafinsoli (Katsina), Yandev (Benue), Maiduguri (Bornu), Bauchi and Bida (Niger) and others are to come into operation shortly.

The work of the agricultural department of the Native Authority may include:

(1) Advice to farmers;
(2) Encouragement and management of mixed farming in areas where this is possible. That is to say, issues on repayment to farmers of work bulls, ploughs and carts and the training of bulls to the plough;
(3) Distribution of approved seed and seed multiplication;
(4) Soil conservation and prevention of soil erosion;
(5) Assistance in distributing fertilisers and seed dressings;
(6) Operation of citrus and other tree-crop nurseries.

Cotton and groundnut marketing is controlled through the board concerned. The cost of operating and staffing approved markets for cotton is borne by the Northern Nigeria Marketing Board and is 100 per cent reimbursable. The lists of approved markets for cotton, and buying stations for groundnuts together with the dates on which each may open are published annually in the Regional *Gazette*, whilst the operation of these markets is laid down in Rules made by the Native Authority under section 37 of the Law.

The claims for reimbursement of operating costs are submitted by Native Authorities to the Principal Produce Officer concerned for payment. The Marketing Boards give further assistance through the medium of grants for the maintenance of approved produce evacuation roads. Assistance is also given for the construction and permanent improvement of produce evacuation roads.

Almost all Native Authorities run agricultural shows to encourage improvement in the quality of farm produce and animals. These shows are held between December and March and are extremely popular throughout the North. Other agricultural activities organised by the Native Authorities include:

(1) Maintenance of irrigation schemes—the Government hands over any such scheme to the Native Authority concerned three years after completion to continue maintenance;
(2) Mechanical ploughing;
(3) Bonemeal production for fertilisers;
(4) Pasture development;
(5) Small coffee and oil palm plantations;
(6) Pest control (including control of baboons in many areas);
(7) Dry-season farming.

All of which are conducted in close co-operation with agricultural officials of the Central Government.

2. Forestry

All Native Authorities operate a forestry department in co-operation with the Forestry Division of the Ministry of Animal and Forest Resources. The liaison is once more through the Provincial representative of that Ministry. The main work of this department may be said to be:

(1) The establishment and control of Forest Reserves and Communal Forest Areas;
(2) The establishment of nurseries and plantations;
(3) The preservation of sylvan produce in accordance with the Forestry Ordinance and Native Authority Forestry Rules;
(4) Amenity planting; and
(5) Sale of timber, fuel and minor forest produce.

Forestry staff are either trained at a Provincial level or attend courses at the Forestry School at Jos. No grants are paid to Native Authorities in respect of trained forestry staff, but during training a grant of £3 per student per month (to cover maintenance) is paid to the sponsoring Native Authority.

A Native Authority may conserve its forest resources in one of two ways:

(1) It may create Forest Reserves; or
(2) It may set up Communal Forest Areas.

Forest Reserves. These are set up under section 22 of the Forestry Ordinance[31] and are areas set aside for long-term development of forest produce. The procedure for setting them up is complicated and includes an inquiry held with the local native community affected to ensure that farming rights, compensations, etc., are arranged satisfactorily before the reserve is delineated and published by *Gazette.* Covering authority to set up a reserve is given by the Provincial Commissioner and the Minister of Animal and Forest Resources. Once gazetted[32] a Forest Reserve attracts an annual grant of £1 per square mile to the Native Authority concerned. Rights of way are limited, no timber may be cut therein and no farming is permissible. Persons are entitled to enter the reserve as a rule only to hunt or to gather specified forest produce.

Communal Forest Areas. These are also set up under the Forestry Ordinance (section 34) and differ from Forest Reserves in that they are operated through a committee of a District or equivalent council known as the Management Council, by means of Rules made by the Native Authority concerned.[33] These Rules are of a model type and include provision to prevent injury to forest

---

[31] Cap. 75 of the Laws of Nigeria, 1948.
[32] Or awaiting "Gazetting" on April 1.
[33] With the approval of the Provincial Commissioner.

produce and control of timber. As the name suggests the area is for the benefit of the native community in which it is situated.

Animal Health and Husbandry

The veterinary services provided by a Native Authority vary enormously in size and extent. In the tsetse-infested areas of the Riverein Province the services are strictly limited, but in the cattle-breeding areas of the northern emirates where the animal cattle tax forms an important part of the Native Authority's revenue, veterinary services may concern themselves with:

(1) Prevention of animal diseases, *e.g.*, rinderpest and black-quarter in cattle, trypanosomiasis in cattle, rabies in dogs, Newcastle disease in poultry, etc.;

(2) Improvement of trade cattle routes and inspection and control of herds passing through, on behalf of the Regional Government;

(3) Improved breeding strains, *e.g.*, horse stud farm at Sokoto;

(4) Slaughtering of beasts, *e.g.*, modern abattoirs at Maiduguri and Nguru by Bornu Native Authority and at Sokoto by Sokoto Native Authority;

(5) Hides and skins inspection;

(6) Annual cattle inoculation;

(7) Poultry schemes;

(8) Improved grazing and water supplies for cattle.

Native Authority veterinary staff are trained either at Vom or at Kaduna (Mando Road). Native Authorities are reimbursed by the Ministry of Animal and Forest Resources for 50 per cent of the cost of the salaries of any staff given the approved training.

9. WELFARE SERVICES

Social welfare services, although not operated by all Native Authorities, are becoming increasingly important and are organised in close co-operation with the Ministry of Social Welfare and Co-operatives. They include blind rehabilitation centres (*e.g.*, Ilorin and Zaria); remand homes, approved schools and probation services (*e.g.*, Kano, Sokoto, Bornu); provision for paupers; playing fields and stadiums, and guidance to produce marketing, consumer and thrift co-operative societies.

CHAPTER 6

LOCAL GOVERNMENT FINANCE

THE funds of a Native Authority are controlled by means of a Native Treasury. There are *sixty-two* Native Treasuries and a list of these and Native Authorities for whom they operate is given below. Four Treasuries are operated by Joint Committees. Treasuries are classified in two ways by the Ministry for Local Government: (1) by their general administrative efficiency into the classifications of A and B; and (2) by their financial soundness or otherwise by the classifications (i) financially sound, and (ii) not financially sound.

A third classification was added in January 1962 under Group (1) above of "C". This indicates a Treasury which is unable to satisfy requirements of standards of accountancy laid down by Ministry, and so it has to be supervised in detail by an Administrative Officer. A Treasury is said to be financially sound if its budget satisfies the following requirements:

(1) That there is an estimated surplus of not less than 10 per cent of estimated ordinary revenue[1] over recurrent expenditure for the financial year;

(2) That the estimated expenditure on personal emoluments (salaries) is less than 45 per cent of the ordinary revenue;

(3) That the expenditure on general administration[2] is less than 45 per cent of the ordinary revenue;

(4) That recurrent expenditure on the Central, District and Village administration of the Native Authority is less than 25 per cent of ordinary revenue.

These controls are intended to prevent a Native Authority spending an unnecessarily large proportion of its funds on cumbersome administrative machinery or on a large staff at the expense of the services to be provided for the taxpayer.

[1] For a definition of ordinary revenue see below.
[2] Expenditure heads I–VIII and XIV.

THE REVENUE OF A NATIVE TREASURY

1. THE REVENUE OF A NATIVE TREASURY

The Native Authority Law defines what are the revenue and other funds of a Native Authority and specifies some of the sources from whence they arise.[3] It stipulates that these funds are to be applied to the administration and welfare of the area of the Native Authority and to the welfare of the inhabitants of that area.[4] The main sources of revenue are:

Community Tax

Authority to collect tax is given by the Commissioner of Revenue, Northern Region, under the provisions of the Personal Tax Law, 1962. Community tax is payable by all persons not liable for income tax. It is payable by all adult males with certain exceptions.[5] The basic rate is fixed for the community and the 'per capita' contribution agreed upon by the Native Authority and approved by the Provincial Commissioner and the Minister for Local Government. The determination of the tax rate is decided after careful consideration of the following factors:

(1) Rates payable in the neighbouring community areas;
(2) The wealth of the community being assessed;
(3) The financial needs of the Native Authority administering the community; and
(4) Any special factors affecting the community concerned.

Community tax is collected by Native and Local Authorities who are tax collection authorities.[6] The tax collectors are normally the Village Heads; the money is then passed to the District Heads who pay it into the Native Treasury. A strict accounting process has been evolved by all Native Authorities and this is enforced to prevent misappropriation at any of the stages of collection. Individual receipts are issued to all taxpayers and these form a valuable form of identification to the holders in addition to proving payment.

Tax rates in 1962–63 vary from 32s. at the lowest rate to 50s. per adult male taxpayer at the highest.

A tax count at District or equivalent level is begun normally in

---

[3] S. 76 of the Law.
[4] S. 79 of the Law.
[5] S. 50 of the Personal Tax Law, 1962.
[6] Certain N.A.s also have a Fishing Tax payable by these communities almost entirely engaged in fishing for a livelihood, *e.g.*, Tiv N.A.

June of each year. After approval by the Ministry for Local Government taxation rates are announced by the Emir or the Chairman of the Native Authority Council or his representative in all areas in public and assessment notices given to the tax collectors. Tax is collected from November onwards when crops have been harvested and sold.[7] Methods of collection vary slightly from one area to the next. Highly organised Districts will virtually complete tax collection within a month. In poorer rural areas and in areas where communications are difficult it may take much longer. Total tax collected is placed on a deposit account in the Native Treasury. Before the end of the financial year (March 31) $12\frac{1}{2}$ per cent of the account is paid into the Central Government to the Consolidated Revenue Fund. The remaining $87\frac{1}{2}$ per cent is then paid into the revenue of the Native Authority concerned. Late payments are adjusted in the following financial year.

Cattle Tax or Jangali

This is payable by all cattle owners. Nomadic herdsmen, *i.e.*, Fulani, Shiwa Arabs, do not normally pay community tax in addition but settled tribes may be called upon to pay both.[8] The Personal Tax Law now lays down the rates payable on beasts throughout the Region. The details are as follows:

Part I. Bulls, Cows, Oxen, Steers, Bullocks, Heifers, Calves

Area	Rate per Beast	
	s.	d.
Benue, Ilorin and Kabba Provinces . .	6	6
Lowland Division of Plateau	6	6
Jos and Pankshin Divisions of Plataue Province excluding Kanam	7	6
Falinza Plateau in Sardauna Province . .	3	0
All other areas	7	0

Part II. Sheep and Lambs

All areas	2	0

---

[7] Benue and other Riverain Provinces are, in fact, able to begin tax collection earlier.
[8] S. 54 (1) of the Personal Tax Law, 1962.

Herds are counted as from June of each year and collection may begin on July 1. Collection closes on November 30, unless an extension is granted by the Ministry for Local Government.

Income Tax

Income tax and tax collected at source from salaried employees (P.A.Y.E.) when collected by a Native or Local Authority as a Tax Collector appointed by the Commissioner of Revenue will be accounted for by payment of 80 per cent to the Consolidated Revenue Fund and 20 per cent to the Tax Collector for payment into the revenue of the Native Authority.

Rates

Section 77 of the Native Authority Law empowers the Native Authority to levy rates to provide for its public services. Such rates may be classified as:

(1) Special rates—*i.e.*, for a water utility, etc.; or
(2) A general rate; based either on a per capita collection (all paying the same amount) or proportionately to the wealth of the ratepayer as assessed for tax.[9]

Native Authorities have not yet taken advantage of their power to collect general rates, relying as they do on tax for the bulk of their funds. The power has, however, been delegated to Subordinate Councils set up under Instrument, and it is from this source that we may expect the development of a system of rating. Rules for the collection of rates are made under paragraph (50) of section 37 of the Law. Provision is also made in the Law specifically for a special Education Rate provided that the approval of the Local Education Authority[10] is obtained.

Court Dues

A Native Authority may use all moneys collected by Native Courts in its area in respect of (*a*) fees on civil suits, such as divorce, dowries, inheritance, etc., and (*b*) fines and forfeitures inflicted by the court.

[9] Property Rating in N. Nigeria is limited to the Sabon Garis of Kano, Zaria and Jos by Native Authorities.
[10] S. 77 (2) of the Law.

Moneys collected by the Provincial Court, however, are not a perquisite of the Native Authority concerned, but are government revenue.

Interest on Investments

Native Authorities are empowered by the Law[11] to invest surplus funds with the overall approval of the Minister of Finance. Investments are arranged for Native Authorities by agents in the United Kingdom and interest paid half-yearly on a general ledger account through the Accountant-General.

Grants-in-Aid

Assistance is given by the Government and by other public bodies to Native Authorities in a variety of ways to promote and encourage public services of a required standard.

These grants may be either (a) capital grants in respect of new development work or (b) recurrent grants in respect of trained staff, maintenance of equipment and buildings, etc.[12] at varying rates. Grants are awarded by the Ministry dealing in its portfolio with the service concerned. The required standard to be maintained and the method of assessing the grant are also the responsibility of the Ministry. Grants from sources other than government include those from such bodies as the Northern Region Development Corporation and the Northern Nigeria Marketing Board, they may also include contributions from other Native Authorities where a joint service is operated.

Miscellaneous Revenue

This may include such items as:

(1) School fees;
(2) Market fees and dues;
(3) Hospital fees;
(4) Forestry receipts;
(5) Land registration fees;
(6) Bicycle and dog licencing, etc.

[11] S. 80 of the Law.
[12] Details of Grants-in-Aids are given in Chap. 5, *ante,* under the various services concerned.

Details of fees and dues payable are given in the subsidiary legislation made by the Native Authority either under the authority of the Native Authority Law or under other Laws.

2. THE BUDGET OF THE NATIVE AUTHORITY

The Law gives the general directive that the funds of a Native Authority should be applied to the administration and development of its area and to the welfare of the inhabitants.

The financial year of a Native Authority is the same as that of government. That is to say it commences on April 1 and ends on March 31 following. The recurrent budget of a Native Authority is based on its annual estimate which are prepared as follows:

(1) Heads of Departments prepare preliminary proposals of expenditure, containing details of the total expenditure necessary to maintain existing services and details of any proposed extension or capital expenditure.

(2) The Native Treasury prepares a preliminary estimate of revenue.

(3) These estimates are then put before the Finance Committee which reviews the estimates of departments, investigates the "financial soundness" of the Native Authority after taking all departmental requirements into account and if necessary recommends to the Native Authority Council proposals for increasing revenue, *e.g.*, an increase in the rate of community tax.

(4) All changes in salaries; variations in existing staff strengths; new recurrent subheads and proposals for changes in tax rates or assessments require the approval of either the Ministry for Local Government or the Provincial Commissioner. This approval is then requested.

(5) On receiving approval to changes, the final estimates are prepared first at departmental level and then by the Treasury. When complete they are considered by the Finance Committee and the Native Authority Council.

(6) The estimates are approved by the Ministry for Local Government under the provisions of section 86 of the Law.

The expenditure and revenue of the Native Authority estimates are divided in Heads[13] as follows:

Revenue	Expenditure
I Tax	I Central Administration
II *Jangali*	II District Administration
III Court Fees and Fines	III Village Administration
IV Interest on Investments	IV Judicial
V Miscellaneous Revenue	V Treasury
VI Grants from Regional Funds	VI Police
	VII Prisons
VII Grants from other Sources	VIII Miscellaneous
VIII Commercial Undertakings	IX Works, Recurrent
IX Grants: Capital Works	X Veterinary
	XI Education
	XII Survey
	XIII Medical and Health
	XIV Agriculture
	XV Forestry
	XVI Pensions, etc.
	XVII District Council Funds
	XVIII Commercial Undertakings
	XIV Works Extraordinary (Capital Works)

Revenue Heads I–VII are classified as "Ordinary" Revenue and Expenditure Heads I–XVII are classified as "Ordinary" Expenditure.

Each of these Heads is divided into subheads as necessary. The first subhead under each expenditure Head is devoted to salaries and the personal emoluments of permanent staff and is divided into items indicating each post or salary grading. The remaining subheads cover other charges and include provision for daily paid labour, special expenditure is indicated separately. If the expenditure of a Head is complex it may be subdivided into sections, *i.e.*, Head VIII, Miscellaneous Expenditure, may be divided into A. General; B. Social Welfare Services; C. Co-operative Services;

---

[13] Heads of Revenue and Expenditure are always numbered in this order using roman numerals.

D. Information; or Head XIII, Medical and Health, into A. Medical; B. Health.

Once approved the annual expenditure estimates of a Native Authority must not be changed without authority. This authority varies according to:

(1) The grade of the Treasury;

(2) Its financial soundness; and

(3) The type of supplementary expenditure required.

The following table shows the types of authority required by Financial Memoranda.

AUTHORITIES REQUIRED TO INCUR SUPPLEMENTARY
EXPENDITURE OVER AND ABOVE THAT PROVIDED FOR
IN THE APPROVED ANNUAL ESTIMATES OF THE
NATIVE AUTHORITY

All supplementary expenditure on subheads existing in the Estimates and expenditure on new subheads which have to be created after the Estimates are approved require the approval of the Minister for Local Government.

There are exceptions, however, to this rule and these are shown in the table below. Approval by Native Authority itself implies a full discussion in the Finance Committee and approval by the Native Authority Council. If a limit is fixed in terms of money or alternatively a percentage the greater may be taken but such a limit is a gross limit and not the limit for each application.

Symbols in the Table

N.A. = Native Authority

D.O. = Divisional Officer

P.C. = Provincial Commissioner (as soon as appointed)

S.H. = Subhead of Estimates

(f) = Authority is conditional on a surplus of 10 per cent ordinary revenue over current expenditure being assured.

109

EXPENDITURE	PROVISO	GRADE	AUTH-ORITY	AMOUNT
(i) Salaries: Supplementary Expenditure and New Subheads required as a result of an approved authority to vary the establishment	(f)	A(i)	N.A.	Unlimited
	(f)	B(i), C(i)	D.O.	Unlimited
	None	A(ii), B(ii), C (ii)	P.C.	Unlimited
(ii) Increments: Supplementary Expenditure required to pay approved increments not provided in the Estimates	(f)	A(i)	N.A.	Unlimited
	(f)	B(i), C(i)	D.O.	Unlimited
	None	A(ii), B(ii), C(ii)	P.C.	Unlimited
(iii) Percentages to Tax Collectors: Where an increase in tax collected makes the Estimated amount insufficient	(f)	A(i)	N.A.	Unlimited
	(f)	B(i), C(i)	D.O.	Unlimited
	None	A(ii), B(ii), C(ii)	P.C.	Unlimited
(iv) Allowances (in the Personal Emoluments Subhead)	(f) and that there is no increase in allowances to N.A.s District Head, Councillors or Head of Depts.	A(i), B(i)	P.C.	£25 or 10%
(v) Other charges on Head I to XV, except Special Items and the Unallocated Stores Subhead of Head IX	(f)	A(i)	N.A.	£500 or 25% New S.H. £50
	(f)	B(i), C(i)	D.O.	£100 or 10% No New S.H.
	(f)	B(i), C(i)	P.C.	£500 or 25% New S.H. £50
	Equivalent Savings quoted	A(ii), ((ii), C(ii)	P.C.	£500 or 25% No New S.H.
(vi) Head IX: Unallocated Stores Subhead	(f) and that total stocks do not increase	A(i), B(i), C(i)	P.C.	10%

EXPENDITURE	PROVISO	GRADE	AUTH-ORITY	AMOUNT
ii) Head XVI: To pay approved Retiring Benefits	(f)	A(i)	N.A.	Unlimited
	(f)	B(i), C(i)	D.O.	Unlimited
	None	A(ii), B(ii), C(ii)	P.C.	Unlimited
ii) Head XVII: District Council Funds if an increase of taxpayers requires an increased provision or there is increased Central District Council Revenue	(f)	A(i)	N.A.	Unlimited
	(f)	B(i), C(i)	D.O.	Unlimited
	None	A(ii), B(ii), C(ii)	P.C.	Unlimited
x) Head XVIII: Commercial undertakings	5%	All	P.C.	£5,000 or 25%
x) Head XIX and Special Expenditure on other heads	Total of Supplementary Expenditure: on the Head does not exeeed 10% of the approved Estimate	A(i) B(i) C(i)	N.A. D.O.	Unlimited

Development and Capital Work

All works which are not recurrent are classified as special or extraordinary. Special expenditure is shown as a separate section of the Head concerned and works extraordinary are shown under Head XIX and may refer to any department.

Wherever possible Native Authorities co-ordinate their development by assessing the surplus funds available for development and producing a Development Plan to cover a five-year period.

The period of the Plan is fixed throughout the Region and being phased to coincide with that of the Central Government's development plan. Native Authorities are now in a six-year plan, April 1962–March 1968, following that of government, but a five-year period is more usual.

Five-year development plans have the following advantages:

(1) They ensure a balanced development between the departments of the Native Authority;

(2) They enable the Regional Government now to estimate with some degree of accuracy its financial commitments for capital and recurrent grants and the future demands on its staff; and

(3) They assist the Regional Government to plan balanced development throughout the Region by co-ordinating Native Authority plans with its own five-year development programme.

In preparing its Development Plan the Native Authority submits a Project Register showing projects in the following headings:

A. Agriculture   G. Public Buildings

B. Education   H. Urban Development

C. Forestry   J. Rural Development

D. Medical   K. Public Utilities

E. Veterinary   L. Miscellaneous Equipment

F. Communications

The Register is divided into two parts. Part I is all projects in the above form to be financed directly from Native Authority funds with or without government assistance. Part II is all projects in the prescribed form to be financed from loans from loans boards or banks. These projects must be reasonably capable of running themselves in due course and of providing funds to repay the capital borrowed.

Not all surplus funds can be earmarked for development, as a sufficient reserve must be left to meet the demands for working capital and for investments which cannot be realised within the period of the Plan.

Approval of the Plan lies with the Minister for Local Government. It is submitted to him through the Provincial Commissioner of the Province who must satisfy himself that:

(1) The estimates of cost are realistic;

(2) The total estimated cost to the Native Authority of projects financed from its funds is not less than the probable funds available for the five-year period;

(3) That projects financed from loans may be expected to pay their way to provide the funds necessary for repayment of the capital;[14]

(4) That there is a reasonable balance between sections and between urban and rural development; and

(5) That the Provincial Representatives of Ministries have been fully consulted and have given approval to the development which affects their portfolios.

Once the overall Plan is approved by the Minister only major changes[15] in it will be referred to him. Minor changes may be approved by the Provincial Commissioner or in the case of Grade "A" Treasuries by the Native Authority itself.

Each Native Authority operating a five-year Development Plan should appoint a Development or Planning Committee whose duty will be to assess progress annually on the Plan and to decide before the drafting of the annual estimates which items are to be included in Head XIX for the coming year. Projects not completed at the end of one five-year period may be included in the next Plan with the approval of the Minister for Local Government.

Financial Controls. Financial controls by the Central Government and Native Authorities have been tightened during the past year and Native Treasuries are now checked strictly by Administrative Officers each month. Details of these checks are laid down in a booklet known as *Financial Directions.* These include surprise checks on the cash and current accounts of the Native Treasury and checks on the principal books of account.[16] A recent directive from the Ministry for Local Government stipulates that the Finance Committee of the Native Authority must meet monthly and investigate:

(1) The monthly statement of accounts as submitted by the Native Treasurer;

(2) The position with regard to tax outstanding from the annual collection;

---

[14] A Native Authority with the approval of the Provincial Commissioner may raise loans within Nigeria under s. 78 of the Law.

[15] Major changes are those which affect the funds of a section by over 20 per cent of its total estimated expenditure.

[16] Financial Memoranda also lay down checks on cash to be carried out by senior N.A. officials.

(3) Repayment of personal and other advances outstanding in the Native Treasury;

(4) Outstanding audit inquiries in reports submitted by the Director of Audit;[17]

(5) The Revenue Collector's chart which shows the reconciliation of Revenue Collector's records with Treasury records and receipts;

(6) Applications by the Treasury to incur supplementary expenditure in excess of that approved in the annual estimates.

At all the monthly meetings of the committee the Divisional Officer should be in attendance unless the Treasury is graded as "A".

Under a recent directive not more than 5 per cent of either community tax or *Jangali* may be outstanding at the close of the financial year. Any excess will result in automatic down-grading of the Treasury.

Native Treasury accounts are audited by the Regional Audit service as often as the staff position will permit. In practice for the average Native Authority this means a biannual check of all its central and departmental accounts. It has not been possible to date to hold a detailed check into the accounts of Subordinate Councils. In addition, where it is possible to post a Provincial Supervisor of Accounts[18] the routine accounting is checked in each Native Treasury of the Province about once per quarter. The Native Authority Law lays down in detail the procedure to be followed by the Department of Audit. After every financial year the Native Treasury compiles a comprehensive statement of its accounts for submission to the Ministry for Local Government and to the Director of Audit.

These annual accounts include:

(1) A statement of Revenue received;

(2) A statement of Expenditure incurred under every Head;

(3) A statement of the Assets and Liabilities of the Treasury as at March 31;

---

[17] Audit queries must be acknowledged within two weeks of receipt and fully answered within three months.

[18] This is a government appointment of executive grade. Normally the P.S.A. holds a Diploma in Native Treasury Accounting.

(4) Details of all "below the line" accounts, *i.e.*, Advance and Deposit accounts;

(5) A list of all investments held by the Treasury;

(6) Details of all commercial undertakings;

(7) Notes on major variations of Revenue and Expenditure from the approved estimates.

Auditors are empowered by Law to investigate any documents or books of account as they consider fit to ascertain the true position of the Native Authority finances, and they are empowered to call before them and examine witnesses if necessary. Anyone refusing to attend before an auditor or to answering his questions may be taken before a court and may be liable on conviction to a fine of up to £25 or to imprisonment up to two years.[19]

At the conclusion of an audit inspection the auditor prepares a report on the state of the Native Treasury accounts.[20] A copy of this report is sent to the Ministry for Local Government (this is submitted to and discussed in the Executive Council) and also to the Native Authority itself. It is the duty of the latter to answer any queries raised in the report within three months. In the case of expenditure being disallowed as irregular or improper or a recommendation made that an official be surcharged either for a deficiency or for improper expenditure of funds the Native Authority must recover this amount from the official concerned.

Officials and employees of the Native Authority, however, are protected in law[21] from liability to surcharge if the expenditure or loss incurred was the result of their acting in good faith on the written instructions of the Native Authority or as the result of a resolution passed by the Native Authority Council or one of its committees. Appeals to the Ministry against disallowance or surcharge may be made within thirty days. Payment of every sum certified to be due must be paid within sixty days. If it is not paid the amount is recoverable by court action as a civil debt by the Native Authority.

[19] S. 90 (2) of the Law.
[20] S. 93 (1) of the Law.
[21] S. 92 of the Law.

3. SUBORDINATE COUNCIL FINANCES

Subordinate Councils may be classified into:

(1) Those who do not manage their own finances, but have control of District Council Funds (D.C.F.);[22] and

(2) Those who are sufficiently advanced as to be able to operate their own sub-estimates of revenue and expenditure.

1. District Council Funds are an annual grant to a Subordinate Council by the Native Authority based on a fixed amount per taxpayer of the area concerned. These fixed amounts vary at present from 1s. per taxpayer to 2s. 6d. Thus if the capitation rate is 2s. and there are 5,000 taxpayers in the Subordinate Council area the District Council Funds for the year will be £500. Unlike recurrent expenditure the District Council Funds may be put on deposit in the Treasury and will not die at the end of the financial year with other expenditure.

Subordinate Councils may, therefore, accumulate funds over a period of years if they so desire.

The District or equivalent Council may in theory spend the money as it thinks fit but in practice until the Native Authority sets up its Subordinate Council by Instrument (and in some cases even afterwards) it keeps a strict watch on how the Subordinate Council spends its funds and all resolutions to use District Council Funds must be sent to the Native Authority for approval. A list of the services on which District Council Funds may be used is included in the Instrument of a Subordinate Council. At the first meeting in a financial year the Council prepares a list of the projects that it wishes to undertake in the course of the year with the funds at its disposal. The Council scribe prepares a Project List and opens an Expenditure Abstract for each Project. A record is kept of expenditure on each Project and a comprehensive Meeting Report is prepared for each Council meeting to show members the progress achieved and the present state of the finances. Monthly reports are also sent to the Native Authority.

Payment for work and materials is effected either (a) by the Native Treasury itself from the Deposit account of the Council on payment vouchers submitted by the Council or (b) in those distant

---

[22] First introduced in 1948. Included as Head XVII of the Expenditure estimates of the Native Treasury.

from the Treasury by means of an Imprest account held by the Chairman of the Subordinate Council.

2. Councils with enhanced financial delegation are those with assigned sources of revenue other than District Council Funds and who may operate through sub-estimates of the Native Treasury. They may be classified into:

(1) Those whose estimates are completely incorporated with those of the Native Authority, and

(2) Those who prepare separate estimates of their own and who appear in the Native Treasury estimates as one line items of Revenue and Expenditure only. The sources of Revenue for such Councils are:

(a) Share of direct taxes, which may include:

(i) A capitation share. ⎫
(ii) All strangers tax and any special ⎬ Head "A" in Council estimates
assessments. ⎭

(iii) A share of Cattle Tax. ⎫
⎬ Head "B"
(iv) Sheep Tax. ⎭

(b) Fees and fines from Native Courts. Head "C"

(c) Fees and dues from bicycle licencing, ⎫
hawkers' licences, market and slaugh- ⎬ Head "D"
tering dues and other miscellaneous ⎪
revenue. ⎭

(d) Rates either general or special as re- ⎫
quired. ⎬ Head "E
(e) Grants-in-aid from the Native Author- ⎪
ity which may be either: ⎭

(i) A Recurrent grant to assist in Head "F"
carrying out a public service, or

(ii) A Capital grant to assist in de- Head "G"
velopment.

Expenditure is shown as Heads as in Native Authority Estimates but numbered as follows:

Head "A" — Council Administration

Head "B" — Village Administration

Head "C" — Miscellaneous

Head "D" — Works Recurrent

Head "E" — Veterinary

Head "F" — Education

Head "G" — Survey

Head "H" — Medical and Health

Head "J" — Agriculture

Head "K" — Forestry

Head "Z" — Special and Works Extraordinary

Each Head is subdivided into (a) Allowances and (b) Other Charges.

If the estimates of a Council are to form part of the Native Treasury Estimates then the provision made under the Revenue Heads of the Native Treasury will include the Subordinate Council's estimates of revenue in its own without any indication of the Council's share. Only under Head I Community Tax there will be shown subdivision, however, of:

(1) Central Share;

(2) Subordinate Councils' Share.

Under expenditure Head XVII, District Council Funds, will appear the total estimated revenue of each Council. In this manner the Native Treasury may open a deposit account for each Council covering its total estimated revenue and pay all revenue acquired straight into Native Treasury revenue heads. Shortfall or excess of the Council's revenue can be adjusted into or out of the deposit account at the end of the financial year.

If a Subordinate Council has completely separate estimates then only grants to that Council will appear in the Native Treasury Estimates. The Council has its own printed estimates and the Native Treasury only acts as a banking agent. These Councils may also operate "below the line" accounts.

Subordinate Councils may be considered "financially sound" only if they have 15 per cent or more surplus of ordinary revenue over recurrent expenditure. This 15 per cent surplus is divided in 10 per cent for reserve, held towards new capital projects and 5 per cent which may be spent if necessary on supplementary expenditure to the approved estimates during the financial year.

SUBORDINATE COUNCIL FINANCES

NATIVE TREASURIES OF NORTHERN NIGERIA

1962–63

NO.	NAME OF NATIVE TREASURY	GRADE	TOTAL ORDINARY REVENUE	NO.	NAME OF NATIVE TREASURY	GRADE	TOTAL ORDINARY REVENUE
1	Adamawa	A(1)	246,840				
2	Muri	B(11)	135,535	35	Katsina	A(1)	963,290
3	Numan	B(1)	89,260	36	Abuja	A(1)	66,830
4	Bauchi			37	Agaie	B(1)	26,075
	(incl. Dass)	A(11)	359,076	38	Bida	A(1)	192,430
5	Gombe	A(1)	277,240	39	Gwari	B(1)	114,470
6	Jama'are	B(1)	17,960	40	Kamuku	B(11)	22,335
7	Katagum	A(1)	276,720	41	Kontagora		
8	Misau	A(1)	86,340		(incl.		
9	Ningi	B(1)	44,730		Wushishi		
10	Tangale-				N.A.)	B(1)	102,815
	Waja	C(11)	78,215	42	Lapai	B(1)	26,740
11	Idoma	B(1)	185,870	43	Zuru	B(1)	79,470
12	Keffi	C(11)	61,975	44	Akwanga	B(1)	60,340
13	Lafla (incl.			45	Jos	C(1)1	265,955
	Awe N.A.)	B(1)	108,970	46	Kanam	C(1)	30,845
14	Nasarawa	B(1)	77,850	47	Lowland	C(11)	73,110
15	Tiv	B(11)	490,095	48	Pankshin	C(1)	130,405
16	Wukari	C(1)	90,400	49	Wase	B(11)	26,915
17	Bedde	A(1)	52,775	50	Yergam Re-		
18	Biu	B(1)	107,040		settlement		
19	Bornu	A(1)	1,043,735		N.T. (com-		
20	Fika	B(1)	95,875		prising		
21	Borgu	B(11)	68,640		Yergam &		
22	Ilorin	A(1)	374,915		Resettle-		
23	Lafiagi	B(11)	27,590		ment N.A.s)	B(1)	21,390
24	Pategi	B(11)	20,151	51	Chamba	C(1)	71,130
25	Igala	A(1)	299,232	52	Dikwa	A(11)	151,570
26	Igbirra	B(1)	115,280	53	Gashaka/		
27	Kabba (incl.				Mambilla	C(1)	87,310
	Bunu and			54	Gwoza	C(11)	31,740
	Ijumu	B(11)	44,660	55	Mubi	B(11)	95,505
28	Kwara	C(1)	64,280	56	United Hills	C(11)	9,965
29	Yagba			57	Argungu	A(1)	109,270
	(comprising			58	Gwandu	A(1)	270,470
	W. Yagba			59	Sokoto	A(1)	1,004,365
	& E. Yagba			60	Yauri	B(1)	66,615
	N.A.s)	B(11)	41,895	61	Jema'a	B(1)	95,015
30	Gumel	A(1)	91,245	62	Zaria (incl.		
31	Hadejia	A(1)	176,985		Birnin		
32	Kano	A(1)	1,965,545		Gwari		
33	Kazaure	A(1)	65,880		N.A.)	B(1)	566,306
34	Daura	A(1)	105,215				

CHAPTER 7

LOCAL GOVERNMENT STAFF

THE Native Authority Law, 1954,[1] gives the general authority for a Native Authority to employ such staff as are necessary for the efficient discharge of its functions, *i.e.*, of its services and general administration, and to dismiss such staff. The Central Government controls the Native Authority's use of staff in two main ways:

(1) By allowing major posts in the service of the Native Authority to be filled only with the approval of the Premier; and

(2) By dictating conditions of service for local government staff throughout the North by staff Regulations issued by the Ministry for Local Government.

Control of Senior Posts

The Law stipulates that the following Native Authority staff posts must receive the Premier's approval of the selected candidates before they can be appointed as:

(1) A secretary (*i.e.*, the senior secretary of the Native Authority);

(2) A clerk to the Native Authority Council;

(3) A Native Treasurer;

(4) A Chief of Police;

(5) A Supervisor of Works;

(6) Any officer whose salary is in excess of a prescribed limit fixed by the Governor. At the moment this limit is fixed at £450 per annum.[2]

The Premier has the further overall right to disallow or revoke the creation of any office set up by a Native Authority and to disallow or revoke the appointment of any person by a Native Authority to any post. Should a Native Authority fail within a reasonable time to fill any of its approved posts when vacant then the Premier may himself appoint a person to that post.

---

[1] S. 36 (1) of the Law.
[2] S. 36 (2A) of the Law and N.A. Legal Notice No. 12 of 1961.

Control by Staff Regulations

These are laid down by the Ministry for Local Government for use in all Native Authorities. New staff regulations were worked out in April 1962 by the Ministry for Local Government in consultation with an advisory committee composed of selected officials from certain Native Authorities.

Native Authorities employ large numbers of officials to carry out their services and general administration. The following gives some idea of the numbers of Native Authority established staff in three of the largest Native Authorities in the Region in 1962.

HEAD	KANO	SOKOTO	BORNU
Central Administration . .	199	117	104
District Administration . .	262	218	249
Village Administration . .	1,284	380	320
Judicial Administration . .	211	188	208
Treasury Administration .	43	34	32
Police Administration . .	742	571	611
Prisons Administration . .	270	133	194
Public Works . . .	142	93	87
Miscellaneous (*i.e.*, Social Welfare, Co-operatives, Markets, etc.)	140	148	112
Commercial Undertakings .	154	21	—
Veterinary	81	85	95
Education	931	406	331
Survey	57	18	55
Health	686	342	218
Agriculture	66	89	43
Forestry	53	147	53
TOTAL . . .	5,331	2,990	2,762

In addition to permanent staff the Native Authorities employ large numbers of daily paid labour. Daily paid labour does not enjoy the benefits of established staff. It can be dismissed at any time by being given notice of seven days and it is not pensionable however long its continuous service may be. Native Authorities in the past have tended to overstaff their services with non-technical staff. Governmental control of excessive recurrent expenditure on employees has been necessary and no Native Authority if it is to be considered financially sound may spend more than 45 per cent of its ordinary revenue on established staff in any financial year, or more than 25 per cent of it on staff for Central, District and Village Administration.

1. PAYMENT OF STAFF

Salary scales for established staff are laid down by the Premier or by the Native Authority concerned with the approval of the Premier. These salary scales are laid down for all Native Authorities and the Ministries concerned with the various Native Authority departments lay down the scales payable for staff who have technical qualifications. The education scales, for example, lay down the scale payable for any grade of teacher. The technical departments of Veterinary, Agriculture, Forestry and Survey specify the scales to be used in accordance to the technical training and experience of the employee concerned.

The police and prisons staff of Native Authorities are also paid on special scales.

In 1960 the revision of Government service salary scales in accordance with the Mbanefo Report led to a similar revision of Native Authority salary scales. Revised scales were submitted to all Native Authorities by the Ministry for Local Government based on the Mbanefo recommendations in so far as incremental scales were affected, but with innovations in respect of staff on fixed salaries and certain special posts.

No major objections were raised and Native Authorities adopted the new scales with effect from September 1, 1959 (back-dated to bring the new scales into operation at the same time as those of the Government). Changes for daily paid labour rates were fixed by the Ministry for Social Welfare and Co-operatives. The salaries of staff on a fixed remuneration per annum were reorganised *vis-à-vis* the responsibility of the post and the wealth of the Native Authority concerned. The system ensured that:

(1) It would directly link in varying degree the salaries of all fixed salary holders to the revenue of the Native Authority.

(2) It would correct old and long-standing anomalies and injustices in reward for service both between posts within one Native Authority and another.

(3) It would make possible in the future more frequent revisions as the procedure would be extremely simple.

(4) It would give an incentive to fixed salary holders to see that the assessments and collection of general tax were as accurate as possible. The future salaries of District Heads, etc., would depend upon this.

Salaries of District, Village, Clan and Ward Heads

These are worked out by means of a table which gives a fixed salary in accordance with the number of taxpayers in the area concerned, and the current rate of Community Tax collected by the Native Authority. There are three such tables for Village and Ward Heads (X, Y and Z) and the Native Authority chooses the table that it will use in accordance with its wealth. Three of the tables worked out in the same way (XX, YY and ZZ) give comparative salaries for District and Clan Heads.

Native Authority Full-time Councillors

The salaries of Native Authority full-time Councillors were revised by comparison to the salary of the highest paid District Head of the Native Authority under the old rates. The same portion was applied to the new salary of the District Head as worked out above to give the new salary of the Councillors:

e.g., Councillors' old rate   £600
      Highest paid District Head   £400
      New rate for District Head is, say   £560
∴ Councillors' new salary is $3/2 \times 560 = £840$

Alkali and Full-time Court Presidents

The salaries of *Alkalai* and full-time Court Presidents were revised as follows:

(1) The Chief *Alkali* of the Native Authority should receive a salary:

   (a) Not less than the salary of the ninth most highly paid employee in the Native Authority;

   (b) Not less than £25 more than the highest paid District *Alkali*; and

   (c) Not less than his salary at the old rates.

(2) The salaries of *Alkalai* and full-time Court Presidents were revised to ensure that:

123

(a) Salaries were not less than £189 p.a.;

(b) Salaries were not less than 50 per cent of the salary of the District Head of the same District;

(c) If the person concerned was a graduate of Kano Law School a personal allowance would be paid to ensure total emoluments were not less than £216 p.a.;

(d) Court Presidents, members and *Alkali* who passed a course of instruction at the Institute of Administration, Zaria, would be granted a personal allowance of £15 in addition to a basic salary of £189.

Other Employees on Fixed Salaries

Other employees on fixed salaries included market overseers, pound keepers, etc., and increases in such salaries was left to the discretion of the Native Authorities with the proviso that a maximum increase on the old salary would be 15 per cent.

The Salaries of Emirs and Chiefs

The salaries of Emirs and Chiefs are fixed by the Premier on their appointment, and are based on their responsibilities and status. They vary from the Sultan of Sokoto on a salary of £8,400 p.a. to Chiefs on less than £200 p.a.

2. CONTROL OF STAFF

There is no unified system of local government staff in Northern Nigeria. Each Native Authority appoints its own staff and administers them in accordance with model Staff Regulations common to all Native Authorities. Staff are not transferable by Government from one Native Authority to another.

Section 36 (6) of the Law gives the Premier power to direct any Native Authority to set up a committee to deal with matters generally affecting the appointment and dismissal of staff and to give that committee any such functions as he sees fit. A recent Government direction[3] stipulates that all Native Authorities must form Establishment Committees except for those Native Authorities which, with the agreement of the Minister for Local Govern-

---

[3] Ministry for Local Government circular No. 56 of 1962 to all Provincial Commissioners and Native Authorities.

ment, are too small to form them and whose Councils normally themselves handle staff matters.

Staff Discipline

If any information reaches the Government that a Native Authority is not observing fairness and impartiality in its appointments or its terms of service to its staff then there is provision in the Law for the Governor to set up an impartial inquiry to investigate the truth of the allegations. If the inquiry shows that the allegations are true the Governor-in-Council may direct that staff affected or aggrieved by this treatment may appeal direct to him for justice and if necessary the Governor himself will take over control of its staff from the Native Authority.

Approved disciplinary measures for Native Authority staff are detailed in Staff Regulations. Normal forms of discipline on staff are:

(1) Reprimands: these must be in writing and are entered on the official's service sheet.
(2) Deferment of an increment—normally for three or six months.
(3) Withholding an increment—for one year.
(4) Dismissal.

If it is the intention of the Native Authority to dismiss an official for misconduct they must so inform him in writing and he shall be requested to state any grounds for exonerating himself by a specified date.

The discipline of senior staff is dealt with by the Native Authority Council itself. For junior staff decisions are normally taken by a disciplinary committee which is often the Establishment Committee. The Native Authority, if it hands over discipline and control of its police force to the Chief of Police permits him to inflict disciplinary measures for offences against discipline on members of the force in accordance with Native Authority Police Regulations. These may include:

(1) Reduction in rank or grade.
(2) Imprisonment for not more than seven days (168 hours).
(3) A fine of 10s. (in the case of an N.C.O. it may be up to 30s.).
(4) Confinement to barracks for a period up to fourteen days.
(5) A reprimand.

Dismissal from the force is dealt with through a discipline committee.

Similar disciplinary powers are delegated to the Chief Warden under the Native Authority Prison Rules in respect of prison staff.

In the event of a serious charge involving court action or any other inquiry an employee may be interdicted pending the result of the court action or other inquiry. During the period of his interdiction the employee is taken off all duties by the Native Authority and his pay is normally reduced to 50 per cent. If the inquiry acquits him his back pay is repaid in full as if he had not been interdicted.

Employees of a Native Authority may not indulge in political activities in any of the following forms:

(1) Standing as a political party representative for election to the Native Authority Council.

(2) Standing as an independent representative for election to the Native Authority Council if he has already stood as a political representative to a Subordinate Council of the Native Authority.

(3) Acting as an active member of a political party if he is an *Alkali*; a Native Court President or a member of such a court; a member of the Native Authority Police staff, or a member of the Native Authority Prison staff.

(4) Receive any pay from his Native Authority if he is a member of the Federal or Regional Legislature during such period as he is on the business of either of these Legislatures. For convenience of calculation this period is taken as one-twelfth of the year and the salary for this period is not payable by the Native Authority.[4] Employees may, however, receive full pay while on duty with any type of Regional or Federal Committee or Board.

(5) No District Head or any member of a Native Authority Council who is (a) appointed by name; (b) named as the holder of an office; or (c) nominated to that position by the Minister, may stand as a member for a Subordinate Native Authority Council but he may exercise his right to vote.

[4] Members of the Legislative Houses receive an allowance of £800 p.a.

(6) No employee other than a District or a Village Head may stand for election to a Provincial Council. Native Authority staff are also required to observe the following controls:

    (i) Not to engage in trade, agriculture, or industry to such an extent as to cause him to neglect his duties to the Native Authority;

    (ii) To inform the Native Authority of any investments or shares held in any company carrying on business within the area of jurisdiction of the Native Authority;

    (iii) Not to operate any private agency without express permission;

    (iv) Not to contribute to, edit or manage any newspaper without express permission;

    (v) Not to give professional assistance to private individuals outside his specified duties without the written permission of the Native Authority;

    (vi) Not to commence any legal proceedings for defamation relating to matters arising out of his official duties;

    (vii) Not to withhold information concerning discovery of what appears to be a valuable mineral;

    (viii) Not to give interviews on matters affecting public policy;

    (ix) Not to collect subscriptions from subordinates to cover the cost of testimonials and representation to senior employees or Heads of Departments; and

    (x) Not to bring petitions except in accordance with the regulations laid down concerning them.

3. APPOINTMENT OF STAFF AND CONDITIONS OF SERVICE

Native Authorities should not appoint staff to any post unless the candidates have first completed successfully an appropriate course of instruction.[5] If such a course cannot be undertaken at once, however, staff can be employed pending a vacancy on a course which the newly appointed official may fill. All staff except Councillors, District Heads and Village Heads are appointed on

---

[5] Messengers and similar posts are exempt from this provision and so are recruits to N.A. Police and Prison Staff.

probation for three years and until the probationary period is
completed there is no security of tenure in the post. All staff must
be medically examined before appointment. Persons applying for
posts must also:

(1) Complete the standard application form of Native
Authority appointments;[6] and

(2) On receiving an offer of appointment on either pensionable
or contract terms sign an acceptance and a standardised
form of Agreement and Declaration of Secrecy.[7]

The Law provides (section 100) that a Native Authority may bond
its staff if it so desires but this is not a common practice. The
salaries applicable to posts in a Native Authority are controlled:

(1) By Ministries who lay down minimum scales for specified
technical posts;

(2) By the Ministry for Local Government which lays down
minimum educational standards for posts; and

(3) By the Native Authority itself which limits the salary
scales for posts to those which it can afford, in order to
remain financially sound. For example, the Clerk to the
Native Authority Council in Ilorin Native Authority
(Scale "A") earns £468 p.a. and in Borgu Native
Authority (Scale "F") earns £195 p.a.

On appointment a service card is made out for every official
which records:

(1) All disciplinary action;

(2) All promotions;

(3) Scale of salary and increments awarded;

(4) Educational qualifications, and courses attended, etc.;

(5) Awards and commendations;

(6) Any other material pertinent to the conditions of service
or promotion of the official concerned.

The normal retirement age for Native Authority officials is 55.
This may be increased with the consent of the employer and an
official employed until such time as the Native Authority feels that

[6] Agreement to terms offered and agreement to be subject to the conditions
of N.A. staff Regulations.
[7] Agreement not to divulge any confidential matter concerning the policy or
administration of the N.A.

he may no longer fulfil his duties efficiently. An employee may retire or the Native Authority dispense with his services on his reaching the age of 45 subject to six months' notice on either side or payment of six months' salary in lieu of notice.

An official who wishes to resign from the service of the Native Authority may do so by giving one months' notice or one month's salary in lieu. On the same terms the Native Authority may dispense with the services of an official on the grounds of economy or inefficiency on the part of the official.

The privileges of established Native Authority staff include the following:

(1) Annual salary increments within the limits of the salary scales concerned;

(2) Annual leave with pay;[8]

(3) Sick leave;

(4) Pilgrimage leave (after completion of one year's continuous service and subsequently after every five years' service) with pay not exceeding three months;

(5) Uniforms for certain posts;

(6) Travelling allowances when on duty;

(7) Transport allowances for motor vehicles, bicycle or horses;

(8) Advances to purchase transport;

(9) Leave transport grants;

(10) Warm clothing allowance where necessary, for officials travelling abroad;

(11) Acting allowances for those acting in higher posts;

(12) Overtime for certain classes of employee;

(13) Free medical, dental and optical treatment for officials and their families;

(14) Medical and mental allowances to officials dealing with 100 per cent tubercular, meningitis or mental patients;

(15) Retiring benefits. These may be either in the form of an annual pension (commutable if so desired) or a gratuity.[9] Details of these benefits are given in the Retiring Benefits (Native Authorities, Northern Region) Rules, 1948, and are applicable to all persons in the continuous service of a

---

[8] The leave period is based on the salary scale and ranges from forty-two days p.a. for salaries of £1,020 and above to fifteen days p.a. for salaries below £239 p.a.

[9] The payment of retirement benefits is provided for in s. 36B of the Law.

Native Authority. For the purpose of the Rules Native Authority personnel are divided into:

(a) Native Authority Officials. All persons on a salary scale in excess of £153 or on a fixed salary exceeding £153 (Scale F and below);

(b) Native Authority Employees. All persons on a salary scale of £153 or less or on a fixed salary of £153 or less (Scale G and below).

Native authority officials may be granted after ten years' continuous service:

(a) A pension; or

(b) A reduced pension and a retiring gratuity according to the formula laid down. After five years but not up to ten they may be awarded a gratuity. Native Authority employees, however, receive gratuities after five years' continuous service according to a prescribed formula. In addition to these a Native Authority with the approval of Ministry of Local Government may make ex-gratia compassionate allowances in exceptional circumstances.

Daily Paid Staff

Conditions affecting daily paid staff are naturally different from those affecting established staff. Daily paid staff are eligible for annual leave after twelve months' continuous service according to their wage rate per diem or in proportion to the length of continuous service. They are not normally eligible, however, to a leave transport grant. Sick leave on full pay is permissible under certain conditions. Labour rates vary according to the standard of living in different areas.

Normal retirement benefits are not applicable to daily paid staff but a Native Authority will participate in the National Provident Fund with effect from April 1, 1963. This is a compulsory saving scheme in which both the Native Authority and its non-pensionable employees[10] will contribute in equal proportions for the benefit of the employee. The contributions are placed to the credit of the employee monthly and will earn interest on his behalf. The con-

---

[10] In addition to daily paid labour the scheme will embrace all employees on £153 p.a. or less.

tribution rate of the employee is 3d. per 5s. of wages or salary. The employee may draw against the sum standing to his credit:

(1) Upon retirement at 55 years of age;
(2) If sick, when he may draw 3s. 6d. per day.

If the employee dies then his family may benefit from the credit in his name on application through a court.

Women Employees

Native Authorities employ women as teachers, nurses, community attendants, midwives, public enlightenment supervisors, wardresses, policewomen, etc. They are subject to normal staff regulations with the following exceptions:

(1) A woman employee who marries may be asked to retire on or after marriage, but is not normally required to do so. She must, however, inform the Native Authority of her impending marriage;
(2) If pregnant a woman employee may leave her work up to six weeks before confinement and shall not be permitted to resume duty until six weeks after confinement. This period will be on full pay;
(3) Pregnancy leave is in addition to normal leave entitlement;
(4) An unmarried woman who becomes pregnant may be liable for dismissal but disciplinary proceedings will not be instituted until after her confinement.

CHAPTER 8

LOCAL GOVERNMENT ELECTIONS

1. ELECTED BODIES

LOCAL government elections in Northern Nigeria may be divided into:

(1) Elections to Native Authority Councils;
(2) Elections to Subordinate Councils of a Native Authority;
(3) Elections to Outer Councils; and
(4) Elections to Provincial Councils.

1. Native Authority Councils

Elected representatives on Native Authority Councils are elected under the provisions of Regulations made by the Governor in accordance with section 6 (4) of the Native Authority Law, 1954. Elections are indirect in 74 per cent of the Regulations in force at July 1, 1962, the electorate being made up of the members of Subordinate Councils. Election with one exception now is by means of a secret ballot. The names of the Returning Councils who are to elect representatives are given as a schedule to the Regulations.

2. Subordinate Councils

Elections to Subordinate Councils of a Native Authority are conducted in accordance with Rules made by the Native Authority under section 37 paragraph (20) of the Native Authority Law with the approval of the Governor. These Rules may be either made (*a*) for a specific local Council only or (*b*) be model Rules applying to all local Councils of the Native Authority. In this case a schedule to the Rules gives the electoral units and the numbers to be returned in respect of each local Council. These Rules are normally introduced at the same time as the local Councils are set up by Instrument and they now almost always stipulate election by secret ballot. They are almost all (95 per cent) direct elections. Tenure of office of elected members is normally three years.

3. Outer Councils

The Outer Council of a Native Authority is set up by Instrument and this contains provision for a majority of elected members. These are elected also by Rules made under the authority of

132

paragraph (20) of section 37 of the Native Authority Law. The election is indirect, the electoral colleges being Subordinate Councils of the Native Authority. The term of office is normally three years.

4. Provincial Councils

Provincial Council elections are held in accordance with Electoral Regulations made by the Governor-in-Council under the authority of section 8 of the Provincial Councils Law, 1959. These provide for indirect elections, the electoral colleges being the elected representatives of the Subordinate Councils of the Native Authorities of the Province. The term of office of an elected member is that of the electoral college who elected him.

2. CONDUCT OF ELECTIONS AND FRANCHISE

Although the secret ballot is a comparatively recent innovation in the North in local government elections it has gained hold very rapidly, due to political party activity, and is now commonplace. The electorate is still 90 per cent illiterate, however, and this presents difficulties in balloting techniques and in giving the necessary propaganda to forthcoming elections. Local government elections have benefited enormously from the experience gained by Native Authorities and by the electorate themselves in the recent Regional and Federal elections and in the plebiscites held in the Northern Cameroons in 1959 and 1961.

Elections may be direct or indirect. In the direct election the members to be returned to the representative body are elected directly by the people. In indirect elections, however, the people elect representatives to one body which then forms an electoral college and it is this college only which forms the electorate to elect members into the Council concerned. Direct elections are more expensive as they have to embrace the whole electorate of the people, but they possess the important advantage that the size of the voting electorate prevents the danger of undue influence or coercion in voting. There is greater danger in the indirect method where much fewer persons have the right to vote.

Electoral units for direct elections are normally the administrative units of the Native Authority or its tax collection units. These have the valuable advantage of being well defined and well known to the electorate, *i.e.*, the Village area and the District for rural communities and the town Ward in urban areas. Electoral units, however, should be of uniform size as regards the numbers of electors living therein if there is to be fair proportional representation. One method of ensuring proportional representation where the administrative areas vary considerably in population density is to form multiple constituencies (*i.e.*, where the electoral unit returns more than one candidate to conform to proportional representation) but these are very difficult to administer with an illiterate electorate and are avoided by Native Authorities wherever possible. In deciding on the porportionate representation and the division of the area into electoral units the following problems have to be given consideration.

(1) Careful choice of central voting stations; long distances are sometimes unavoidable, but it is unfair to expect voters to walk a long way from their homes to record their votes. It is an advantage if possible and a common practice to hold elections on market days at market centres where the majority of the electorate visit.

(2) Supervision and collection of ballot boxes. If it is necessary to have two or three polling stations in one area there is the common problem of supervision of each polling station in an area where it is difficult to find adequate-educated staff. Collection of ballot boxes at the Central Counting Station is also a difficulty in rural areas lacking motor roads.

(3) The timing of the election. Wherever possible elections should be held in the dry season but after the marketing of crops, *i.e.*, December–April. Travelling is easier at this time and the rural electorate are not taken away from work on their farms.

Details of electoral units are given normally on a schedule to the subsidiary legislation setting up the election. If this legislation is of the model type intended to cover all local Council elections the schedule should be reviewed every two or three years against the details of population shown on the tax assessment returns to ensure that representation remains proportionate.

Registration of the electorate is normally undertaken only in urban areas. In rural areas evidence as to qualification to vote is by the elector's tax receipt for the current year. The basic problem of finding adequately educated staff capable of compiling a "Register of Electors" is the main reason why Native Authorities avoid registration if possible. Qualifications of electors may vary. The common qualifications, however, are:

(1) That he is an adult male;
(2) That he is a taxpayer in the area for one or more years;
(3) That he is over 21 years of age;
(4) That he is not undergoing a sentence for a serious criminal offence;
(5) That he is of sound mind.

A youth may be liable for tax, if he is not a student, from the age of 16 years. It is also very difficult to assess when a man reaches 21 years if he can give no proof as to the date of his birth. In rural areas the District or Village Head will know most of the electors personally and these problems seldom arise. There is often a residential qualification for voting which may be residence in the area (*i.e.*, payment of tax in that area) for the past three years. A common form of qualification in electoral Rules is to give an alternative such as:

(1) Has paid tax in the area for three years immediately preceding the election; or
(2) Was born in the area and has paid tax there for one year immediately preceding the election.

Qualifications of candidates standing for nomination must include the qualification of being an elector of the area. A person must be proposed for nomination by an elector and seconded by one. He must express his willingness to stand for election either verbally or in writing. In some local government elections he may be called upon to place a deposit of money before he can be accepted as a candidate. If in the subsequent poll he obtains less than one-tenth of total votes cast (in some Rules it may be one-eighth of the total votes) then the deposit is forfeited and is paid into Native Treasury Revenue. Deposits vary from £1 to £5.

There are disqualifications to holders of certain posts in Native Authorities standing for election:

(1) No *Alkali*, Native Court judge or full-time member of a Native Court may stand for election to any local government body.

(2) No member of the Native Authority police or prison staff may stand for election to any local government body.

(3) No Native Authority employee may stand for election to his Native Authority Council as the representative of a political party.

(4) No Native Authority employee may stand as an independent member to a Native Authority Council if he has already stood as a political party representative to a Subordinate Council.

(5) No District Head or a traditional or nominated member of a Native Authority Council may stand as a member of a Subordinate Native Authority Council.

(6) District and Village Heads are the only employees of a Native Authority who may stand for election to a Provincial Council.

Qualifications of candidates for election to Provincial Councils are as follows:

(1) They are male citizens of Nigeria and of the age of 21 years or more;

(2) They must either:

(a) have been resident in the Province for a continuous period immediately preceding the date of election of at least three years; or

(b) have been born in the Province or whose fathers were born in the Province provided they have paid tax for the past year in Northern Nigeria or were exempted from tax;

(3) They must not be undergoing a sentence of imprisonment;

(4) They must not be of unsound mind;

(5) They must not have been convicted under the Penal Code to six months' imprisonment or more the sentence having expired within one year prior to the date of the election.

If the nominations are equal to or less than the number of persons to be returned then there is no election and the names of the persons nominated are announced to the public as the members who will represent them. If a place is to be contested, however, there is an announcement made of this fact together with the names of the contestants and the date and place of the poll.

Methods of voting in direct elections vary but in the majority of cases now a secret ballot is held. There are still certain areas where the "public acclamation" system is used in both direct and indirect elections by Native Authorities for elections to Subordinate Councils. This may be either by a show of hands for each candidate in turn or by supporters standing behind the candidate of their choice to be counted. Public voting in this form, of course, possesses the danger of intimidation by powerful candidates of the voters and it is the policy of the Ministry for Local Government that all remaining Native Authorities will adopt the secret ballot as soon as possible.

Bearing in mind that the majority of the electors cannot read polling may be organised either by (a) the single box method; or (b) the multiple box method. Type (b) is the most widely used although type (a) has been used with success with an illiterate electorate.[1]

Single Box Method

In the single box method the procedure is as follows:

(1) The voter enters the polling station and comes to the Returning Officer. The entrance is guarded by a policeman or guard to see that electors enter one by one.

(2) The voter either:

    (a) has his name checked on the Electoral Register if registration has taken place; or

    (b) produces proof that he is a qualified person to vote, *i.e.*, his tax receipts. The Returning Officer should mark the receipt (but not deface it or them) to prevent use a second time. In doubtful cases as to eligibility to vote the Returning Officer must use his discretion.

(3) The voter is given a ballot paper which is stamped in his presence. On the paper are the names of the candidates and against each a symbol[2] and/or a colour. Photographs of the candidates are also, if possible, displayed in the

---

[1] Akwanga, Daura, Katsina.
[2] The symbol may be (a) a shape—square, circle, triangle, etc.; (b) a political symbol; or (c) a symbol selected for the candidate by the Electoral Officer.

polling station and in the voting booth. If there is only one polling station for the electoral unit then the candidates will be present themselves and can hold copies of their symbols. If there is more than one polling station then a representative of each candidate will be present at each polling station in the unit to ensure that the voting is completely impartial.

(4) The voter takes his card and retires to the screened voting booth. Here he marks the card against the name and symbol of his choice with a pencil provided and folds the card.

(5) The voter returns and puts his folded card in the box in front of the Returning Officer and the candidates or their representatives.

(6) The voter then leaves the station by a separate exit (not the entrance).

Advantages	*Disadvantages*
(1) Vote is recorded before Returning Officer.	(1) Voter may not understand how to mark paper.
(2) Voting paper cannot be taken out and sold.	(2) Voter may not mark paper.
(3) Fewer boxes for Returning Officer to deal with than in multiple box method.	(3) Voter may deface paper.

Multiple Box Method

In the multiple box method each candidate again has a colour and/or symbol which is associated with him. The procedure is as follows:

(1) The voter enters the polling station by the guarded entrance.

(2) The voter is checked by the Returning Officer as in the single box method.

(3) The voter is given a ballot paper. This is a plain white paper with a serial number (for checking purposes; counterfoils of papers are tallied at the time of the count) and the name of the election.

(4) The voter enters the screened polling booth where there is a box for every candidate. Each box is clearly marked with the symbol and/or colour of its candidate. The voter places his card in the box of his choice and leaves the booth.

(5) The voter leaves the polling station by a separate exit.

Advantages	*Disadvantages*
(1) More simple to understand than the single box method.	(1) Voter records vote in private so that it is possible to keep his card and sell it.
(2) Voters do not have to mark cards in any way.	(2) Voters may try to tamper with boxes in booth.

(The diagrams of polling stations at the end of the chapter illustrate the details of voting by each method.)

Multiple Constituency. Mention should be made of the multiple constituency, that is to say an electoral unit which is to return more than one representative.

This means that each voter will have more than one vote. He must therefore:

(1) In the single box method mark his card for each vote (*i.e.*, twice for two votes) but not give two votes to any one candidate;[3] or

(2) In the multiple box method to record his votes in different boxes and not give all his votes to one box. To check this the same serial number is on each of his ballot cards and if two cards of the same serial number appear in one box only one is counted.

Certain Native Authorities give a choice of the type of voting to be used in their subsidiary legislation[4] allowing a simple procedure for backward areas and a more complicated form for sophisticated units.

The mechanics of an election after the necessary legislation has been approved are shown in the following chart.

---

[3] If he marks the paper in this way the paper will be considered defaced and not counted.
[4] *e.g.*, N.R.L.N. 391 of 1957.

STAGE	ACTION TO BE TAKEN	OFFICER RESPONSIBLE	TIMINGS	REMARKS
1	Area divided into electoral units and published in electoral Rules	Native Authority	One month before proposed election	Details published i Rules but these should be made known to electora
2	Appointment of Electoral Officer, Returning Officers and Registration Officers	Native Authority	Immediately after publication of Rules	Staff should be appointed as early as possible to allo for training, etc.
3	Announcement of Elections and registration	Native Authority Chief Reg. Officer	2/3 weeks before elections	To be given as mu publicity as possib
4	Training of election and Registration Officials	Electoral Officer	Before Registration begins	It is most importa that all officials kn the legislation and the details of their own duties
5	Registration begins	Registration Officers	At least a fortnight before proposed election	Each electoral uni should have a registration office
6	Registration ends	Registration Officers	As soon as possible after it has begun	Arrangements mu be made for publishing Electoral Roll as quickly as possible
7	Appeals on registration	Electoral Officer	Within 3 days of publication of Roll	Appeals against R must be made by electors only
8	Nominations	Electoral Officer	Not less than 7 days before proposed polls	Candidates must qualified and confirm that they wis to stand
9	Notice of poll (if necessary)	Electoral Officer	Not less than 7 days before polls (minimum)	Electorate must know time and pl where it should vo
10	Polling day	Returning Officers	Election day	All voting station open and close at the same time
11	Counting of poll and announcement of result	Returning Officers, Electoral Officer	Election day	Held before all candidates or thei reps. announceme made immediately
12	Appeals	Electoral Officer	Within 48 hours of election	May be to the Ele toral Officer or th Divisional Officer to a special committee
13	Consideration of appeals	Appeals Committee or Electoral Officer	As soon as possible	If an appeal is allowed it may b necessary to hold new election

Details of Election Officials

Electoral Officer	Responsible for the overall organisation and conduct of the election as a whole.
Registration Officers	Officials responsible under the Electoral Officer for compiling the Electoral Roll.
Returning Officers	In charge of electoral units. They will run the polling and counting of votes.
Polling Officers	In an electoral unit with more than one polling station a Polling Officer is in charge of each station, responsible to the Returning Officer concerned.

The success or failure of an election depends on the standard of its officials. Their training therefore is most important. Native Authorities have evolved very efficient forms of temporary polling stations and the procedure of casting votes is widely known by the more sophisticated electorates. Where a local government election is fought on political grounds (more common in urban areas) the political parties concerned can assist the Native Authority in making sure that their supporters are familiar with the electoral procedure.

By-elections

A by-election is necessary if a member:

(1) Dies;

(2) Tenders his resignation in writing to the Chairman of the Council concerned;

(3) Becomes involved in circumstances which would prevent his election;

(4) Leaves the Council for any other reason.

Care must be taken that the vacancy does not invalidate any business of the Council before it is filled, *i.e.*, by preventing the quorum to validate the meeting.

When a by-election is held the successful candidate holds his office only for the same length of time as that remaining to the other elected members already in office so that fresh elections for all elected seats on the Council may be held at the same time.

When a Council is dissolved after its tenure of office the elected members may stand for re-election if they so desire.

Electoral Offences

Section 62 of the Native Authority Law, 1954, empowers the Governor to make Rules setting out election offences and their punishment. These Rules apply to all elections to Subordinate Councils of Native Authorities throughout Northern Nigeria. These were made as the Native Authority Subordinate Councils (Election Offences) Rules, 1957,[5] and are still applicable.

Parties to the election offences are stated in these Rules as (*a*) all persons actually commiting the act or making the omission which constitutes the offence; (*b*) any person enabling another to commit an offence; (*c*) any person aiding or abetting an offence; (*d*) any person who commits or procures another person to commit an offence.

The offences themselves are listed as:

(1) Personation, *i.e.*, voting in the name of another person or recording more than one vote in his name.[6]

(2) Undue influence, *i.e.*, force, threats, fraud or oaths.

(3) Bribery which means the promise of any benefit or reward whatsoever[7] to influence a vote.

(4) Interference with the secrecy of the vote.

(5) Canvassing for votes at the place of poll.

(6) Destruction or mutilation of election documents including ballot papers.

(7) Making false statements in order to interfere with the conduct of the elections.

(8) Voting when prohibited or disqualified from voting.

(9) Inpugning the character of a candidate to influence voters.

(10) Generally behaving in a disorderly manner at an election.

The punishment upon conviction of any of these offences is imprisonment up to six months or a fine up to £50 or both such imprisonment and fine as the court sees fit. Conviction of an

---

[5] N.R.L.N. 427 of 1957.
[6] Two or more credible witnesses required for conviction.
[7] Except lawful legal expenses.

election offence will also mean disqualification for some time of exercising the privilege of voting in local government elections.

Appeals against Results

The persons responsible for hearing complaints after the results of a poll have been made known may be:

(1) The Electoral Officer.

(2) The Divisional Officer.

(3) The Provincial Commissioner.

(4) An Appeals Committee.

The decision of the person or persons responsible is always final.

The appellant may be either an elector or a candidate. He must appeal in the form laid down in the electoral legislation and this may require:

(1) The appeal to be in writing giving reasons.

(2) The appeal to be made in the time limit stated.

(3) A deposit to be given to cover the expenses of witnesses to be called.

An appeal against a result of a poll may not include an allegation of irregularity in the preparation of the Election Register (appeals for which having already been heard). Appeals will be dismissed without hearing if the hearer is satisfied that the complaint, even if substantiated, would in no way affect the result of the election.

If a complaint is upheld then the election must be declared void and another election must be held as soon as possible using the same legislation.

EXAMPLES OF POLLING STATIONS USING SINGLE AND MULTIPLE BOX SYSTEMS

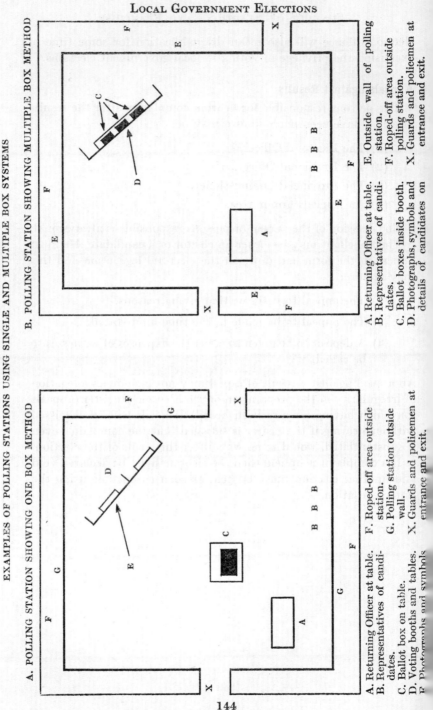

A. POLLING STATION SHOWING ONE BOX METHOD

B. POLLING STATION SHOWING MULTIPLE BOX METHOD

A. Returning Officer at table.
B. Representatives of candidates.
C. Ballot box on table.
D. Voting booths and tables.
E. Photographs and symbols
F. Roped-off area outside station.
G. Polling station outside wall.
X. Guards and policemen at entrance and exit.

A. Returning Officer at table.
B. Representatives of candidates.
C. Ballot boxes inside booth.
D. Photographs, symbols and details of candidates on
E. Outside wall of polling station.
F. Roped-off area outside polling station.
X. Guards and policemen at entrance and exit.

LIST OF NATIVE AUTHORITIES' ELECTORAL RULES AND REGULATIONS

NO.	NATIVE AUTHORITY	N.A. COUNCILS	OUTER COUNCILS	DISTRICT COUNCILS	VILLAGE COUNCILS	TOWN COUNCILS
1	Abuja	I	—	D	—	D
2	Adamawa	I	I	D	—	D
3	Agaie	D	—	—	—	—
4	Akwanga	I	—	D	D	—
5	Argungu	I	I	D	—	D
6	Awe	D	—	—	—	—
7	Bauchi	I	I†	D	—	—
8	Bedde	I	—	—	—	D
9	Bida	I	—	D	—	Revoked
10	Birnin Gwari	D	—	—	—	—
11	Biu	—	—	—	—	—
12	Bornu	—	I	D	—	D
13	Borgu	I	—	I	D	—
14	Bunu	D	—	—	—	—
15	Chamba	I	—	D	—	—
16	Dass	D†	—	—	—	—
17	Daura	—	I	D	—	D
18	Dikwa	I	D	D	—	D
19	East Yagba	I	—	D†	—	—
20	Fika	I	—	I	D	D
21	Gashaka-Mumbilla	I	—	D	—	—
22	Gombe	I	I	D	—	D
23	Gumel	—	D	D	—	—
24	Gwandu	I	I	D	—	D

LIST OF NATIVE AUTHORITIES' ELECTORAL RULES AND REGULATIONS—*continued*

NO.	NATIVE AUTHORITY	N.A. COUNCILS	OUTER COUNCILS	DISTRICT COUNCILS	VILLAGE COUNCILS	TOWN COUNCIL
25	Gwari	I	—	D	—	D
26	Gwoza	D	—	—	—	—
27	Hadejia	—	I	D	—	D
28	Idoma	I	—	D	—	D
29	Igala	I	—	D	—	—
30	Igbirra	I	—	D	—	—
31	Ijumu	D	—	—	—	—
32	Ilorin	I	—	I	D	D
33	Jema'a	I	—	D	—	D
34	Jema'are	I	I	—	D	—
35	Jos	I	—	D	—	D
36	Kabba	D	—	—	—	—
37	Kamuku	D	—	D	—	—
38	Kanam	I	—	D	—	—
39	Kano	—	I†	D	—	D
40	Katagum	—	I†	D†	—	D
41	Katsina	—	I†	D	—	Revoke
42	Kazaure	—	I†	D	—	D
43	Keffi	I	—	D	—	D
44	Kontagora	I	—	D	—	D
45	Kwara	I	—	D	—	—
46	Lafia	I	—	D	D	D
47	Lafiagi	I	—	D	—	—
48	Lapai	D	—	—	—	—

NO.	NATIVE AUTHORITY	N.A. COUNCILS	OUTER COUNCILS	DISTRICT COUNCILS	VILLAGE COUNCILS	TOWN COUNCILS
49	Lowland	I	—	D†	—	—
50	Misau	—	I†	D	—	D
51	Mubi	I	—	D	—	D
52	Muri	I	I	D	—	D
53	Nassarawa	I	—	D	—	D
54	Ningi	I	—	D	—	—
55	Numan	I	I	I	D	I
56	Pankshin	I	—	D	—	—
57	Pategi	I	—	D	—	—
58	Sokoto	—	I	D	—	D
59	Tangale-Waja	D	—	—	—	—
60	Tiv	I	—	D	—	D
61	United Hills	D	—	—	—	—
62	Wase	—	—	D	—	D
63	Wukari	I	—	D†	—	D
64	Wushishi	D	D	—	—	D
65	West Yagba	I	—	D	—	—
66	Yergam	I	D	D	—	—
67	Yauri	D	I†	D	—	D
68	Zaria	—	I	D	—	D
69	Zuru	I	—	D	—	D
70	Resettlement	D	—	—	—	—
71	Kaduna	—	—	—	—	—

NOTE: D — Direct elections.
I — Indirect elections.
† — Non-secret ballot elections.

CHAPTER 9

PROVINCIAL ADMINISTRATION

NORTHERN Nigeria is divided administratively into thirteen Provinces, each of which is divided into Divisions. There are forty-one Divisions in all. The officer of the Central Government responsible for the good order and government of a Province in the past was the Resident who was assisted by Divisional Officers who might be Senior District Officers or District Officers. The Resident has, however, been replaced by the Provincial Commissioner (see below). The Divisions and Divisional Officers still remain. There are one or more Native Authorities to each Division. The present division is as follows:

PROVINCE	SIZE IN SQ. MILES	DIVISIONS	NATIVE AUTHORI-TIES	PRESENT ADMINIS-TRATIVE STRENGTH[1]
Adamawa .	20,821	3	3	8
Bauchi . .	26,120	3	8	9
Benue . .	29,318	5	7	12
Bornu . .	40,584	4	4	11
Ilorin . .	17,719	3	4	8
Kabba . .	10,953	4	8	7
Kano . .	16,630	2	4	11
Katsina . .	9,466	1	2	5
Niger . .	28,666	4	9	10
Plateau . .	11,253	4	8	8
Sardauna[2] .	16,114	3	6	9
Sokoto . .	36,338	3	4	7
Zaria . .	17,243	2	3	7
TOTAL .	281,225	41	70	112

The constitution of Northern Nigeria as defined by the Nigeria (Constitution) Order in Council, 1960, provides that either (a) the

[1] Includes leave reliefs.
[2] Formerly the Northern Cameroons, made a Province of Northern Nigeria for the first time in June 1962.

Governor may by Instrument set up a Provincial Administration for any Province consisting of:

(1) A Provincial Commissioner;

(2) A Provincial Authority under the Chairmanship of the Administrator; and

(3) A Provincial Council set up by the Governor;

or (b) the Provincial Administration of a Province may be set up by the Legislature of the Region.

The Provincial Administration Law[3] is an example of action taken by the Legislature under the second alternative. It was passed by the Legislature in March 1962 and is expected to be put into operation in September 1962. It provides for the appointment by the Premier of a political appointment of an official of the status of Minister with portfolio to each Province to be known by the title of Provincial Commissioner.[4] The Provincial Commissioner will be assisted by the Senior Administrative Officer in the management of the Province. This official will be known as the Provincial Secretary. The relationship between the Commissioner and his Provincial Secretary will be the same as that between a Minister of the Cabinet and his Permanent Secretary. That is to say he will be subject to the directions of his Provincial Commissioner in the same way as a Permanent Secretary is subject to the directions of a Minister from the Central Government. All powers formerly vested in a Resident will now be vested in the person of the Provincial Commissioner. The latter and the Premier may, however, delegate any of these powers either to the Provincial Secretary or to any other administrative officer of the Province.

Should no Commissioner be appointed to a Province his duties will be carried out by the Provincial Secretary.

Finally, provision is included in the Law for the Premier through the Provincial Commissioner concerned to direct any Native Authority in that Province to carry out its functions as laid down by statute law or by native law and custom. The Native Authority must then comply with these instructions.

The idea of an executive arm of the Central Government in each Province and the co-ordination of departments at Provincial level

[3] No. 2 of 1962.
[4] This presupposes that Provincial Commissioners must be appointed from among the members of the elected legislature.

149

is not a new one in the Region, although until 1959 there was no legislation for it. In 1948 Provincial Development Committees were set up to co-ordinate development between departments in each Province. Niger Province set up a Provincial Council with representatives from all authorities and departments in 1947 and Bauchi set up a similar Council in 1954. In June 1956 the Northern Nigeria Government requested the Colonial Office to send out an impartial Commissioner with following terms of reference:

"Having regard to the great size of the Northern Region of Nigeria and to the widely differing customs and traditional systems of local government practised within the Region, to advise how best a measure of authority can be devolved on provincial authorities so as to provide an effective and acceptable link between the Regional Government and the Native Authorities, and to make recommendations regarding the composition and functions of such authorities."

The Commissioner selected was Mr. R. S. Hudson, C.M.G., and during his investigations he was advised by (a) a Senior Resident; (b) a District Head of Kano Native Authority; and (c) a Northern Civil Servant of the Riverain Areas.

The subsequent report advised in detail on the setting up of twelve Provincial Administrations each consisting of a Provincial Council and a Provincial Authority. The Council was to be a deliberative as well as a consultative body with defined powers and duties. The members were to be representative of "Chiefs, Native Authorities and the people". The authority was to be a small executive body charged with the execution of Provincial policy as defined by the Council. A White Paper by the Northern Government supporting these proposals was laid before the Northern legislature in 1957 but the necessary legislation was shelved due to opposition by the larger Native Authorities of the Region, and by administrative difficulties. As a preliminary step, however, the Provincial Councils Law, 1959, set up provision for Councils for each Province by Instrument.[5] These Councils are purely advisory in character. The Instrument is made by the Governor-in-Council and must contain the following provisions:

(1) The name of the Council.

(2) The functions of the Council.

[5] Section 3 of the Provincial Councils Law.

These are stated in existing Instruments as:

(a) To debate and make recommendations on any matter which has been referred to it by the Minister for Local Government.

(b) To appoint committees under the provisions of section 10 of the Law and to make Standing Orders for the conduct of business of such committees. (Committees may be set up by a Provincial Council with the approval of the Minister.)[6]

(c) To make Standing Orders for business in respect of section 9 of the Law. These *must* include provisions for

   (i) a quorum;

   (ii) a minimum voting majority;

   (iii) method of assent to Council documents;

   (iv) Vice-Chairmanship;[7]

   (v) control of public and Press;

   (vi) notices of meetings and the form of agenda.

They *may* include also any other provisions that the Council may think proper for the efficient discharge of its duties and to discuss and make recommendations to the Regional Government on any matters brought before it in accordance with its Standing Orders.

(3) The composition of the Council, as specified in sections 5 and 6 of the Law.

(4) The tenure of office of nominated members.

Provincial Councils are large bodies as can be seen from the table below. There is an elected majority in each case; these members being elected in accordance with electoral Regulations set up by the Governor-in-Council. In all cases these are indirect elections; the electoral colleges being formed by (a) the elected members of Subordinate Councils of the Native Authorities or (b) Subordinate Native Authorities of the Native Authorities or (c) Outer Councils of the Native Authorities. In addition each Council has nominated members who are nominated (a) by the Native Authorities of the Province; or (b) by the Minister to represent special interests. The term of office of nominated members is three

---

[6] No committees have as yet been set up by any Provincial Council.
[7] The Chairman is the Provincial Commissioner.

years, the term of office of an elected member is that of the persons who elected him.

Members of Provincial Councils are not disqualified for election or appointment to the House of Assembly. The Council Instruments have been amended to include provision in the Council for one-third of the total number of members of the Regional and Federal legislatures in the Province as nominated members. The members themselves elect in the presence of a senior administrative officer which of them shall sit on the Council. Their term of office is three years or to the date that they cease to be members of the legislative body concerned.

(5) The summoning and frequency of meetings of the Council. Provincial Councils hold normal meetings at least twice per year. Extraordinary meetings may be called, however, by the Chairman within fourteen days on receipt of a request in writing by not less than one-half of the members of the Council.

(6) The appointment of a Secretary to the Council. This is done by the Chairman but requires the approval of the Minister. The Secretary must be an experienced administrative officer who should normally be the rank of Senior District Officer. The duties of the Secretary have been laid down by the Ministry for Local Government in detail.

Although all the Provincial Councils with the exception of Sardauna Province were set up in 1960 the first meetings of these bodies were postponed until 1962 when all were formally opened by the Minister for Local Government. It is, therefore, not possible at this stage to assess the value of the Councils as advisory bodies.

PROVINCE	INSTRU-MENT	INSTRUMENTS AMENDMENTS	ELEC-TORAL REGS.	TOTAL MEMBER-SHIP	NO. OF NOMINATED MEMBERS OF LEGISLATURE
AMAWA	70/60	56/61; 169/61	71/60	36	6
UCHI	29/60	71/61	30/60	67	9
NUE	46/60	72/60			
		25/61; 79/61	47/60	54	8
RNU	58/60	57/61; 154/61	59/60	45	9
RIN	48/60	58/61	49/60	35	4
BBA	50/60	34/62	35/61		
		24/61; 75/61	51/60	46	5
NO	73/60	59/61	74/60	64	20
TSINA	33/60	72/61	34/60	35	9
GER	31/60	73/61	32/60	60	5
ATEAU	52/60	74/61; 138/61	53/60	39	5
RDAUNA	88/62	—	/62	25	5
KOTO	107/60	61/61	108/60	57	16
RIA	56/60	60/61	57/60	46	5

Model Standing Orders have also been made by the Ministry for Local vernment.

CHAPTER 10

CONTROL OF NATIVE LANDS

ON July 1, 1962, the control of the Native Lands was governed by the Land and Native Rights Ordinance.[1] A new Law governing land usage, however, was passed by the Northern Legislature in April 1962 and will come into effect on October 1, 1962. This is the Land Tenure Law, 1962. This Law is based largely on the former Ordinance with the following main changes:

(1) The powers of the Governor under the Ordinance are now vested in the Minister of the Northern Nigeria Government responsible for Lands (*i.e.*, the Minister for Land and Survey);

(2) The power to control titles to land either by customary titles or by statutory titles may be delegated to Native Authorities by the Minister if he so wishes; and

(3) All matters dealing with the issue and control of Wayleave Licences are now the subject of a separate Law (the Waylcave Licences Law, 1962).

The Land Tenure Law defines "Native Lands" as the whole of the lands of Northern Nigeria, whether occupied or unoccupied, with the following exceptions:

(1) Interest by non-natives[2] in land prior to February 25, 1916 (on February 4, 1927, in the case of the former trust territory of Sardauna Province);

(2) Rights of persons over lands specified in the Second and Third Schedules of the Niger Lands Transfer Ordinance.

Land may be held in one of three ways:

(1) Under customary rights of occupancy, *i.e.*, a native or native community using or occupying land in accordance with native law and custom;

---

[1] Cap. 105 of the Laws of Nigeria, 1948.
[2] Non-natives are those who are not persons whose fathers are or were members of any tribe indigenous to Northern Nigeria.

(2) Under statutory rights of occupancy granted by the Minister under the provisions of the Law;

(3) Under statutory rights of occupancy granted by a Native Authority or Local Authority under powers delegated to them by the Minister.

All such rights may, however, be revoked by the Minister if the land concerned is needed for public purposes.[3] If this is done, however, compensation will be payable on improvements to the land (*i.e.*, buildings, crops, utilities, etc.). If the occupier of the land is in fact the local native community then compensation may be paid:

(1) To the native community; or

(2) To the Chief or headman of the community to dispose of for the benefit of the native community in accordance with native law or custom; or

(3) Into a specific fund named by the Minister to be used for the benefit of the community.

Both the Ordinance and the new Law are specific in the control of the use of native lands by non-natives. No non-natives may hold land now without the specific consent of the Minister and the statutory Right of Occupancy when given will contain in its Certificate such controls as:

(1) Payment of rent;

(2) Insistence on specific development to the land within a stated period of time;

(3) Occupancy limited in any one certificate to a specified number of years;

(4) Inability to alienate land without special permission from the Minister.

Failure to conform to these controls makes the holder liable to lose his right of occupancy over the land.

The customary right of occupancy depends upon the native law or custom of the community concerned. In many places it is the Native Authority or its representative who is the guardian of customary rights. A native of a local community requiring land

[3] S. 34 of the proposed Land Tenure Law, 1962.

will normally apply to (*a*) the head of the family; or (*b*) the village or hamlet head; or (*c*) to the Chief of the area himself.

If there is implied general consent of the community that the individual (if a native) may obtain land, his request is granted. There is normally no written document or certificate to prove right of occupancy. It is therefore impossible to obtain a mortgage under a customary right of occupancy.

In Muslim areas, even in the far north, local law and custom is mixed in with Muslim doctrines regarding land usufruct. Local law varies in these areas from place to place and is jealously preserved.

Civil cases involving land and inheritance of land are heard by Native Courts. In respect of natives the new Law directs that in cases involving inheritance of land devolution shall be governed by:

(1) In cases involving occupancy of a native, by the native law and custom which he observes;

(2) In the case of a non-native, by the law or custom of that non-native at the time of his death.

A statutory right of occupancy may not be divided up by inheritance on the death of the occupier without the consent of the Minister.

Customary rights of occupancy may be revoked:

(1) When the land is required by the Government of Northern Nigeria or the Federal Government for public purposes;

(2) When the land is required by the Native Authority for public purposes;

(3) When the land is needed for a statutory right of occupancy;

(4) When the land is needed for mining;

(5) When the occupier has alienated his land to a non-native without the permission of the Minister.

POWERS OF NATIVE AUTHORITIES

The traditional Chiefs are still in most Native Authority areas the custodians of the land. The Land Tenure Law gives the power to the Governor-in-Council or the Minister for Land and Survey to delegate any of the powers of the latter under that Law to Native Authorities subject to any conditions or restrictions that they may think fit. These powers may include the power to issue Certificates of Occupancy to non-natives.

As seen in the above paragraph Native Authorities may enter upon land held under a customary right of occupancy if they wish to use it for public purposes. They may not occupy land, however, which is subject to a statutory right of occupancy or subject to investigation or exploitation of minerals or mineral oils; or which is required by the Government for public purposes.

Under the Land Tenure Law Native Authorities will be given powers under two sets of Regulations for the control of land.

1. The Land Tenure (Native Authority Control of Settlements) Regulations, 1962[4]

These Regulations provide for the appointment of settlement areas and the control of all lands therein.[5] They have the advantage of:

(1) Providing for resettlement out of over-populated or unproductive areas;

(2) Resettling communities which have lost their former lands, *e.g.*, in the mining areas of Jos.

The Regulations provide for Native Authorities with the approval of the Provincial Commissioner to establish settlement plans which will zone specific surveyed areas into:

(1) Agricultural holdings;

(2) Residential and trading areas;

(3) Fuel and forest reserves;

(4) Communal grazing areas;

(5) Reservoirs, catchment areas and other works of a like nature; and

(6) Areas for future development;

and provide for the detailed development of these zones.

2. The Land Tenure (Native Authority—Right of Occupancy) Regulations, 1962[6]

These apply to the whole of Kaduna Capital Territory, and to certain specified areas at Kano, Zaria, Kafanchan, Jos, Bukuru,

---

[4] Formerly Regulation 1 of 1950 under the former Ordinance.
[5] They are designed to establish settlements in unpopulated areas.
[6] Formerly Regulation 40 of 1951 under the former Ordinance.

Minna, Sokoto, Gusau and Bauchi. They provide for the Native Authorities concerned to grant certificates of occupancy to natives of Nigeria for specified periods (not exceeding thirty years) in thickly populated urban areas where there is a large immigrant population. The land is divided into equal plots which can be sold by auction to the highest bidder, but are more usually allocated by the Native Authority to the most deserving applicants.

They have the advantage
(1) Of developing urban residential and commercial areas to required minimum standards of public hygiene, building and public utilities.
(2) Imposing a rent on plots which provide funds for development, *i.e.*, Kano Native Authority Revenue from plots in the current year is about £9,000.
(3) Giving holders of plots better security of tenure than under a customary right of occupancy.
(4) Of ensuring that native lands are not alienated illegally to non-Northerners.

There are also the Land Tenure (Local Authority Right of Occupancy) Regulations, 1962.[7] These apply to Jos and will apply to New Bussa.[8] They are exactly the same as the Native Authority Right of Occupancy Regulations except that they are applied by a Local Authority, *i.e.*, an officer appointed by Government to administer a certain specified area instead of by a Native Authority.

Under the control of Settlement Regulations, the Native Authority Right of Occupancy Regulations and Local Authority Regulations, the Minister has directed that in any one year the allocation of plots by grant, transfer or sale shall be in the proportion 80 per cent to natives and 20 per cent to non-natives. This direction does not affect allocations of plots by grant, transfer or sale made up to 1961.

---

[7] Former Regulation 38 of 1951.
[8] A new Township to be established in connection with the proposed Niger dam and hydro-electric scheme.

APPENDIX A

Schedule of Local Government Training Courses run by the Northern Nigeria Government for the benefit of Native Authorities

DEPARTMENT MINISTRY	TYPE OF COURSE	DURATION	EDUCATIONAL QUALIFICA-TION	REMARKS
CAL VERNMENT INISTRY R LOCAL VERNMENT)	Progressive "A" for Secretaries and N.A. Officials	4 months	Secondary II	Held at Institute of Administration, Zaria
	Progressive "B"	4 months	Successful completion of Progressive Course "A"	Gives Diploma in Local Government
	Native Treasury Accounting Preliminary	10 months	Literacy in English Language	Held at Provincial centres (commencing Nov. '62)
	Native Treasury Intermediate	6 months	Secondary II	Institute of Administration, Zaria
	Native Treasury Diploma	5 months	1st Class Pass on Intermediate Course	Institute of Administration, Zaria
	Provincial Training Course Provincial Local Government Training Scheme)	4–10 days	None	Held in Provinces at N.A. levels for lower grade officials
	Refresher Courses	10 days–2 weeks	Literacy in English	Institute of Administration
	Chiefs' Courses	3 weeks	None	Annual Course held in Kaduna. Courses conducted in Hausa

APPENDIX A—*continued*

DEPARTMENT MINISTRY	TYPE OF COURSE	DURATION	EDUCATIONAL QUALIFICATION	REMARKS
JUSTICIAL (MINISTRY OF JUSTICE)	Judicial Course for Native Courts' Presidents and Members	3 months	Literate in English or Hausa	Held at Institut of Administration. Candidate chosen by Ministry of Justice
	Advanced Judicial Course	1 month	1st or 2nd Class Certificate in Judicial Course	Held at Institut of Administration
	Judicial Scribes' Course	1 year	W.A.S.C.† or equivalent	Institute of Administration
POLICE (MINISTRY OF INTERNAL AFFAIRS)	N.A. Police Recruits' Course	6 months	Literacy in English or Hausa	Held at Nigeria Police College, Kaduna
	Specialist and Refresher Training	As required	Literacy in English or Hausa	Held by S.P.O. in conjunction with the N.P.F
PRISONS (MINISTRY OF INTERNAL AFFAIRS)	Warders' Course	2 months	None	Held at Warde School, Kadun
AGRICULTURE (MINISTRY OF AGRICULTURE)	Agricultural Instructors' Course	9 months	Secondary II	At Provincial Farm Centres
	Agricultural Assistants' Course	2 years	Secondary IV	At School of Agriculture, Samaru, Zaria
	Assistant Agricultural Superintendents, and Assistant Agricultural Superintendents (Mechanical)	1 year	Secondary IV	At School of Agriculture, Samaru, Zaria (Promotion Course)

† West African School Certificate.

DEPARTMENT MINISTRY	TYPE OF COURSE	DURATION	EDUCATIONAL QUALIFICA-TION	REMARKS
GRICULTURE IINISTRY OF GRICULTURE) –*continued*	Short Courses in Agricultural Machinery	(Not fixed)		Held at Samaru as need arises
	Young Farmers' Courses	Not fixed	School Leavers	Run at Kafinsoli by Katsina N.A.
ETERINARY IINISTRY OF NIMAL AND OREST ESOURCES)	N.A. Livestock Assistants	9 months	Secondary II	Held at Mando Road, Kaduna
	Livestock Assistants	2 years	Secondary IV	Held at Kaduna. This is a higher grade than above and for both N.A. and Govern-ment Staff
	Hides and Skins Assistants	6 months	Secondary II	1 month Kaduna and 5 months at Hides and Skins Depot, Kano
	Poultry Husbandry	6 weeks	Middle II	At Kaduna as required
RESTRY INISTRY OF NIMAL AND REST SOURCES	Forest Guard	6 months	Middle II	School of Forestry, Naragunta, Jos. Either in English or Hausa as necessary
	Forest Super-visors	6 weeks	Middle II	
	Foresters	9 months	Middle II	
RVEY INISTRY OF ND AND RVEY)	Land Settle-ment Officers' Course	6 months	Middle II	Held at Survey School, Zaria
UCATION INISTRY OF UCATION)	Teachers' Elementary Certificate (Grade III)	3 years / 1½ years	Class VII full Primary Education. Vernacular Teachers Grade IV	Held at Grade III Teacher Training Colleges (Bridge Course to up-grade Class IV Teachers)

DEPARTMENT MINISTRY	TYPE OF COURSE	DURATION	EDUCATIONAL QUALIFICATION	REMARKS
EDUCATIONS (MINISTRY OF EDUCATION) —*continued*	Teachers' Higher Elementary Certificate (Grade II)	(i) 2 years (ii) 4 years (iii) 5 years	(i) after obtaining Grade II or (ii) full Secondary Education, (iii) after Class VII Primary	Held at Grade I T.T. Colleges
	Arabic Teachers' Grade II	3 years	Secondary II	School of Arabic Studies, Kano
	Arabic Teachers' Grade III	2 years	Primary VII or Korank Schools	School of Arabic Studies, Kano
	English Ministry of Education Certificate full Domestic Science Course	2 years	Grade II Teachers' Certificate or Higher School Certificate	Held in United Kingdom
	Arabic Teachers' Certificate Bakhtar Ruda Institute of Education	1½ years	Arabic Grade II Teachers' Certificate	Bakhtar Ruda College, Sudan
	Teachers' Associateship Course in Education	1 year	Grade II Certificate	University College of Ibadan
	Teachers' Professional Certificate of Dept. of Education in Tropical Areas	1 year	Grade II Certificate	Institute of Education at London, Bristol and Edinburgh
	Manual Training Instructors	—	—	Appointed after a recognised course at a Government Trade Centre

DEPARTMENT MINISTRY	TYPE OF COURSE	DURATION	EDUCATIONAL QUALIFICA- TION	REMARKS
EALTH MINISTRY OF EALTH)	Health Inspectors' Course	2 years	Middle II	Held at School of Hygiene, Kano
	Dispensary Attendants	2 years	Middle II	Medical Auxiliary Training School, Kaduna
	Nurses Training	6 months + 2 years in training hospitals	Middle II	Nurses Preliminary Training School, Kaduna
	Midwives' Grade II	1½ years	Middle II	
	Midwives' Grade I	1 year	Holders of Grade II	
	Community Nurses	1½ years	Grade II Midwife	Community Nurses Centre, Kaduna
	N.A. Leprosy Inspectors	Not fixed.		
ORKS INISTRY OF ORKS)	Assistant Works Superintendents (Building and Water)	1 year Theory 1 year Practical	Middle II + Trade Tested as Grade I, II or III Artisan	Mainly for M.O.W. Staff but N.A.s may sponsor candidates
	Assistant Works Superintendents (Mechanical)	1 year Theory 1 year Practical	As above	Held at Regional Mechanical Workshop, Kaduna, open to both Government and N.A.
	Road Overseers	2 months	Literacy Selection by Provincial Engineer concerned	Road Overseers' School, Zaria

DEPARTMENT MINISTRY	TYPE OF COURSE	DURATION	EDUCATIONAL QUALIFICATION	REMARKS
WORKS MINISTRY OF WORKS) —*continued*	Road Overseers (Advanced Courses)	6 months	Nomination by Provincial Engineers	Training in improved methods with particular reference to bituminous surfacing
	Pump Operators' Courses	3 months	Middle II	Held at Pump Operators' School, Zaria
	Stores Staff Trainings (Primary Course)	3 months	Middle II + 1 year's experience of Stores Accounting	Held at M.O.W. Regional Stores Kaduna

APPENDIX B

The Native Authority Law, 1954

A Law to Consolidate and Amend the Statute Law relating to Native Authorities.

[July 31, 1954][1]

(Reprinted, with the authority of the Governor of the Northern Region of Nigeria, in accordance with section 42 of the Interpretation Ordinance, with all additions, omissions, substitutions and amendments effected by any Law and all adaptations, modifications and additions effected by any Order made under section 57 of the Nigeria (Constitution) Order in Council, 1954, and section 3 of the Nigeria (Constitution) Order in Council, 1960, until and including the 4th day of May, 1961.)

PART I

PRELIMINARY

Short Title and Commencement

1. This Law may be cited as the Native Authority Law, 1954, and shall come into operation upon such date as the Governor may, by notice in the Regional *Gazette*, appoint.

(Adaptation by L.N. 131 of 1954)

Interpretation

2. Definitions:

"administrative sub-area" means one of the sub-areas into which the area under the jurisdiction of a Native Authority, or part thereof, is divided under the provisions of section 54;

"Advisory Council" means a Council established under the provisions of section 63;

"Chief" means any person recognised as a Chief by the Governor;
(Adaptation by L.N. 131 of 1954)

"Chief and Council" means a Chief associated with a Council in accordance with the provisions of section 8; *(Inserted by N.R. No. 37 of 1960)*

"Chief in Council" means a Chief associated with a Council in accordance with the provisions of section 7; *(Inserted by N.R. No. 37 of 1960)*

"Council" means a Council which is appointed to an office of Native Authority, a Council which in association with a Chief or other person comprises a Native Authority, an Advisory Council, an Outer Council, a Local Council or a Town Council;

"functions" include powers and duties;

"Local Council" means a Council established under the provisions of section 55;

[1] N.R.L.N. 131 of 1954.

165

"market" means a concourse of buyers and sellers having stalls or occupying places exceeding twenty in number;

"member of a Native Authority" means a Chief or other person who is appointed, either alone or in association with a Council, to an office of Native Authority; or a member of a Council which with or without a Chief comprises a Native Authority; or a member of a Council or group of persons which is appointed to an office of Native Authority;

"Minister" means the Minister to whom is assigned under section 37 of the Constitution of Northern Nigeria responsibility for Local Government; (*Adaptation by L.N. 131 of 1954; substituted by N.N.L.N. 7 of 1961*)

"native" means any native of Nigeria who is ordinarily subject to the jurisdiction of a Native Court;

"Native Authority" means a Native Authority appointed or deemed to be appointed under this Law in respect of the specified area for which such Native Authority is appointed and includes unless the context otherwise requires a Subordinate Native Authority;

"Native Authority Council" means a Council which, with or without a Chief, comprises a Native Authority;

"native liquor" means palm wine and any kind of description of fermented liquor usually made by natives of Nigeria or of the adjacent territories;

"Outer Council" means a Council established under the provisions of section 57;

"Resident" means the officer appointed by the Premier to be in charge of the province concerned; (*Adaptation by N.R.L.N. 144 of 1960*)

"sub-area head" means a person appointed by a Native Authority under the provisions of section 54 to be head of an administrative sub-area;

"Subordinate Native Authority" means a Native Authority directed by the Governor to be subordinate to any other Native Authority.

(*Adaptation by L.N. 131 of 1954; amended by N.R. No. 37 of 1960*)

PART II

ESTABLISHMENT AND APPOINTMENT OF NATIVE AUTHORITIES
Establishment of Office of Native Authority

Establishment of Native Authorities

3. (1) The Governor may by notice in the Regional *Gazette* constitute the office of Native Authority for any specified area.

(2) The Governor may grant to a Native Authority a suitable symbol of office.

(*Adaptation by L.N. 131 of 1954*)

Limitation of Powers of Native Authorities

4. When constituting the office of a Native Authority, or at any time thereafter, the Governor may by notice in the Regional *Gazette* direct

that such authority shall exercise only such of the powers conferred upon Native Authorities by this Law as he may specify, and when any such direction shall have been given this Law shall be deemed to confer upon such authority only such powers as the Governor shall have specified.

(*Adaptation by L.N.* 131 *of* 1954)

Native Authorities to be Bodies Corporate

5. (1) Every Native Authority shall be a body corporate by the name designated in the notice constituting such authority, and shall have perpetual succession and a common seal and power to acquire, hold, demise and alienate all movable and immovable property and to sue and be sued.

(2) Any contract or instrument, other than an instrument having legislative effect, which, if entered into or executed by a person not being a body corporate, would not require to be under seal, may be entered into or executed on behalf of a Native Authority by any person generally or specially authorised by the Native Authority for that purpose.

Appointment to Native Authorities

6. (1) The Premier in respect of paragraphs (*a*) and (*d*) and the Minister in respect of paragraphs (*b*) and (*c*) may appoint to any office of Native Authority constituted under section 3—

(*a*) any Chief or other person associated with a Council either—
　　(i) as a Chief or other person in Council; or
　　(ii) as a Chief or other person and Council;
(*b*) any Council;
(*c*) any group of persons;
(*d*) any Chief or other person.

(2) Where a Chief or other person associated with a Council, or a Council, or a group of persons is appointed to any office of Native Authority, the Minister shall either—

(*a*) specify the composition of the Council or group of persons; or
(*b*) direct that the composition of the Council or group of persons be regulated in accordance with the native law or custom of the community concerned.

(3) Where, in accordance with paragraph (*a*) of subsection (2) the Minister specifies the composition of a Council or group of persons, he may direct that the Council or group of persons shall be composed of members of any one or more of the following classes—

(*a*) persons named or approved by the Minister;
(*b*) the holders of offices named by the Minister;
(*c*) persons nominated in such manner and for such term as the Minister may prescribe;

(*d*) persons elected in such manner and for such term as the Minister may prescribe;

(*e*) persons selected to be members in accordance with the native law and custom of the community concerned. (*Inserted by N.R. No. 3 of 1955*)

(4) The Governor may make regulations providing for the method of election to a Native Authority Council of persons whom the Minister has under the provisions of paragraph (*d*) of subsection (3) prescribed shall be elected in any manner other than according to native law and custom, and such regulations may provide (without prejudice to the generality of the foregoing power) for all or any of the following matters, that is to say—

(*a*) the qualifications and disqualifications of electors;

(*b*) the registration of electors;

(*c*) the ascertainment of the qualifications of persons who submit themselves for election;

(*d*) the holding of elections, direct or indirect;

(*e*) the establishment of electoral areas (by whatever name called) for the purpose of returning members to the Councils;

(*f*) the determination of any question which may arise as to the right of any person to be or remain a member of a Council or to take part in any election;

(*g*) the disqualification of any person for membership of a Council;

(*h*) the definition and trial of offences relating to elections and the imposition of penalties therefor;

(*i*) the co-option of members to a Council and the appointment of *ex-officio* members.

(*Adaptation by L.N.* 131 *of* 1954; *N.R.L.N.* 144 *of* 1960; *amended by N.N. No.* 23 *of* 1961)

Provisions affecting Chiefs-in-Council

7. Where the Premier has appointed to any office of Native Authority a Chief associated with a Council as a Chief-in-Council, the following provisions shall have effect—

(1) in the exercise of the functions conferred upon the Native Authority by this or any other Law or by any Ordinance the Chief shall, subject to the provisions of paragraph (3), consult with the Council;

(1A) the Chief shall preside at all meetings of the Council:

Provided that when the Chief is absent from the area of his jurisdiction or is temporarily incapacitated through illness or any other cause from fulfilling his functions there shall preside at all meetings of the Council such other person as may be specified in the Standing Orders of the Native Authority made under section 52;

(*Inserted by N.R. No.* 37 *of* 1960)

(1B) in any matter arising for decision by the Native Authority; the Chief shall not have a vote:

Provided that in the event of an equality of votes the Chief shall have a casting vote;
(*Inserted by N.R. No. 37 of 1960*)

(2) the Chief shall, subject to the provisions of paragraph (5), act in accordance with the advice of the Council (which in case of divided opinion shall be by majority vote) in any matter in which he is by this section obliged to consult with the Council;

(3) the Chief shall consult with at least two members of the Council in any case—

(*a*) in which the matters to be decided are in his judgment too unimportant to require the advice of the Council or a quorum thereof; or

(*b*) in which the matters to be decided are in his judgment too urgent to admit of the advice of the Council or a quorum thereof being given by the time within which it may be necessary for him to act;

(4) in any case falling within sub-paragraph (*b*) of paragraph (3) the Chief shall, as soon as is practicable communicate to the Council the measures which have been adopted, with the reasons therefor;

(5) if in any case in which he consults with the Council the Chief considers it expedient in the interests of order and good government in the area over which the jurisdiction of the Native Authority extends that he should not act in accordance with the advice of the Council, then he may act otherwise than in accordance with that advice;

(6) whenever the Chief acts otherwise than in accordance with the advice of the Council—

(*a*) he shall report the matter to the Governor or to the Divisional Officer for transmission to the Governor at the earliest opportunity, with the reasons for his action; and

(*b*) any member of the Council may require that there be recorded in the minutes of the Council any advice or opinion which he may give upon the question with the reasons therefor;

(7) when the Governor receives such a report he shall either—

(*a*) inform the Chief that he does not intend to intervene; or

(*b*) call upon the Chief to consult with the Council further upon the question and if, after further consultation, the Chief still considers it expedient for the purposes aforesaid that he should not act in accordance with the advice of the Council, the Governor shall either—

(i) inform the Chief-in-Council that he does not intend to intervene further; or

(ii) give such direction as he may deem expedient, and the Native Authority shall comply with the direction of the Governor.

(*Adaptation by L.N. 131 of 1954 and N.R.L.N. 144 of 1960*)

Provisions affecting Chiefs-and-Council

8. Where the Premier has appointed to any office of Native Authority a Chief associated with a Council as a Chief and Council, the following provisions shall have effect—

(*a*) the Chief shall preside at all meetings of the Council:

Provided that where the Chief is absent from the area of his jurisdiction or is temporarily incapacitated through illness or any other cause from fulfilling his functions there shall preside at all meetings of the Council such other person as may be specified in the Standing Orders of the Native Authority made under section 52; (*Substituted by N.R. No. 3 of 1955 and N.R. No. 4 of 1957*)

(*b*) in any matters arising for decision by the Native Authority, the Chief shall have an original vote, and in the event of an equality of votes a second or casting vote;

(*c*) in any matters arising for decision by the Native Authority, the decision of the majority of members, including the Chief, present and voting shall, subject to the provisions of any Standing Orders made by the Native Authority in accordance with paragraph (*a*) of subsection (1) of section 52 be the decision of the Native Authority;

(*d*) in the exercise of any function conferred upon the Native Authority by this or any other Law or by any Ordinance the Chief shall have no power to act otherwise than in accordance with the decision of the Chief and Council.

(*Adaptation by L.N. 131 of 1954 and N.R.L.N. 144 of 1960*)

Provisions affecting Persons, other than Chiefs, Associated with Councils

[2] **9.** Where the Minister has appointed to any office of Native Authority a person associated with a Council other than a Chief associated with a Council, the provisions of section 7 or section 8, as the case may be, shall apply as though the person so appointed were a Chief save that where the word "Premier" occurs in either of these sections for the purpose of this section the word "Minister" shall be substituted.

(*Adaptation by L.N. 131 of 1954 and N.R.L.N. 144 of 1960*)

Temporary appointments as Native Authority or Member thereof

10. A person may be appointed as a Native Authority or as a member of a Native Authority for a specified period of time and such person shall upon the expiration of that period cease to be a Native Authority or a member of a Native Authority, as the case may be, but may thereafter be appointed as a Native Authority or as a member of a Native Authority and either for a specified or for an unspecified period of time.

Provision for Temporary Absence or Illness of Chief and for Associated and Advisory Councils to Function as Native Authorities

11. (1) Where a Chief or any other person appointed to any office of

---

[2] This section is under consideration for amendment.

THE NATIVE AUTHORITY LAW, 1954

Native Authority in accordance with the provisions of paragraph (*d*) of subsection (1) of section 6 is temporarily absent from Nigeria or is absent from the area of his jurisdiction, but within Nigeria, for a prolonged period, or is temporarily incapacitated through illness or any other cause from fulfilling his functions, the Premier may (unless the provisions of subsection (2) hereof are applicable) by notice in the Regional *Gazette* appoint a person in place of such Native Authority during his absence or incapacity.

(2) Where the Native Authority for any area is either a Chief-in-Council or a Chief-and-Council or a Chief who, under the provisions of section 63 has appointed an Advisory Council, and such Chief is temporarily absent or incapacitated in the circumstances mentioned in subsection (1), the Native Authority Council or the Advisory Council, as the case may be, shall be deemed to be the Native Authority for the area during the absence or incapacity of the Chief.

(3) Notwithstanding the provisions of section 6 where the Native Authority appointed for any area is either a Chief-in-Council or a Chief-and-Council or a Chief who, under the provisions of section 63, has appointed an Advisory Council, and such Chief dies or for any other reason whatsoever ceases to be Chief then, until a successor to such Chief has been appointed and approved under the provisions of the Appointment and Deposition of Chiefs Ordinance or until another Native Authority is appointed for the area, the Council or the Advisory Council, as the case may be, shall be the Native Authority for the area and shall perform all the duties and shall have and may exercise all the powers of a Native Authority under this Law as if it were a Native Authority duly appointed under the provisions of section 6. (*Amended by N.R. No. 4 of 1957*)

(4) Any such Council or Advisory Council becoming a Native Authority under the provisions of subsection (3) shall make interim Standing Orders for the conduct of its business in accordance with the provisions of section 52 and when such Council or Advisory Council ceases to function as a Native Authority under the provisions of subsection (3) such Standing Orders shall lapse.

(*Adaptation by L.N. 131 of 1954; N.R.L.N. 144 of 1960*)

Power of Premier to Appoint Administrative Officer to Office of Native Authority

12. Where the office of Native Authority constituted for any area is for the time being vacant, the Premier may by notice in the Regional *Gazette* appoint any administrative officer to such office.

(*Adaptation by L.N. 131 of 1954 and N.R.L.N. 144 of 1960*)

Application of Law to Administrative Officers Functioning as Native Authorities

13. When a Premier has appointed an administrative officer to act

171

under section 12 the relevant provisions of this Law shall apply *mutatis mutandis* save that section 47 shall, for the purposes of this section, be construed as if for the words "a court presided over by a magistrate" there were substituted the words "a court presided over by a judge".

(Adaptation by L.N. 131 of 1954 and N.R.L.N. 144 of 1960)

Validity of Exercise of Powers from without Area of Appointment

14. No act done by an administrative officer appointed under section 12 in the exercise of any power conferred upon him in virtue of this Law with reference to the area for which he is appointed, shall be deemed to be invalid by reason only of the fact that the act was not done within such area.

General Provisions relating to the Appointment of Members of Native Authorities

Presumptions where Person Discharging Specified Function is Appointed

15. Where the person or persons for the time being discharging specified functions, or being a member of a specified group, is appointed to be a Native Authority or a member of a Native Authority a person shall be deemed to be lawfully discharging such functions or to be lawfully a member of such group if and so long as he is so recognised by the Premier or Minister as the case may be or by such person as the Premier or Minister as the case may be may direct.

(Adaptation by L.N. 131 of 1954 and N.R.L.N. 144 of 1960)

Revocation of Orders and Appointments

16. The Governor, Premier or Minister as the case may be may at any time revoke, suspend or vary any constitution, appointment, direction, or Order made under sections 3, 4, 6, 10, 11 and 12:

Provided that nothing contained in this section shall be deemed to authorise the removal of an elected member of a Native Authority otherwise than in accordance with the provisions of section 19 or 19A.

(Adaptation by L.N. 131 of 1954 and N.R.L.N. 144 of 1960; amended by N.R. No. 37 of 1960 and N.N. No. 23 of 1961)

Disposal of Property on Revocation of Constitution

17. Upon the revocation of the constitution of a Native Authority, all immovable property of that Native Authority shall vest in the authority by which the area in which such property is situated is thereafter to be administered, and all other property shall vest in such person or authority as the Governor may direct.

(Adaptation by L.N. 131 of 1954)

Retirement of Individual Members of a Native Authority

18. (1) Where a Chief associated with a Council, a Council, any group of persons, or any Chief or other person is appointed as such to be a Native Authority the Chief and any individual member or members of the Native Authority Council, the Council, the group of persons, or the Chief or other person may retire from membership of such Native Authority at any time on giving notice in writing to the Premier or Minister, whoever of the two made the appointment, of his intention so to retire.

(2) No notice referred to in subsection (1) may be withdrawn after it has been received by the Premier or the Minister as the case may be.

(Inserted by N.R. No. 37 of 1960)

(Adaptation by L.N. 131 of 1954 and N.R.L.N. 144 of 1960)

Removal of Individual Members where a Body of Persons is Appointed a Native Authority

19. Where a Chief associated with a Council, a Council or any group of persons is appointed as such to be a Native Authority the Governor may at any time direct that any Chief and any individual member or members of the Native Authority Council, the Council or the group of persons, whether he or they have obtained membership personally or in a representative capacity, shall cease to be a member or members of the Native Authority:

Provided that whenever the Governor proposes to make a direction under this section in respect of any person who is a member of a Native Authority by reason of his having been elected thereto in pursuance of the provisions of paragraph (*b*) of subsection (2) of section 6 or of paragraph (*d*) of subsection (3) of the same section the Governor shall give to such person notice in writing of his proposal to make such direction and such person shall be entitled within one calendar month from the receipt by him of such notice to make representations in writing to the Governor touching such proposal.

(Adaptation by L.N. 131 of 1954)

Removal of Members of a Native Authority in Cases of Misconduct or Neglect

19A. (1) Where a Chief associated with a Council, a Council or any group of persons has been appointed as such to be a Native Authority and, after due and impartial inquiry, it has been shown to the satisfaction of the Governor that such Native Authority has misconducted or neglected the affairs of the Native Authority in such a way as to bring about a situation prejudicial to the interests of the inhabitants of the area of the Native Authority or of the Region generally the Governor-in-Council may by Order—

(*a*) direct that any Chief or any member or members of the Native Authority Council, the Council or the group of persons whether he or they have obtained membership personally or in a representative capacity shall forthwith cease to be a member or members of the Native Authority; and

(*b*) appoint any person or persons in their place.

173

(2) For the avoidance of doubts it is hereby declared that for the purposes of this section a Native Authority shall include a Subordinate Native Authority. (*Inserted by N.R. No. 5 of 1958*)

Constitution of Subordinate Native Authorities

Constitution of Subordinate Native Authorities

20. (1) The Governor may by notice in the Regional *Gazette* direct that any office of Native Authority constituted for any specified area shall be subordinate to another office of Native Authority.

(2) (*Deleted by N.R. No. 37 of 1960*)

(3) Every Subordinate Native Authority shall (subject to any vesting of powers made under section 22) obey the Orders of the Native Authority to which the Governor has directed that it shall be subordinate.

(*Adaptation by L.N. 131 of 1954; amended by N.R. No. 17 of 1960*)

21. (*Repealed by N.R. No. 37 of 1960*)

Powers of Subordinate Native Authorities

22. (1) A Native Authority may, subject to the provisions of any direction made under section 4, by Order vest in a Native Authority which is subordinate to it such of the functions which it may itself exercise as may seem to it expedient and may at any subsequent time by Order increase, restrict or vary the functions of any such Subordinate Native Authority.

(2) A Subordinate Native Authority shall, subject to the terms of any Order made under the provisions of subsection (1) or to any directions given in accordance with section 4, have exercise and perform all the functions of a Native Authority under this Law.

(*Substituted by N.R. No. 37 of 1960*)

Application of Section 15

23. The provisions of section 15 shall apply to all Subordinate Native Authorities.

Powers of Governor in Relation to Directions under Section 20

24. The Governor may at any time revoke, suspend or vary any direction made in respect of a Subordinate Native Authority under the provisions of section 20.

(*Substituted by N.R. No. 37 of 1960; adaptation by L.N. 131 of 1954*)

Removal of Members of a Subordinate Native Authority

25. (*Repealed by N.R. No. 37 of 1960*)

Existing Native Authorities

Existing Native Authorities deemed Constituted under this Law

26. Every office of Native Authority constituted under the Native

Authority Ordinance, and existing at the coming into operation of this Law shall be deemed to have been constituted under and in accordance with the provisions of this Law.

Existing Appointments Deemed Appointments under this Law

27. Every—
   (a) Chief associated with a Council;
   (b) Council;
   (c) group of persons;
   (d) Chief or other person,

who or which at the coming into operation of this Law was appointed as a Native Authority or as a member of a Native Authority within the meaning of the Native Authority Ordinance, shall be deemed to be appointed as a Native Authority or as a member of a Native Authority under and in accordance with the provisions of this Law for the area for which he or it was appointed the Native Authority or was a member of the Native Authority on the coming into operation of this Law.

Existing Subordinate Native Authorities to Remain as Such under this Law

28. (1) Every Native Authority which was a Subordinate Native Authority on the coming into operation of this Law shall remain subordinate to the Native Authority to which it was then subordinate and the provisions of sections 22, 23, and 24 shall apply to such Subordinate Native Authority. (*Amended by N.R. No. 37 of 1960*)

(2) (*Deleted by N.R. No. 37 of 1960*)

PART III

POWERS AND DUTIES OF NATIVE AUTHORITIES

Jurisdiction of Native Authorities

General Powers and Duties of Native Authorities

29. (1) Every Native Authority shall have and exercise over all persons residing or being in the area over which its authority extends—
   (a) all the powers conferred upon or vested in it by or under this Law;
   (b) all such powers as are or may hereafter be conferred upon or vested in it by any other Law or by any Ordinance; and
   (c) all such powers as it may possess or as may be vested in it by any native law or custom:

Provided that a Native Authority shall not exercise any powers which it may possess or which may be vested in it solely by native law or custom except over persons to whom, or matters to which, the native law or custom applies. (*Amended by N.R. No. 37 of 1960*)

(2) It shall be the duty of every Native Authority—
   (a) to perform the duties and obligations imposed upon it—
      (i) by this Law;

(ii) by any other Law or by any Ordinance;

(iii) by any native law or custom; and,

(b) generally to maintain order and good government in the area over which its authority extends.

Duties of Native Authorities relating to Crime

Prevention of Crime

30. (1) It shall be the duty of a Native Authority to interpose for the purpose of preventing, and to the best of its ability to prevent, the commission of any offence within the area of its authority.

(2) (a) A Native Authority knowing of a design by any person to commit an offence within the area of its authority may arrest or direct the arrest of such person, if it appears to the Native Authority that the commission of the offence cannot be otherwise prevented;

(b) Any person so arrested shall, unless he be released within twenty-four hours of his arrest, be taken forthwith before a court having jurisdiction over him.

(3) Every Native Authority receiving information that any person who has committed an offence for which he may be arrested without a warrant by a police officer or a private person or for whose arrest a warrant has been issued, is within the area of its authority, shall cause such person to be arrested and taken forthwith before a court having jurisdiction over him.

(4) Every Native Authority receiving information that property of any description which has been stolen, whether within or without the area of its authority, is within such area, shall cause such property to be seized and detained pending the order of a court having jurisdiction in the matter, and shall forthwith report such seizure and detention to such court.

(5) Where a Native Authority consists of more than one person the functions vested by this section in a Native Authority shall be exercisable by each member of the Native Authority.

Powers of Native Authorities to Trade
and provide Public Services

Power to Trade and Provide Public Services

31. A Native Authority may, with the approval of the Minister engage in any form of trade, industry or commerce for the purposes of directly furthering the administration, development and welfare of the area of its jurisdiction and of satisfying a public need which cannot otherwise be adequately satisfied, and may provide any public services for the same purpose.

(*Adaptation by L.N.* 131 *of* 1954 *and N.R.L.N.* 144 *of* 1960)

176

Establishment, Management and Closing of Markets

Power to Establish Markets

32. A Native Authority may—
(a) establish markets;
(b) provide all such matters and things as may be necessary for the convenient use of the market;
(c) take stallages, rents, tolls, fees and dues in respect of the use by any person of any market;
(d) demolish, reconstruct, abolish, close or move any market;
(e) appoint inspectors of markets.

Management of Markets

33. All markets other than those established in townships shall be under the control and management of the Native Authority within whose jurisdiction they are situated.

Markets not to be Established without Authority

34. (1) In any area for which an office of Native Authority has been constituted, no person other than the Native Authority shall, without the consent of the Minister—
(a) establish any market;
(b) being the occupier of land, permit a market to be established thereon;
(c) maintain, conduct or manage a market established in breach of the provisions of this section.

(2) Any person who contravenes the provisions of subsection (1) shall be liable to a fine of fifty pounds or to imprisonment for three months or to both such fine and imprisonment and also to a penalty of five pounds in respect of every day on which the offence is continued after conviction for such offence. (*Substituted by N.R. No. 4 of 1957*)

Markets not to be Continued after Closing Order

35. Whenever a Native Authority shall have ordered any market, whether established before or after the commencement of this Law, to be closed, any person who having control over the market or the land on which the market is held shall keep the market open or permit it to be used as a market after he has been notified of such order, shall be liable to the penalties prescribed in section 34, and any person who shall sell or purchase any goods in such market after having been notified of such order as aforesaid shall be liable to a fine of one pound.

Officers and Staff of Native Authorities

Power to Engage Staff

36. (1) Subject to the provisions of subsection (2) a Native Authority shall appoint a secretary or a clerk to its Council and may appoint such other officers and employ such other persons as it shall consider

necessary for the efficient discharge of the functions of the Native Authority, and may, subject as aforesaid, dismiss any person so appointed or employed.

(2) A Native Authority shall not appoint, engage, employ or dismiss or reduce the salary of—

(a) a secretary, clerk to the Council, treasurer, Chief of Police or supervisor of works; or

(b) any officer whose salary is equal to or in excess of the prescribed salary,

without the approval in writing of the Premier. (*Substituted by N.R. No. 37 of 1961; amended by N.N. No. 23 of 1961*)

(2A) The Governor in Council may by order determine the prescribed salary for the purposes of subsection (2). (*Inserted by N.R. No. 37 of 1960; substituted by N.N. No. 23 of 1961*)

(3) The Premier shall have power to disallow or revoke the creation of any office by a Native Authority and to disallow or revoke the appointment of any person by a Native Authority to any office.

(3A) If a Native Authority fails within a reasonable time to make an appointment to any vacant office or to any vacancy in the staff of the Native Authority the Premier may make such appointment. (*Inserted by N.R. No. 37 of 1960*)

(4) (*Deleted by N.R. No. 37 of 1960*)

(5) Subject to the provisions of subsection (2) a Native Authority may pay to any officer or person so employed such remuneration as is provided for in the standard salary scales for the employees of Native Authorities prescribed from time to time by the Premier or as the Native Authority may with the approval of the Premier otherwise determine.

(6) The Premier may—

(a) direct a Native Authority to establish a committee for purposes connected with the appointment and dismissal of staff;

(b) allocate to any such committee such functions as he may think fit. (*Inserted by N.R. No. 4 of 1957*)

(*Adaptation by L.N. 131 of 1954 and N.R.L.N. 144 of 1960*)

Governor's Control of Native Authority Staff

36A. (1) If at any time it shall appear to the Governor after due and impartial inquiry that a Native Authority or any member thereof has by act or default to show due impartiality or fairness towards the officers or members of the staff of such Native Authority or any of them or has refused or neglected impartially or fairly to administer any written law or administrative or other regulation relating to the appointment or terms of service of any such officer or member of its staff the Governor in Council may by order direct that—

(a) any officer or member of the staff may appeal to the Governor from any decision of the Native Authority or member thereof in relation to any matter affecting the appointment or terms of service of such officer or member of the staff; or

(b) all or any of the functions of such Native Authority in relation to its officers or the members of its staff shall forthwith and until further order vest in the Governor and shall be exercisable by him.

(2) On any appeal made under the provisions of paragraph (a) of subsection (1) the Governor may make such order as he shall consider just.

(*Inserted by N.R. No. 5 of 1958*)

Retiring Benefits for Native Authority Staff

36B. A Native Authority may pay to any officer or person appointed, engaged or employed by it such retiring benefits as are provided for in the standard directions for retiring benefits for the employees of Native Authorities prescribed from time to time by the Minister or as the Native Authority may with the approval of the Minister otherwise determine.

(*Inserted by N.R. No. 37 of 1960*)

Legislative Powers of Native Authorities

Powers of Native Authorities to Make Rules

37. Subject to the provisions of any written law for the time being in force a Native Authority, with the concurrence of the Native Authority, if any, to which it is subordinate, and save as is provided in sections 146 and 146A, subject to the approval of the Governor, may make rules—

Agriculture

(1) prohibiting, restricting or regulating the cutting or destruction of trees growing on communal or native lands;

(2) requiring and regulating the planting, tending protection and preservation of trees or plantations of trees (including amenity trees) on communal or native lands or in towns or villages;[3]

(3) (*Repealed by N.R. No. 3 of 1955*)

(4) for the purpose of controlling, preventing and destroying any plant or insect which may be harmful to crops;[4]

(5) requiring the cultivation of land for the production of crops and for regulating and controlling the processing, sale, delivery and marketing of crops;

(6) regulating and controlling whether by prohibition or otherwise the borrowing and lending of money or money's worth secured either wholly or in part on standing crops;

Animals

(7) (a) prohibiting cruelty to animals or specified acts of cruelty to animals; and

[3] *e.g.*, Control of Grazing Rules.
[4] *e.g.*, Close Season for Cotton Rules.

(*b*) authorising the detention for treatment, or destruction without compensation to the owner, of any animal suffering from the effects of cruelty and the recovery of the expenses of treatment or of destruction;

(8) prohibiting, restricting and regulating the keeping of livestock of any description and for the prevention of any payment of compensation for damage done by straying animals;[5]

(9) providing for the protection and prevention of the premature slaughter of animals, livestock or any species thereof;

(10) regulating and controlling communal hunting;

(11) (*a*) for the appointment, management and control of pounds;
(*b*) prescribing the powers and duties of pound masters;
(*c*) for the seizing and impounding of stray animals, and the recovery of expenses incurred in connection therewith; and
(*d*) for the sale of impounded animals and the disposal of the proceeds of any sale;

(12) prohibiting or regulating the capture, killing or sale of fish or any specified kind or kinds of fish;

(13) prohibiting, restricting or regulating the movement in or through the area of its authority of livestock of any description;

Buildings and Similar Matters

(14) (*a*) providing for the demolition of dangerous buildings;
(*b*) enabling some person or persons to carry out such demolition at the expense of the owner in default of the owner so doing, to remove and sell the materials of any buildings so demolished; and
(*c*) regulating the procedure by which such expenses may be recovered;

Advertisements

(15) (*a*) the control of the siting of advertisements and of hoardings or other structures designed for the display of advertisements;
(*b*) the removal of any advertisement the siting of which does not conform to any rule made under sub-paragraph (*a*); and
(*c*) applying the provisions of paragraph (14) to any hoarding or other structure designed or used for the display of advertisements which is so sited as to conduce to the danger of road-users or other members of the public;

(16) prohibiting or regulating the making of borrow pits or excavations;

[5] *e.g.*, Control of Domestic Animals Rules.

Children and Young Females

(17) regulating and controlling the movement of children and young females from or within the area of the Native Authority;[6]

(18) regulating child betrothals within the area of its authority and prescribing safeguards to be taken—

(*a*) when the child betrothed leaves the place in which her parents or guardians reside but does not leave the area of authority of the Native Authority making the rule;

(*b*) when the child betrothed leaves the area of authority of the Native Authority making the rule;

Education

(19) (*a*) requiring persons who have been or may become enrolled as pupils in any Native Authority school or any other school in the Northern Region which has been approved for the purpose of rules under this paragraph by a Local Education Committee established under section 25 of the Education Ordinance, 1952, or under section 24 of the Education Law, 1956, to attend at such school in accordance with the directions of the headmaster or head teacher thereof during the period for which such pupils have engaged for themselves or through their parents or guardians or consequent upon rules made under the provision of sub-paragraph (*b*) herein to attend such school; (*Amended by N.R. No. 4 of 1957*)[7]

(*b*) empowering heads of administrative sub-areas to select suitable children from among those in their sub-areas and to require them to become enrolled as pupils in specified Native Authority schools for such period they may think fit in each particular case;

(*c*) requiring the parents or guardians of persons to whom the provisions of sub-paragraphs (*a*) or (*b*) herein apply to ensure that the provisions of any rules made under the provisions of the said sub-paragraphs (*a*) or (*b*) are complied with; (*Amended by N.R. No. 4 of 1957*)

Elections to Subordinate Councils

(20) making provisions for the election of members to Councils other than Native Authority Councils, including (without prejudice to the generality of the foregoing power) the following matters, that is to say—

(*a*) the qualifications and disqualifications of electors;

(*b*) the registration of electors;

(*c*) the ascertainment of the qualifications of persons who submit themselves for election;

---

[6] *e.g.*, Control of Juveniles accompanying Koranic Mallams.
[7] *e.g.*, School Attendance Rules.

(d) the holding of elections, direct or indirect;

(e) the establishment of electoral areas (by whatever name called) for the purpose of returning members to the Councils;

(f) the determination of any question which may arise as to the right of any person to be or remain a member of a Council or to take part in any election;

(g) the disqualification of any person for membership of a Council;

(h) the co-option of members to a Council and the appointment of *ex-officio* members;[8]

Fires and Fire Brigades

(21) (a) for the prevention of fires;

(b) providing for the establishment of fire brigades;

(c) prescribing the duties of the members of such brigades; and

(d) generally in connection with any matters relating to the extinguishing of fires and to the custody and use of appliances provided for such purpose;

Land

(22) relating to the use and alienation whether upon devolution by will or otherwise of any description whatever of interests in land within the area of jurisdiction of the Native Authority and without derogation from the generality of these provisions specially in respect of any or all of the following matters—

(a) the control of any or all powers of alienation of land or of any interest therein to strangers or to persons other than strangers;

(b) the control and use of communal land and of family land either generally or specifically and with special reference to the cultivation thereof and the type of crops which may be grown thereon;

(c) the control of mortgaging with special reference to the approval of the mortgagee and the use to which the land may be put when mortgaged;

(d) making the purchaser at any sale, whether such sale is by order of any court whatsoever or not, subject to the approval of the Native Authority or of a specified individual or individuals and providing, in the case of a sale by a court, that the land shall again be sold if the purchaser is not approved under the rules;

(e) for the recording or filing of documents relating to the alienation of land or any interest therein;

(f) for the control either generally or specifically of the size or extent of communal land or family land over which any individual or group of persons may exercise rights or be permitted to exercise rights; and

(g) the regulating of the allocation of communal land or family land and specifying the person or persons who may allocate such communal land subject to such special or general directions as the Native Authority may require.

[8] *e.g.*, Elections to Subordinate Councils Rules.

In this paragraph—

"land" means all land (including everything attached to the earth) other than the categories of land referred to in proviso (a) to this section;

"stranger" means any native of Nigeria or native foreigner who is not eligible by native law and custom to inherit land or the use of land within the area of jurisdiction of the Native Authority making the rule;

(23) (a) prohibiting farming on land within a stated distance of, or in areas which are, badly eroded areas, areas reclaimed or treated with anti-erosion measures or areas the farming of which is likely to cause erosion or is unsuitable save with the permission of the Native Authority concerned;

(b) prohibiting, restricting, controlling or regulating the grazing of stock on areas or land the subject of sub-paragraph (a);

(c) controlling and regulating the treatment of land and methods of farming in order to prevent erosion and particularly with regard to the erection and maintenance of walls and fences, the making and maintenance of drains, trenches, gullies or similar works, the clearance of under growth, bushes or trees, the planting and maintenance of windbreaks and the building and maintenance of terraces; and

(d) the appointment of overseers of farms and areas;

(24) providing for the fencing of land or any particular land and for the maintenance and repair of such fences;

Public Health

(25) prohibiting, regulating or prescribing such matters or things as may be deemed necessary or advisable in the interest of the public health;[9]

(26) preventing the spread of infectious or contagious disease, whether of human beings or animals, and for the care of the sick;

(27) for the purpose of exterminating or preventing the spread of tsetse fly;

(28 providing for—

(a) the maintenance of public latrines, urinals, dustbins and manure and nightsoil depots in a sanitary condition;

(b) surface scavenging, and the removal and disposal of nightsoil and of other refuse;

(c) the cleansing of streets;

(d) the provision and proper construction of rubbish receptacles on private premises;

(e) the erection and construction, demolition, re-erection and reconstruction, conversion and reconversion, alteration, repair, sanitation and ventilation of public and private buildings;

[9] *e.g.*, Prohibition of Non-Iodised Salt Rules.

(*f*) the prevention of overcrowding in premises or rooms either in respect of human beings or animals, including the designation of an officer to fix (subject to a right of appeal by any person affected to the Native Authority) the maximum number of human beings or animals which may occupy any particular premises or room;

(29) for preventing in any place where an infectious disease exists, the holding of public meetings or the performance of native customs likely to tend to the dissemination of such infectious disease;

(30) for the destruction of rats, mice and other kinds of vermin, and of fleas, bugs, or any other such parasites as it may be deemed advisable to destroy and for rendering houses rat-proof;

(31) providing for the regulation and sanitary maintenance of factories, workshops, breweries and places of public instruction, recreation or assembly;

(32) providing for the regulation of bakehouses, dairies, aerated water manufactories, eating houses and food-preparing or food-preserving establishments;

(33) regulating laundries or wash-houses;

(34) regulating the admission into any town or part of a town of cattle or other animals;

(35) providing for the construction, position and proper sanitary maintenance of all places where animals are kept, and the methods to be adopted in cleansing and disinfecting places which have been occupied by any animal suffering from a contagious or infectious disease;

(36) licensing slaughter-houses and regulating the slaughter of animals intended for the food of man, and the management and use of slaughter-houses;

(37) providing for the inspection of such animals;

(38) regulating the preparation and sale of meat;[10]

(39) preventing unnecessary pain or suffering before or in the process of slaughtering animals, and prescribing the methods of slaughtering;

(40) prescribing charges for the use of slaughter-houses, and fees for inspections and licences;

(41) declaring any area specified in any such rules to be a public burial ground, requiring the burial of all persons who die within the jurisdiction of the Native Authority making the rules in such burial ground, requiring the burial of a dead body within a specified period after death, and imposing on any person named in the rules the duty of causing any dead body to be buried;

(42) preventing the pollution of water in any stream, water-course or water-hole, and preventing the obstruction of any stream or watercourse;

[10] *e.g.*, Preparation of Dried Meat Rules.

(43) prohibiting or regulating the sinking of wells and providing for the closing of wells;

Public Order

(44) prohibiting any act or conduct which in the opinion of the Native Authority might cause a riot or a disturbance or a breach of the peace;[11]

(45) providing for the peace, good order and welfare of the persons within the area of its authority;[12]

(46) prohibiting, restricting or regulating the migration of natives from or to the area of its authority;

Registration, Licensing and Rates

(47) (a) requiring the marriage, birth or death of any persons subject to its jurisdiction to be reported to it or to such person as it may direct;

    (b) providing for the registration of births and deaths occurring amongst natives in any area in which such births and deaths are not registrable under the Births, Deaths and Burials Ordinance and for the imposition of fees in respect of such registration; and

    (c) appointing registration offices and registrars for the purposes of any such registration;

(48) (a) for the licensing of buildings or other places for the performance of stage plays or the display of cinematograph films;

    (b) prescribing the building materials thereof and the mode of building, seating accommodation, entrances, exists and all other matters appertaining to the same;

    (c) prescribing against overcrowding and for the control and prevention of fire; and

    (d) prescribing for the maintenance of good order therein and for the entry and inspection during any performance or display or at any time by any police officer or person authorised so to do;

(49) (a) requiring bicycles and vehicles other than motor vehicles to be licensed, authorising the exaction of fees for licences issued in respect of bicycles and such vehicles;

    (b) specifying the equipment with which bicycles and such other vehicles must be fitted, and generally for regulating and controlling the riding of bicycles and the use of such other vehicles; and

    (c) generally for all purposes incidental to sub-paragraphs (a) and (b);

[11] *e.g.,* Control of Assemblies and Processions Rules.
[12] *e.g.,* Control of Traffic and Motor Parks.

(50) providing for the method of assessment of rates and the conditions under which such rates are to be made and collected;
(Substituted by N.R. No. 37 of 1960)

(50A) providing for the naming of public thoroughfares, open spaces and buildings and the numbering of buildings; *(Inserted by N.R. No. 37 of 1960)*

Roads, Streets and Open Spaces

(51) (a) regulating the repairing, improving, stopping or diverting of streets, water-courses, or drains preventing obstructions thereto and prescribing the mode of objection to the stopping or diverting thereof;

    (b) regulating the construction of new streets, water-courses or street drains and building lines;

    (c) regulating the cutting, uprooting, topping, injuring or destroying of any tree growing in any street;

    (d) requiring and regulating the planting, tending, protection and preservation of trees in streets; and

    (e) regulating traffic in any street;

(52) regulating animal traffic along highways;

(53) protecting vegetation along any road or path;

(54) declaring any land to be an open space and the purposes for which such space is to be used or occupied and regulating such use or occupation;

Trade and Industry

(55) for the regulating, controlling or promoting of trade or industry and regulating the carrying on of any offensive trade;[13]

(56) prohibiting or regulating the hawking of wares, or the erection of stalls on or near any street;

Miscellaneous

(57) prohibiting, restricting or regulating the manufacture, distillation, sale, transport, distribution, supply, possession and consumption of native liquor;

(58) prohibiting or regulating the removal from any place of African antique works or art and generally for the protection and preservation thereof;

(59) governing the establishment and administration of schemes of rural development or settlement;

(60) with regard to public services provided by the Native Authority in any capacity whether under the provisions of section 31 or otherwise;

---

[13] *e.g.*, Cotton and Groundnut Marketing Rules.

Duties of Employees: Fees, Penalties, etc.

(61) prescribing the duties of any person employed in connection with any of the purposes of rules made under this section;

(62) specifying fees or charges in respect of any matter or act for which provision is made in any rule;

(63) (*a*) imposing as penalties for the breach of any rule, a fine not exceeding one hundred pounds or imprisonment not exceeding six months or both such fine and imprisonment;

(*b*) providing for the service of notice upon any person who has committed or is committing an offence against or breach of any rules made under the provisions of this section requiring such person to take such action in relation to the offence or breach as may be specified in the notice and in default of compliance with such notice enabling the Native Authority concerned itself to take the necessary action and recover the expenses of so doing and for regulating the procedure therefor;

(*c*) providing for the disposal whether by way of forfeiture or otherwise of any property, article or thing in respect of which an offence has been committed or which has been used for the commission of an offence:

Provided that this sub-paragraph shall apply only to an offence of which any person has been convicted by a native court.

(*Adaptation by L.N. 131 of 1954; amended by N.R. No. 37 of 1960*)

Application of Rules made under Section 37

38. Subject to any exception specified in such rules, all rules made under section 37 shall apply to all persons who are within the area of the jurisdiction of the Native Authority.

Power of Governor to Revoke Rules made under Section 37

39. (1) The Governor may at any time revoke any rule made by a Native Authority under section 37 and such revocation shall be made known in the manner therein prescribed for the promulgation of such rule and shall thereupon have effect.

(2) Where the Governor has revoked a rule in accordance with this section he may—

(*a*) require the release from custody of any person sentenced to imprisonment by a court for the contravention of such rule;

(*b*) require the repayment of any fine imposed by a native court; and

(*c*) require the repayment by a Native Authority whose rule has been revoked as aforesaid to a person upon whom a fine has been imposed by the High Court or a magistrate's court of a sum of money not exceeding the amount of such fine by way of compensation for such fine, whether such sentence of imprisonment or fine was imposed before or after the revocation of such rule by the Governor. (*Inserted by N.R. No. 37 of 1960*)

(*Adaptation by L.N. 131 of 1954*)

Power to Arrest with Warrant

40. Any person who may be accused of an offence against rules made under section 37 may be arrested in accordance with a warrant obtained under section 108.

Power to make Rules Concerning Markets

41. (1) For or in relation to any market established under this Law or established before the commencement of this Law a Native Authority, subject to the approval of the Minister, may make rules for any of the following purposes—

(*a*) for regulating the use of markets and market buildings, and for keeping order, preventing obstructions, and maintaining cleanliness therein or in the approaches thereto;

(*b*) prescribing the goods which may be sold in any market;

(*c*) prohibiting the sale of any specified kind of goods within any specified area except in a market established under this Law;

(*d*) for regulating stallages, rents, tolls, fees and dues and the collection thereof;

(*e*) for fixing the days and the hours during each day on which a market may be held and for preventing the sale and purchase of goods in the markets on any days or at any hours except those fixed;

(*f*) prescribing the charges which may be made for the carriage by land or water of goods to or from the market within the limits named in the rules;

(*g*) prescribing the weights, scales and measures to be used in the sale of any particular produce and regulating the use thereof;

(*h*) for the examination of produce or articles of food;

(*i*) for controlling the sale of native liquor;

(*j*) for fixing the maximum price which be demanded on the sale by retail of any article of food in a market;

(*k*) for regulating the duties and conduct of inspectors and other persons appointed for the purposes of this Law.

(2) Any rule made under this section may provide that any breach thereof shall be punishable with such penalty not exceeding a fine of five pounds or imprisonment for one month as the Native Authority may think fit.

(*Adaptation by L.N. 131 of 1954 and N.R.L.N. 144 of 1960*)

Powers of Governor in relation to Rules which may be made by Native Authorities

42. Wherever in the opinion of the Governor it is expedient for the good order and government of the area of a Native Authority that any rules should be made which such authority is empowered to make by section 37 or section 41 the Governor may direct the Native Authority to make and enforce any such rules, and if the Native Authority shall neglect or refuse to make the rules which it is so directed to make the Governor may himself make such rules and thereupon such rules, when made known in the manner prescribed by section 146, shall have the same force and effect as if they had been made by the Native Authority and approved by the Governor.

(Adaptation by L.N. 131 of 1954)

Power of Native Authorities to Issue Orders

43. Subject to the provisions of any written law for the time being in force in the Region, a Native Authority, may subject to the general or specific directions of the Native Authority, if any, to which it is subordinate, issue orders, to be obeyed by all persons within its area to whom the orders relate, for all or any of the following purposes—

(1) prohibiting, restricting or regulating gambling;[14]

(2) prohibiting, restricting or regulating the carrying and possession of weapons;

(3) prohibiting, restricting or regulating the burning of grass or bush, and the use of fire or lights in any manner likely to ignite any grass or bush in contravention of any law or regulation;

(4) prohibiting, restricting, controlling or regulating noise in public places (whether the noise emanates from a public place or emanates from a private place and can be heard in a public place) including (without prejudice to the generality of the foregoing powers) the following matters:

(a) prohibiting, restricting, controlling or regulating—

    (i) the sounding of horns or other similar appliances fitted to vehicles other than motor vehicles;

    (ii) the playing of gramophones, phonographs, musical-boxes, automatic musical instruments, wireless loudspeakers or any other form of mechanical reproduction of sound;

    (iii) the use of loudspeakers, loudhailers, megaphones and all forms of public address equipment whether mechanical or otherwise;

    (iv) singing, shouting, drumming and the playing of instruments of all kinds.[15]

(b) the licensing of any persons, buildings, places, vehicles or instruments in connection with any of the matters mentioned in paragraph (a) and the grant of permits to any persons in respect of the same;

(5) prohibiting the hindrance or interruption of the free passage of any person transporting goods or produce along any path or road leading to any town or village;

[14] *e.g.*, Beggar Minstrel Orders.
[15] *e.g.*, Control of Noise Orders.

(6) requiring people to carry lamps during such hours and within such places or areas as may be specified in the order; (*Amended by N.R. No. 3 of 1955*)

(7) prohibiting, restricting, controlling or regulating the dressing of ore;

(7A) requiring any native to cultivate land to such extent and with such crops as will secure an adequate supply of food for the support of such native and of those dependent on him; (*Inserted by N.R. No. 3 of 1955*)

(8) requiring persons to report the presence within the area of its authority of any person who has committed an offence for which he may be arrested without a warrant or for whose arrest a warrant has been issued, or of any property stolen or believed to have been stolen within or without the area of its authority;

(9) prohibiting, restricting or regulating or requiring to be done any matter or thing which the Native Authority, by virtue of any native law or custom for the time being in force and not repugnant to morality or justice, has power to prohibit, restrict, regulate or require to be done;

(10) specifying fees or charges to be paid in respect of any matter or act for which provision is made in any order.

Powers of Governor in Relation to Orders which may be Issued by Native Authorities

44. (1) Whenever in the opinion of the Governor it is expedient for the good order and government of the area of a Native Authority that any order should be issued which such authority is empowered to issue by section 43, the Governor may direct the Native Authority to issue and enforce any such order, and if the Native Authority shall neglect or refuse to issue the order which it is so directed to issue, the Governor may himself issue such order and thereupon such order, when made known in the manner prescribed by section 146, shall have the same force and effect as if it had been issued by the Native Authority.

(2) When the Governor is of opinion that any order issued by a Native Authority should not have been issued or should not be enforced, he may direct the Native Authority to revoke such order, or may himself revoke such order and after the order has been revoked may—

(*a*) require the release from custody of any person sentenced to imprisonment by a court for contravention of such order;

(*b*) require the repayment of any fine imposed by a native court; and

(*c*) require the payment by a Native Authority whose order has been revoked as aforesaid to a person upon whom a fine has been imposed by the High Court or a magistrate's court of a sum of money not exceeding the amount of such fine by way of compensation for such fine, whether such sentence or imprisonment or fine was imposed before or after the Governor's direction to revoke or his revocation of such order was issued.

(*Adaptation by L.N.* 131 *of* 1954)

Breaches of Orders under Sections 43 and 44

45. (1) When a Native Authority issues an order under section 43 or the Governor issues an order under section 44, the Native Authority or the Governor, as the case may be, may by the same order specify a penalty for the breach thereof and may specify different penalties in the case of successive breaches:

Proved that the penalty shall not exceed a fine of one hundred pounds or imprisonment for six months or both such fine and imprisonment.

(2) Any person accused of the breach of such an order may be arrested in accordance with a warrant obtained under section 108.

(*Adaptation by L.N.* 131 *of* 1954)

Jurisdiction of Courts

Courts before which Proceedings to be Brought

46. Without prejudice to the powers of transfer conferred by sections 32 and 34 of the Native Courts Law, 1956, any proceedings arising under a rule made under section 37, 41 or 42 or an order issued under section 43 or 44 or for an offence contrary to section 34 or section 35 shall be brought—

(i) if all the parties are subject to the jurisdiction of a native court, before a native court having jurisdiction in the area;

(ii) if any of the parties is not subject to the jurisdiction of a native court, before a magistrate's court.

(*Amended by N.R. No.* 37 *of* 1960)

Other Powers of Native Authorities

Power of Native Authority to Order Stranger to leave its Area

47. (1) A Native Authority may order any native who is not a member of the native community living in the area of its authority, and who fails, when so required by the Native Authority, to produce reasonable proof to the Native Authority that his means and legitimate labour are sufficient for the adequate support of himself and his dependants, to leave such area within such time after the order has been communicated to him, not being less than fourteen days, as the Native Authority may direct:

Provided, however, that any person so ordered to leave such an area may appeal against the order to a court presided over by a magistrate, but the court shall not set aside the order unless such person satisfies the court that his means and legitimate labour are sufficient for the adequate support of himself and his dependants.

(2) Any person who fails to obey an order made under this section, or who, having left the area which he was directed by the order to leave, returns to such area without the consent of the Native Authority, shall be liable to a fine of twenty-five pounds or to imprisonment for six months, or to both such fine and imprisonment.

Declaration and Modification of Native Law and Custom

48. (1) A Native Authority may, and where the Governor so requires, shall, record in writing a declaration of what in its opinion is the native law or custom relating to any subject either as applying throughout the area of authority of the Native Authority or in any specific part thereof or as affecting specified persons or classes of persons in such area or in any part thereof and submit such declaration to the Governor.

(2) A Native Authority may if it considers it expedient for the good government and welfare of the area of its authority submit for the consideration of the Governor a recommendation for the modification of any native law or custom, relating to any subject either as applying throughout the area of its authority or in any part thereof or as affecting certain specified persons or classes of persons or any part thereof whether or not a declaration has been submitted and an order made under the provisions of this section in respect of such native law or custom.

(3) If the Governor is satisfied that a declaration submitted under the provisions of subsection (1) accurately records the native law or custom with respect to the subject to which it relates or that a modification submitted under the provisions of subsection (2) is expedient and that the native law or custom or modification thereof is not repugnant to justice, equity or good conscience nor incompatible either in its terms or by necessary implication with any Ordinance or Law, he may by order direct the native law and custom set out in the declaration or the modification thereof to be the native law and custom in respect of the subject to which it relates and to be in force in the area concerned.

(*Adaptation by L.N.* 131 *of* 1954)

Special Provisions relating to Subsidiary Legislation
under different Enactments made by different
Native Authorities

Subsidiary Legislation made under One Authority may in Certain Cases be varied under Another

49. (1) Where a Native Authority has enacted any rule or bye-law or issued any order in accordance with the provisions of any law and subsequently such Native Authority is authorised under a different enactment to enact any rule or issue any order in respect of substantually the same or the same subject-matter as that previously made or issued such Native Authority may—

(*a*) amend, vary modify or repeal such previous enactment by means of the legislative authority subsequently vested in the said Native Authority even though such previous enactment is being amended, varied, modified or repealed by an enactment of a different kind;

(b) declare, by means of an enactment under the subsequent legislative authority, that the prior enactment shall be deemed to be a rule or order, as the case may be, made or issued under the provisions of the subsequent authority; and thereupon such rule, bye-law or order as aforesaid shall be deemed to be a rule or order, as the case may be, made or issued under the latter legislative authority and be in full force and effect, save in so far as the same may be in conflict with any of the provisions authorised to be made or issued by the subsequent legislative authority.

(2) Without prejudice to the generality of the foregoing, the provisions of sub-section (1) shall apply to all rules made under the authority of the enactments set out in the first column of the First Schedule as though it had been declared in accordance with paragraph (b) of subsection (1) that the said rules should be deemed to have been made under the authority of the provisions of this Law set out in the second column of the said Schedule.

Effect on Subsidiary Legislation where another Native Authority is Substituted

50. Where any bye-law has been made, or where any rule or order has been made or issued, by a Native Authority and another or two or more Native Authorities are substituted for such Native Authority aforesaid and such substituted Native Authority or Authorities is or are authorised to make or issue similar rules or orders; then all such existing rules, bye-laws or orders shall, in so far as they relate to the area under the jurisdiction of such substituted Native Authority or Authorities, be deemed to have been made by such substituted Native Authority or Authorities, and may be amended, varied modified, and repealed by such substituted Native Authority or Authorities in so far as they relate to the area within the jurisdiction of such substituted Native Authority or Authorities.

Section 49 to Apply to Original and Substituted Native Authorities

51. The provisions of section 49 shall apply not only in respect of the Native Authority which originally made or issued such rule, bye-law or order but also, where another or two or more Native Authorities are substituted for the Native Authority which originally made or issued such rule, bye-law or order, to such substituted Native Authority or Authorities in respect of the area within the respective jurisdiction of such substituted Native Authority or Authorities.

PART IV

CONDUCT OF BUSINESS, SUBORDINATE COUNCILS,
DELEGATION OF FUNCTIONS AND JOINT COMMITTEES AND
JOINT SERVICES

Conduct of Business

Standing Orders of Native Authorities with a Membership of more than One Person

52. (1) Where a Native Authority consists of a Chief associated with a Council, a Council or a group of persons such Native Authority—

(*a*) shall make Standing Orders in respect of the following matters—

(i) the minimum number of members necessary to constitute a meeting of the Native Authority;

(ii) the minimum number of members comprising the said Native Authority whose assent, recorded at any one meeting of the Native Authority, shall be necessary to validate a resolution or any other act of the said native Authority; Native Authority whose assent, recorded at any one meeting of the Native Authority, shall be necessary to validate a resolution or any other act of the said Native Authority;

(iii) by whom and in what manner the assent or other action of the Native Authority shall be signified on documents;

(iv) the person who shall preside either permanently or temporarily or on special occasions at the meetings of the Native Authority when such Authority consists of a Council or group of persons;

(v) the design and custody of the common seal of the Native Authority;

(vi) procedure at meetings of the Native Authority;

(vii) the manner in which notices should be given of meetings and the subject to be considered thereat;

(viii) the times at which meetings shall be held and the notices therefor;

(ix) the control of the general public within the vicinity of the place where meetings are being held by the Native Authority; and

(x) for the due, proper and orderly conduct of the business of the Native Authority;

(*b*) may make Standing Orders generally for enabling decisions of the Native Authority to be made effective in the simplest, speediest and most efficient manner.

(*Amended by N.R. No. 37 of 1960*)

(2) Any Standing Order made under this section and any amendment of any such Order shall be subject to the approval of the Minister and require his counter-signature before it shall take effect.

(3) After a Standing Order or any amendment thereof has been countersigned by the Minister such Standing Order shall be binding upon the proceedings of the Native Authority which made it until such time as the Order shall be revoked or varied and any decision or act of a Native Authority made or taken in accordance with such Standing Orders shall be of the same force and validity as an act of all the members of the Native Authority acting together and in unity.

(4) When a Native Authority making a Standing Order is a Subordinate Native Authority it shall obtain the approval of the Native Authority to which it is subordinate before submitting the Order for the approval of and counter-signature of the Minister.

(5) A copy of all Standing Orders made under this section shall be deposited with the Minister.

(6) The Minister may make Standing Orders for any Native Authority to which this section applies—

(a) where no Standing Orders exist for the Native Authority; or

(b) where he considers that the Standing Orders of the Native Authority are for any reason unsatisfactory,

and Standing Orders made under this subsection shall be binding on the Native Authority for whom they are made. (*Inserted by N.R. No. 4 of 1957; substituted by N.R. No. 37 of 1960*)

(*Adaptation by L.N. 131 of 1954 and N.R.L.N. 144 of 1960*)

Standing Orders of a Chief or Other Person Appointed Native Authority

53. (1) Where a Chief or other person is appointed as a Native Authority such Chief of other person may make Standing Orders in respect of the conduct of the business—

(a) of the Native Authority to which he has been appointed; and

(b) of any Advisory Council duly appointed by him under the provisions of section 63.

(2) Such Standing Orders may include provisions similar to those which a Native Authority consisting of a Chief associated with a Council, a Council or a group of persons is required to make or may make under section 52 and shall come into force and effect upon their approval in writing by the Minister.

(3) A copy of all Standing Orders made under this section shall be deposited with the Minister.

(*Adaptation by L.N. 131 of 1954 and N.R.L.N. 144 of 1960*)

Subordinate Councils

Administrative Sub-Areas

54. (1) For the purposes of this Law, a Native Authority may—

(a) with the approval of the Minister, divide the area under its jurisdiction or any part of that area into districts, village areas, wards, or such other administrative sub-areas as it may consider expedient; and

(b) subject to the provisions of subsection (2) of section 36, appoint a person to be head of any district, village area, ward or other administrative sub-area. (*Substituted by N.R. No. 3 of 1955*)

(2) Any such division or appointment which is in force on the date upon which this Law comes into operation shall be deemed to have been made under the provision of this Law.

(*Adaptation by N.R.L.N. 144 of 1960*)

Establishment of Local Councils

55. A Native Authority may, and shall if so directed by the Minister by instrument establish a Local Council for any district, town village area, ward or other administrative sub-area, whether or not any person has been appointed to be head of the administrative sub-area, or for a combination of administrative sub-areas.

(*Adaptation by L.N. 131 of 1954 and N.R.L.N. 144 of 1960; amended by N.R. No. 37 of 1960*)

56. (*Repealed by N.R. No. 37 of 1960*)

Outer Councils

57. (1) In addition to the powers conferred by section 55, a Native Authority shall have power by instrument to establish a representative and consultative body to be known as the Outer Council to perform such duties on behalf of and to render such assistance and advice to the Native Authority as may be specified in the instrument establishing the Council. (*Amended by N.R. No. 37 of 1960*)

(2) The Outer Council shall have no executive powers or functions and shall not form part of the Native Authority. (*Substituted by N.R. No. 3 of 1955*)

Power of Minister to Extend Life of Local Councils and Outer Councils

57A. Notwithstanding the provisions of sections 55 or 57 or of any rules made under paragraph (20) of section 37 the Minister may dissolve any Local Council or Outer Council or extend the life of any such Council for such period as he may specify.

(*Inserted by N.R. No. 37 of 1960*)

Contents of Instruments Establishing Councils

58. The instrument establishing a Local Council, a Town Council or an Outer Council shall be subject to the approval of the Minister and shall provide for—

(a) the name of the Council;

(b) the functions of the Council, including, in the case of a Local Council or Town Council, any powers delegated to the Council under the provisions of section 64; (*Amended by N.R. No. 3 of 1955*)

(c) the composition of the Council, which shall be subject to the provisions of section 59;

(d) the chairmanship of the Council;

(e) the summoning and frequency of meetings of the Council.

(*Adaptation by L.N.* 131 *of* 1954 *and N.R.L.N.* 144 *of* 1960)

Composition of Councils

59. (1) A Local Council, a Town Council or any Outer Council shall be composed of—

(a) elected members, being persons elected in such manner as the Native Authority may either by rules made under the provisions of paragraph (20) of section 37 or otherwise prescribe;

(b) such *ex-officio* members as the Native Authority may prescribe as aforesaid; and

(c) if the Native Authority so directs, persons nominated in such manner as the Native Authority may prescribe as aforesaid:

Provided that the elected members shall form a majority of the Council.

(2) A Council may, if the Native Authority so directs, invite persons to attend for any particular purpose.

Standing Orders for Councils

60. When a Native Authority has established a Local Council, a Town Council or an Outer Council, it shall provide for the making of Standing Orders for the conduct of the business of the Council and for their amendment and, if it empowers the Council to make or amend Standing Orders, may direct that any orders or amendments made by the Council shall be subject to the approval of the Native Authority.

Method of Dissolution of Certain Councils

61. Any Council established under the provisions of sections 55 or 57 may be dissolved by the same method by which it was established.

Removal of Individual Members of Subordinate Councils

61A. (1) The Minister may at any time direct that any member of a Local Council or an Outer Council, whether he has obtained membership personally or in a representative capacity, shall cease to be a member of such Local Council or Outer Council, as the case may be.

(2) Whenever the Minister proposes to make a direction under this section in respect of any person who is a member of a Local Council or an Outer Council by reason of his having been elected thereto in pursuance of the provisions of paragraph (a) of subsection (1) of section 59 the Minister shall give to such person notice in writing of his proposal to make such direction and such person shall be entitled within one calendar month from the receipt by him of such notice to make representations in writing to the Minister touching such proposal.

(*Inserted by N.R. No.* 37 *of* 1960)

Election Offences Rules for Subordinate Councils

62. The Governor may make rules for the definition and trial of offences relating to elections to Councils other than Native Authority Councils and for the imposition of penalties for such offences.

(Adaptation by L.N. 131 of 1954)

Appointment and Duties of Advisory Councils

Appointment and Duties of Advisory Councils

63. (1) Where a Chief or other person is appointed a Native Authority such Chief or other person may, subject to the approval of the Premier in the case of a Chief and the Minister in any other case, appoint certain persons to be an Advisory Council.

(2) The constitution of any such Council shall not be altered save with the prior approval of the Premier if a Chief makes the appointment of an Advisory Council and the Minister if any other person makes the appointment of an Advisory Council.

(3) The Chief or other person appointed a Native Authority as aforesaid may require any such Council to perform such duties on behalf of, and to render such assistance to, the Native Authority as may be specified by Standing Orders made under the provisions of section 53.

(4) The Premier if a Chief makes the appointment of an Advisory Council and the Minister if any other person makes the appointment of an Advisory Council shall have power to dissolve an Advisory Council or to dismiss individual members thereof.

(Adaptation by L.N. 131 of 1954 and N.R.L.N. 144 of 1960)

Delegation of Functions

Delegations to Councils

64. A Native Authority with the approval of the Minister, may delegate to a Local Council,

(a) any of its functions under this Law, other than the powers conferred upon the Native Authority by sections 20, 22, 37, (except paragraphs (50) and (60) thereof), 54, 80, 95, 97 and 98 and Part VIII; and

(b) such of its functions under any other Law or under any of the Ordinances set out in the Second Schedule as the Minister may, by notice in the Regional *Gazette*, prescribe.

(Amended by N.R. No. 3 of 1955 and N.R. No. 37 of 1960; adaptation by L.N. 131 of 1954 and N.R.L.N. 144 of 1960)

Delegations to Committees

65. (1) A Native Authority may, with the approval of the Minister appoint committees for any such general or special purposes as, in the opinion of the Native Authority, would be better regulated or managed by means of a committee, and may, with the approval of the Minister, delegate to any committee so appointed, with or without restrictions or conditions, as the Native Authority thinks fit, any functions exercisable by the Native Authority with respect to the whole or part of the area of the Native Authority, except—

(a) the power to make subsidiary legislation;

(b) the powers to raise money under the provisions of sections 77 and 78;

(c) (*Deleted by N.R. No. 37 of 1960*)

(d) the power to make Standing Orders for the conduct of the business of the Native Authority; and

(e) the powers of a Native Authority under this section.

(2) A committee appointed under the provisions of this section may include persons who are not members of a Native Authority:

Provided that at least one-third of the members of every such committee shall be members of the Native Authority. (*Substituted by N.R. No. 4 of 1957*)

(3) The number of members of a committee appointed under the provisions of this section, their term of office, and the area within which the committee is to exercise its authority, shall be determined by the Native Authority.

(4) The member presiding shall, when the votes on any question are equal, have a casting vote in addition to his original vote.

(5) It shall be lawful for a committee with the approval of the Native Authority by whom it is appointed to invite any person whose advice or assistance such committee desires to obtain to attend for such period or such purposes as it deems fit, and a person so invited and attending shall have all the rights of a member except that he shall not be entitled to vote.

(6) Where a Native Authority has, pursuant to the powers conferred upon it by subsection (1), appointed a committee for any purpose, such Native Authority shall make Standing Orders for the conduct of the business of the committee, and the provisions of section 52 shall apply to the making of such Standing Orders in so far as such provisions are applicable, and with such verbal modifications not affecting the substance as are necessary to make them applicable to the circumstances.

(*Adaptation by L.N. 131 of 1954 and N.R.L.N. 144 of 1960*)

Other Delegations

66. A Native Authority may, with the approval of the Premier, delegate to any member or group of members of such Native Authority, or to any sub-area head within the area of its authority, such of the functions of the Native Authority under sections 30, 103, and 104 of this Law as it may deem expedient to delegate, and any such delegation shall be notified in such manner as is customary for the native community in the area concerned.

(*Adaptation by 131 of 1954 and N.R.L.N. 144 of 1960*)

APPENDICES

Saving of Powers

67. (1) Any delegation made under the provisions of sections 64, 65 and 66 shall be revocable at will, and no such delegation shall be deemed to prevent the exercise of any delegated power or function by the person by whom such delegation is made.

(2) Any delegation made under the provisions of this Part shall be notified in such manner as is customary for the native community in the area concerned, and the revocation of any such delegation shall be notified in like manner.

Joint Committees and Joint Services

Establishment of Joint Committees to Operate Joint Services

68. (1) Where two or more Native Authorities desire to make provisions for the joint operation of services of any kind (which term shall include police, prisons, a treasury and any other service which a single Native Authority may lawfully operate) they may, with the approval of the Minister, by instrument jointly and severally establish a committee for the purpose (hereinafter referred to as a "joint committee"), to consist of a person or persons appointed in manner agreed between the Native Authorities concerned, and subject to the provisions of sections 70, 73 and 74, jointly and severally delegate to such joint committee all or any of their functions in respect of the operation of such services.

(2) The establishment of a joint committee shall be notified in the Regional *Gazette*.

(3) A joint committee established under the provisions of this section may include persons who are not members of a Native Authority:

Provided that at least one-third of the members if every such joint committee shall be members of the Native Authorities concerned.

(Inserted by N.R. No. 4 of 1957)

(Adaptation by L.N. 131 of 1954 and N.R.L.N. 144 of 1960)

Appointment, Removal and Remuneration of Members of Joint Committees

69. (1) The instrument establishing the joint committee shall contain provision for the appointment and removal of members of the joint committee, and for the duration of their appointments.

(2) The members of a joint committee may receive such remuneration as may be jointly determined by the Native Authorities concerned, with the approval of the Minister.

(Adaptation by N.R.L.N. 144 of 1960)

Functions which may be Delegated

70. The functions delegated to a joint committee may include all such powers as are necessary for the efficient operation of the service

200

concerned, and, without prejudice to the generality of the foregoing may include—

(a) the power to engage employees on such terms as to remuneration or otherwise as the joint committee may think fit, or as the Native Authorities concerned may from time to time jointly direct, and to dismiss employees;

(b) the power to enter into contracts for any purpose connected with the service operated by the committee;

(c) the power to fix, collect or waive fees or charges;

(d) the power to acquire, hold or dispose of property of any kind;

(e) all or any of the powers and duties conferred or imposed upon a Native Authority by Parts VIII and IX, which Parts shall be read in their application to a police force or prison operated by a joint committee as though for the words "Native Authority" there were substituted the words "joint committee" wherever this may be necessary; and

(f) all or any of the functions of a Native Authority under sections 30, 103 and 104 and the power to delegate such functions in accordance with the provisions of sections 66 and 118,

but shall not include the power to impose general or other rates under the provisions of section 77 and paragraph (50) of section 37.

Standing Orders for Joint Committees

70A. When two or more Native Authorities have established a joint committee they shall provide for the making of Standing Orders for the conduct of the business of the joint committee and for their amendment and, if they empower the joint committee to make or amend Standing Orders, may direct that any Orders or amendments made by the joint committee shall be subject to the approval of the Native Authorities.

(*Inserted by N.R. No. 37 of 1960*)

Joint Committees to be Bodies Corporate

71. Every joint committee shall be a body corporate by the name designated in the instrument establishing such committee, and shall have perpetual succession and a common seal and may sue and be sued.

Application of Sections

72. The provisions of sections 109 to 112 inclusive and of subsections (1), (2), (3) and (5) of section 113 shall apply, *mutatis mutandis*, to civil legal proceedings by or against a joint committee.

Exercise of Delegated Powers

73. A joint committee shall exercise the powers delegated to it subject to such joint directions, whether general or particular, as it

may from time to time receive from the Native Authorities concerned but so long as the delegation remains in force none of the Native Authorities concerned shall itself exercise any of the delegated powers, with the exception of the powers referred to in paragraph (*f*) of section 70.

Revocation or Modification of Delegated Powers

74. (1) A Native Authority which has delegated any of its powers to a joint committee shall not revoke or modify the delegation without the prior consent of the Minister, which shall be subject to such conditions, as to financial or other matters, as the Minister may deem just, and, without prejudice to the generality of the foregoing, the Minister may direct that such revocation or modification shall not take effect until the last day of a financial year, as defined in section 84.

(2) Any such revocation or modification shall be notified in the Regional *Gazette*.

(*Adaptation by L.N.* 131 *of* 1954 *and N.L.R.N.* 144 *of* 1960)

Revocation of Delegated Powers by Minister

74A. Where a Native Authority has delegated any of its functions to a joint committee in accordance with the provision of section 68 the Minister may direct that such delegation shall be revoked and thereafter such functions shall be performed by the Native Authority.

(*Inserted by N.R. No.* 37 *of* 1960)

Services Operated by Joint Committees and Employees thereof

75. (1) Where the management of two or more existing police forces or prisons or other services is delegated to a joint committee, the joint force or service shall be deemed to have been constituted by the joint committee.

(2) All persons employed in any service which is operated by a joint committee shall, from the date of the delegation to the joint committee of power to operate the service, be deemed to be employed by the joint committee:

Provided that for the purpose of computing seniority of service, any period of service spent in the employment of any of the Native Authorities concerned shall be deemed to be service in the employment of the joint committee and *vice versa*.

75A. Whenever in the opinion of the Minister it is expedient for the good order and government of the areas of Native Authorities which have established a joint committee in accordance with the provisions of section 68 or any of them that such joint committee should be dissolved the Minister may by direction dissolve such joint committee.

Inserted by N.R. No. 37 *of* 1960)

PART V

FINANCIAL PROVISIONS

Revenue and Funds

Declaration of Revenue and Funds of Native Authority

76. The revenue and other funds of a Native Authority are hereby declared to be as follows—

(1) All such funds as are lawfully in the possession of such Native Authority on the day on which this Law comes into operation;

(2) Revenue accruing to such Native Authority from the following sources—

(a) the amount of tax payable to a Native Authority under the provisions of the Personal Tax Law, 1962;

(b) general or other rates imposed under the provisions of sections 77 and paragraph (50) of section 37;

(c) fees, fines and penalties payable in respect of or as a result of proceedings in Native Courts within the area of a Native Authority and the proceeds of sale of any forfeitures ordered by such Native Courts:

Provided that this paragraph shall not apply to fees, fines and penalties payable in respect of or as a result of proceedings in Provincial Courts;

(d) fees or charges specified by any order or rule made under sections 37, 41, 42, 43 or 44;

(e) moneys payable to a Native Authority under the provisions of any other written law;

(f) receipts derived from any public utility or trading concern belonging to a Native Authority;

(g) grants-in-aid out of the general revenue of Nigeria or of a Region;

(h) any particular revenue of Nigeria or of a Region lawfully assigned to a Native Authority;

(i) the proceeds of loans raised in accordance with the provisions of section 78;

(j) interest on the invested funds of a Native Authority, or upon loans made by a Native Authority;

(*Amended by N.R. No.* 37 *of* 1960)

(3) Any other moneys lawfully derived by a Native Authority from any other source whatsoever not hereinbefore specifically mentioned.

Power to Make Rates

77. (1) A Native Authority or any body to which a Native Authority has delegated its functions under paragraph (50) of section 37 may make general or other rates to provide for, or otherwise in respect of, any public services provided by the Native Authority or such body in any capacity. (*Substituted by N.R. No.* 37 *of* 1960)

(2) A Native Authority may make a special rate to be known as an Education Rate the proceeds whereof shall be paid to the Native Authority:

Provided that where under the provisions of section 25 of the Education Ordinance, 1952, or section 24 of the Education Law, 1956, a Local Education Authority has been established for the area of the jurisdiction of the Native Authority the making of such a rate and the expenditure of the proceeds thereof shall be subject to the approval of such Local Education Authority. (*Amended by N.R. No. 37 of* 1960)

(3) All rates made by a Native Authority or any body to which a Native Authority has delegated its functions under paragraph (50) of section 37 shall be made and collected in accordance with rules under section 37. (*Substituted by N.R. No. 37 of* 1960)

Power to Borrow within Nigeria

78. (1) A Native Authority may, with the consent of the Minister charged with responsibility for finance in writing, raise loans within Nigeria from such sources, in such manner and upon such conditions as the Minister charged with responsibility for finance may approve, of such amounts as may be required for any of the following purposes—

(a) for acquiring any land which the Native Authority has power to acquire;

(b) for erecting any building which the Native Authority has power to erect;

(c) for the execution of any permanent work, the provision of any plant, or the doing of any other things which the Native Authority has power to execute, provide or do, if, in the opinion of the Minister charged with responsibility for finance, the cost of carrying out that purpose ought to be spread over a term of years;

(d) for any other purpose to which the Native Authority is authorised under any enactment to apply its revenue and other funds:

Provided that a Native Authority may, without the consent of the Minister charged with responsibility for finance, borrow by way of temporary loan or overdraft from a bank or otherwise, any sums which it may temporarily require for the purpose of defraying expenses pending the receipt of revenues receivable by it in respect of the period of account in which those expenses are chargeable and taken into account in the estimates made by the Native Authority for that period; and for the purpose of defraying, pending the raising of a loan which the Native Authority has been authorised to raise, expenses intended to be defrayed by means of the loan.

(2) Such loans shall be secured upon the property and revenues of the Native Authority.

(3) Every such loan shall be paid off by equal yearly, half-yearly, or quarterly instalments of principal and interest:

Provided that the period of repayment shall not exceed twenty years.

(4) All sums borrowed by Native Authorities in exercise of the powers conferred by this section shall be regulated, managed and controlled in accordance with section 85 and the expenditure thereof shall be subject to the provisions of section 86.

(*Adaptation by L.N.* 131 *of* 1954 *and N.R.L.N.* 144 *of* 1960)

Powers of Expenditure and Allied Powers

Declaration of General Principle of Expenditure

79. The revenue and other funds of a Native Authority shall be applied to the administration, development and welfare of the area over which its authority extends and to the welfare of the inhabitants thereof.

Power to Invest Moneys

80. A Native Authority may invest any portion of its moneys in such manner as may be approved by the Minister charged with responsibility for finance.

(*Adaptation by L.N.* 131 *of* 1954 *and N.R.L.N.* 144 *of* 1960)

Power to Lend

81. (1) In addition to the power of investment conferred by section 80, a Native Authority shall have power, with the consent of the Minister and upon such terms as may be approved by the Minister to lend money to any corporation operating in Nigeria, or to any person being in Nigeria, for any of the following purposes—

(*a*) the development and improvement of established methods of farming and the introduction of or conduct of experiments in new methods of farming and crop production;

(*b*) the establishment and development of undertakings which in the opinion of the Native Authority, are likely to further the social and economic welfare of the area of its jurisdiction;

(*c*) any other purpose to which the Native Authority is authorised under any enactment to apply its revenue and funds.

(2) The Minister may give a general consent to the making of loans by Native Authorities in general or by any particular Native Authority or Native Authorities up to a stated proportion of the annual revenue of the Native Authority making a loan and may also give a general approval of the terms upon which loans may be made without specific reference to him.

(*Adaptation by L.N.* 131 *of* 1954 *and N.R.L.N.* 144 *of* 1960)

Power to Guarantee Loans

82. A Native Authority may with the approval of the Minister

given generally or in each particular instance guarantee the repayment of any loan made by any other person to any person resident within the area of the jurisdiction of the Native Authority for the purpose of directly furthering the development and welfare of the area of its jurisdiction.

(Adaptation by L.N. 131 of 1954 and N.R.L.N. 144 of 1960)

Management of Finances

Provision Touching Management of Finances

83. (1) A Native Authority shall, if so directed in writing by the Minister, make such provision as may be specified in such direction in relation to the control and management of its finances in accordance with the provisions of this Part.

(2) Without prejudice to the generality of subsection (1), such direction may contain provision touching—

(a) the establishment of a committee (to be known as the Finance Committee) to manage, for and on behalf of and subject to the control of the Native Authority, the financial affairs of the Native Authority; and

(b) such other provision (including the establishment of treasuries or the recognition of existing treasuries) as may, in the opinion of the Minister, be necessary for the due receipt and disbursement of the moneys of the Native Authority.

(Adaptation by L.N. 131 of 1954 and N.R.L.N. 144 of 1960)

Financial Year

84. The financial year for each Native Authority shall begin on the 1st day of April, in one year and end on the 31st day of March in the year next following.

Regulation of Finances

85. (1) Subject to the provisions of subsection (1) of section 86 the Minister may by writing under his hand, either generally or to such extent, during such period, and subject to such conditions as may be specified in the writing, direct that any particular Native Authority shall regulate, control and manage its own finances and may in like manner at any time revoke or vary any direction so given.

(2) Where the Minister directs that any particular Native Authority shall regulate, control and manage its own finances, the Native Authority shall thereafter regulate, manage and control its finances in accordance with the provisions of such direction.

(3) No such direction shall deprive the Minister of the right to disallow or reduce any item of proposed expenditure if he deems it necessary to do so in the interest of the good government of the area of jurisdiction of the Native Authority.

(Adaptation by L.N. 131 of 1954 and N.R.L.N. 144 of 1960)

Estimates

86. (1) Estimates of the revenue and expenditure of every Native Authority shall be submitted annually to the Minister for his approval, and the Minister may, before approving the same, and after consultation with the Native Authority, delete therefrom any item, or reduce the amount of any item, or add thereto any item or increase the amount of any item.

(2) Native Authorities may make advances, operate deposit and suspense accounts within such limits and upon such conditions as shall be approved in writing by the Minister, and such approval may be given either generally or with respect to the Native Authorities in any particular area.

(3) Where no direction has been given under section 85 and save as is provided in subsection (2) of this section and in section 113 no expenditure shall be incurred by a Native Authority, or by any person acting on its behalf otherwise than in accordance with the approved estimates unless the approval of the Minister has been first obtained.

(4) The Minister may by writing under his hand depute any person by name or by office to exercise on his behalf the power of approval referred to in subsection (3), subject to such conditions, exceptions and qualifications as he may prescribe, and thereupon any person so deputed shall have and may exercise such power subject to any prescribed conditions, exceptions and qualifications.

(Adaptation by L.N. 131 of 1954 and N.R.L.N. 144 of 1960)

Joint Treasuries

87. A direction under the provisions of section 83 may be given in respect of two or more Native Authorities jointly, and in such case the direction shall specify—

(a) the extent, if any, to which the funds of such Native Authorities are to be held jointly; and

(b) the extent, if any, to which the services of such Native Authorities are to be provided for by joint estimates.

Financial Memoranda

88. It shall be lawful for the Governor to issue written instructions (to be called Financial Memoranda), not inconsistent with any of the provisions of this Law, for the better control and management of Native Treasuries and of the financial business of Native Authorities, and for the regulation of the procedure of finance committees; and such instructions may be issued either generally or with respect to any particular Native Authority or with respect to the Native Authorities in any particular area.

(Adaptation by L.N. 131 of 1954)

Audit

Audit of Accounts

89. (1) Every Native Authority shall cause to be kept true accounts in accordance with such instructions as may from time to time be issued by the Minister.

(2) Within such period after the end of each financial year as may be prescribed by the Minister every Native Authority shall cause its accounts for the preceding financial year to be compiled and a statement or abstract of such accounts to be prepared.

(3) Such accounts, together with such annual statement or abstract and a copy thereof, shall be laid before an auditor to be appointed by the Minister.

(4) Every Native Authority shall permit the auditor to check any cash, investments or other assets in its possession and to have access at all times to all its accounts and all its books, vouchers and papers relating thereto.

(5) Where in accordance with the provisions of sections 83 and 87, a direction has been given to two or more Native Authorities jointly, the Native Authorities concerned shall make joint provision for the matters referred to in subsections (1) and (2) of this section.

(*Adaptation by L.N.* 131 *of* 1954 *and N.R.L.N.* 144 *of* 1960)

Powers of Auditor to take Evidence and of Native Authority to Issue Summons

90. (1) For the purpose of any examination, the auditor may take evidence and examine witnesses and the Native Authority shall, upon the request of the auditor, by summons require all such persons within its area as the auditor may think fit, to appear personally before the auditor at a time and place to be stated in such summons and to produce all such books and papers, including the minutes of the proceedings of the Native Authority or of any committee thereof, as the auditor may consider necessary for such examination. (*Amended by N.R. No.* 37 *of* 1960)

(2) Any person who, when so required, without reasonable excuse—

(*a*) neglects or refuses to comply with the terms of such summons;

(*b*) having appeared, refuses to be examined; or

(*c*) refuses to answer such questions as are put to him,

shall be guilty of an offence and shall be liable, on conviction therefore, for every such neglect or refusal, to a fine not exceeding twenty-five pounds or to imprisonment for a term not exceeding two years.

Other Powers and Duties of Auditor

91. (1) An auditor appointed by the Minister at every audit held by him or at any other time may recommend—

(*a*) the disallowance of any item of account which is contrary to law;

(b) the surcharge of the amount of any item paid out of account disallowed upon the person responsible for incurring or authorising the expenditure;

(c) the surcharge of any sum which has not been duly brought into account upon the person by whom that sum ought to have been brought into account;

(d) the surcharge of the amount of any loss or deficiency upon any person by whose negligence or misconduct the loss or deficiency has been incurred:

Provided that no item of expenditure incurred by a Native Authority shall be recommended for disallowance by the auditor, if it has been sanctioned by the Minister. (*Amended by N.R. No. 4 of 1957*)

(2) It shall be the duty of any such auditor—

(a) to certify the amount which will become due from any person upon whom he has recommended a surcharge if such surcharge is made; and

(b) to certify at the conclusion of the audit his allowance of the accounts, subject to any disallowance or surcharge which he may have recommended.

(*Adaptation by L.N. 131 of 1954 and N.R.L.N. 144 of 1960*)

Special Relief for Officers and Servants

92. Notwithstanding any of the provisions of section 91, no liability to surcharge shall be incurred by an officer or servant of the Native Authority who can prove to the satisfaction of the auditor that he acted in the pursuance of, and in accordance with, the terms of a resolution of the Native Authority, or of a committee duly appointed by the Native Authority or on the written instructions of any officer of the Native Authority to whom he is subordinate.

Report of Auditor

93. (1) At the conclusion of the audit the auditor shall make and sign a report on such accounts and statement or abstract and shall send—

(a) the original of his report and of such statement or abstract to the Minister; and

(b) a copy of his report and of such statement or abstract to the Native Authority.

(2) A copy of the annual statement or abstract and of the auditor's report shall be furnished by the Native Authority to any inhabitant of the area of the authority of the Native Authority upon the payment of such fee as may be specified by the Native Authority.

(*Adaptation by L.N. 131 of 1954 and N.R.L.N. 144 of 1960*)

Duty of Native Authority to Notify Certain Persons Affected by Recommendations or Certificate of Auditor

94. In any case where the auditor—

(a) has made a recommendation or certificate on any matter with respect to which any person has made an objection at the audit; or

(b) has made a recommendation for the disallowance of any item whereby any person is adversely affected, or for the surcharge of any sum or amount upon any person,

the Native Authority shall, forthwith upon receipt by it of any certificates given in accordance with section 91 (2) (a), give to such person notice in writing of the particulars of any such certificates of the auditor.

Duties of Native Authority as to Disallowance, Surcharge and Certificate

95. The Native Authority shall disallow any item or surcharge any sum or amount upon any person in respect of which or upon whom the auditor has made a recommendation for disallowance or surcharge, and if no notice of appeal has been received by the Native Authority under the provisions of section 99 within thirty days of the receipt by any such person of a notice sent to him under section 94, the Native Authority shall certify the amount due from any person upon whom a surcharge has been made and shall send a copy of the certificate to such person.

Payment of Sums Certified to be Due

96. Every sum certified by the Native Authority to be due from any person shall be paid by that person to the Treasury of the Native Authority concerned within sixty days after a copy of the certificate has been received by that person.

Recovery of Sums Certified to be Due

97. (1) Any sum which is certified by the Native Authority to be due and has become payable shall be recoverable as a civil debt.

(2) In any proceedings for the recovery of such a sum, a certificate signed by the Native Authority shall be conclusive evidence of the facts certified, and a certificate signed by the person authorised to sign on behalf of the Native Authority concerned or by the officer whose duty it is to keep the accounts of the Native Authority that the sum certified to be due has not been paid to him shall be conclusive evidence of non-payment, unless it is proved that the sum certified to be due has been paid since the date of the certificate.

(3) Unless the contrary is proved, a certificate purporting to be signed by the person authorised to sign on behalf of the Native Authority, or by the officer whose duty it is to keep the accounts of the Native Authority, shall be deemed to have been signed by such authorised person.

Duty of Native Authority to Report to Minister and Powers of Minister in Default

98. (1) The Native Authority shall within six months of the receipt by it either of the copy of the auditor's report and statement or abstract sent to it under subsection (1) of section 93 or of any recommendation or certificate made at any time in accordance with section 91 certify to the Minister that the recommendations of the auditor have been complied with and whether all sums or amounts surcharged upon any persons have been recovered from those persons. (*Amended by N.R. No. 37 of 1960*)

(2) If no certificate of the Native Authority has been received by the Minister within the time limited by subsection (1) the Minister may order the Native Authority to take any action which the Minister may, upon consideration of the report of the auditor and the statement or abstract, consider proper and the Native Authority shall thereupon comply with such order.

(*Adaptation by L.N. 131 of 1954 and N.R.L.N. 144 of 1960*)

Appeals to Minister

99. (1) Any person who is aggrieved—

(*a*) by a recommendation or certificate of the auditor on any matter with respect to which such person has made an objection at the audit; or

(*b*) by a recommendation for disallowance or surcharge made by the auditor,

may, within thirty days of the receipt by such person of a notice in writing from the Native Authority under section 94 send to the Native Authority notice in writing of such person's appeal to the Minister against any such recommendation or certificate, and the Native Authority shall forthwith forward such notice of appeal to the Minister. (*Amended by N.R. No. 37 of 1960*)

(2) The Minister on such appeal shall have power to confirm, vary or quash any recommendation or certificate referred to in subsection (1) and may give directions to the Native Authority accordingly.

(3) Where an appeal is made to the Minister under this section, he may at any stage of the proceedings, state in the form of a special case for the opinion of the High Court any question of law arising in the course of the appeal but save as aforesaid, the decision of the Minister shall be final.

(*Adaptation by L.N. 131 of 1954; L.N. 47 of 1955 and N.R.L.N. 144 of 1960*)

Other Provisions

Power to take Security from Employees

100. Where a person is employed in a position of trust either by a Native Authority or by more than one Native Authority, it shall

be lawful for any such Native Authority to take in respect of such employee a fidelity bond to secure the due performance of the duties of such employee and, in the event of any failure of such employee faithfully to discharge any of his duties, to sue on such bond on behalf of such Native Authority or Native Authorities for any loss sustained, notwithstanding that such loss cannot be assigned to any particular Native Authority or Native Authorities.

Method of Pleading Ownership of Moneys in Criminal Proceedings

101. Where the moneys of two or more Native Authorities are deposited in a common treasury the ownership of such funds may be described in the name of any such Native Authority.

(Adaptation by N.R.L.N. 120 of 1960)

PART VI

OFFENCES BY AND AGAINST NATIVE AUTHORITIES

Penalty to which Native Authorities are Liable

102. (1) A Native Authority shall be liable to a fine of fifty pounds upon conviction of any of the following acts or defaults—

(a) if it shall wilfully neglect to exercise the powers by this Law conferred upon it for or in respect of the prevention of offences or the bringing of offenders to justice, or the seizure of property stolen or believed to have been stolen;

(b) if when required by an administrative officer to give a direction to any person under section 104 it shall wilfully neglect to do so;

(c) if when directed by the Governor under subsection (1) of section 44 to issue an order for any of the purposes specified in section 43, it shall wilfully neglect to issue the order directed;

(d) if it shall wilfully neglect to enforce any order lawfully issued by it under section 43 (including any order issued by the direction of the Governor under subsection (1) of section 44 or issued by the Governor under the powers conferred upon him by subsection (1) of section 44;

(e) if it shall wilfully neglect to revoke an order when directed by the Governor under the powers conferred on him by subsection (2) of section 44;

(f) if it shall wilfully neglect to enforce any lawful order issued by a Native Authority to which it is subordinate;

(g) if it shall wilfully neglect to enforce any rules lawfully made by it under this Law or any rules made by the Governor under section 42; or

(h) if it shall be guilty of any abuse of authority conferred on it by this Law or by any other law or by native custom.

(2) When a group of persons is collectively appointed to be a Native Authority proceedings may be taken against all or any members

of such authority, either together or separately, in respect of any act or default punishable under this section, and upon proof of the commission of an offence by such authority every member thereof shall individually be liable to the penalties prescribed unless he shall satisfy the court that he was in no way responsibile for or a party to the commission of the offence.

(3) Subject to the provisions of the proviso to subsection (4) no proceedings shall be taken in respect of an offence under this section without the permission of the Governor.

(4) Proceedings under subsection (3) shall be brought in the High Court:

Provided that where a Native Authority is subordinate to any other Native Authority and the area for which it was appointed is within the jurisdiction of a Native Court of grade A, such Subordinate Native Authority or any members thereof may be tried for such an offence by such Native Court without the permission of the Governor.

(*Adaptation by L.N. 131 of 1954 and L.N. 47 of 1955*)

Duty to Assist Native Authorities

103. (1) It shall be the duty of every person, when thereto required by a Native Authority, to assist in carrying out the duties imposed upon such authority by this or any other Law or by any Ordinance or, in the case of natives, by any native law or custom and to carry out such lawful instructions as he may receive from the Native Authority.

(2) Every person so required by a Native Authority shall be deemed to be empowered to do all that may be reasonably necessary to give effect to any lawful order given by such authority.

Duty to Attend before Native Authority, Certain Officers and Court

104. (1) Every native, being a member of or within the area of, jurisdiction of a Native Authority, shall, when so directed by the Native Authority or by an administrative officer attend before such Native Authority or administrative officer or any other Government officer or before a Native Court having jurisdiction over such person.

(2) Any such person who when so directed to attend before any such authority, administrative officer, other Government officer or court shall, without reasonable excuse, neglect or refuse to attend as and when directed may be arrested in accordance with a warrant obtained under section 108 and taken before such authority, administrative officer, other Government officer or court.

Penalties for Offences

105. (1) Whoever—

(*a*) contravenes or fails to obey any direction which, by this Law he is bound to obey;

(*b*) obstructs or interferes with the lawful exercise by a Native Authority of any powers conferred by this Law, or by any other written law,

shall be liable to a fine of one hundred pounds or to imprisonment for six months or to both such fine and imprisonment. (*Amended by N.R. No. 4 of 1957*)

(2) Whoever, not being a person exercising administrative functions with the approval of the Governor-General, or the Governor, or the Premier, or the Minister, or a Native Authority, or a Chief shall profess to exercise administrative functions, or hold himself out to be a Chief or assume the powers of a Native Authority, shall be liable to a fine of two hundred pounds or to imprisonment of one year or to both such fine and imprisonment:

Provided that no proceedings shall be taken for an offence against this subsection without the consent of the Director of Public Prosecutions. (*Amended by N.R. No. 37 of 1960*)

(3) Any person accused of an offence against this section may be arrested in accordance with a warrant obtained under section 108.

(*Adaptation by L.N. 131 of 1954; L.N. 1 of 1955 and N.R.L.N. 144 of 1960*)

Penalties for Conspiring against Native Authority

106. (1) Everyone who conspires against or in any manner attempts to undermine the lawful power and authority of any Native Authority shall be liable to a fine of four hundred pounds or to imprisonment for one year, or to both such fine and imprisonment.

(2) A person shall not be liable to be convicted of an offence against this section by reason only that he has in good faith and without malice shown or endeavoured to show that a Native Authority has been misled or mistaken in any of its measures or that errors or defects exist in the composition of a Native Authority or in any legislation relating to or enacted by a Native Authority.

(3) No proceedings shall be taken for an offence against this section without the consent of the Director of Public Prosecutions. (*Amended by N.R. No. 37 of 1960*)

(4) Proceedings for offences under this section shall be brought in the High Court.

(*Adaptation by L.N. 1 of 1955 and L.N. 47 of 1955*)

Preservation of Jurisdiction of Courts Concerned in the Issue of Subsidiary Legislation

107. No Native Court shall be precluded from trying an offence under this Law, by reason of the fact that such offence, if committed, was a breach of an order, direction or rule issued or made by any member of the court as a Native Authority or member of a Native Authority.

Procedure for Arrest under Certain Sections

108. (1) Where it is desired that any person should be arrested under—

(a) section 40;

(b) subsection (2) of section 45;

(c) subsection (2) of section 104; or

(d) subsection (3) of section 105;

any member of a Native Authority or any sub-area head shall, if time permits and it is otherwise practicable to obtain a warrant, apply to a court having jurisdiction over such person for a warrant directing the arrest of such person, and such warrant shall be issued if the court considers it is a proper case for the issue of a warrant.

(2) Where time does not permit or where for any reason it is otherwise impracticable to obtain a warrant in accordance with the provisions of subsection (1), any member of a Native Authority or any sub-area head may arrest or cause to be arrested such person and such person shall forthwith be taken before a court having jurisdiction over him to be dealt with according to law.

Part VII

Civil Legal Proceedings By and Against Native Authorities

Definitions in Part VII

109. In this part—

"court" includes the High Court, a District Court and a Native Court;

"suit" means a civil proceeding commenced by writ of summons or in such other manner as may be prescribed by rules of court.

(Adaptation by L.N. 47 of 1955 and N.R.L.N. 120 of 1960)

Limitation of Suits against Native Authorities

110. (1) When any suit is commenced against any Native Authority for any act done in pursuance, or execution, or intended execution of any Ordinance or Law, or of any public duties or authority, or in respect of any alleged neglect or default in the execution of any such Ordinance, Law, duty or authority, such suit shall not lie or be instituted in any court unless it is commenced within six months next after the act, neglect or default complained of, or in a case of a continuance of damage or injury, within six months next after the ceasing thereof:

Provided that if the suit be at the instance of any person for cause arising while such person was a convicted prisoner, it may be commenced within three months after the discharge of that person from prison.

(2) No suit shall be commenced against a Native Authority until one month at least after written notice of intention to commence the same shall have been served upon the Native Authority by the intending

plaintiff or his agent. Such notice shall state the cause of action, the name and place of abode of the intending plaintiff and the relief which he claims.

Mode of Service on Native Authority

111. The notice referred to in the last preceding section, and any summons, notice or other document required or authorised to be served on a Native Authority in connection with any suit by or against such Native Authority, shall be served by delivering the same to, or by sending it by registered post addressed to an officer of the Native Authority at the principal office of the Native Authority:

Provided that the court may with regard to any particular suit or documents order service on the Native Authority to be effected otherwise, and in that case service shall be effected in accordance with the terms of such order.

Representation of Native Authority at Hearing of Suit

112. In any suit pending before a court a Native Authority may be represented in court at any stage of the proceedings by any member or officer of the Native Authority who shall satisfy the court that he is duly authorised in that behalf.

Provisions for Satisfying Judgments against Native Authorities

113. (1) When any judgment has been entered up against a Native Authority, execution shall not issue against such authority, but the court shall certify to the Minister the amount of such judgment together with the sum, if any, awarded as costs and shall state the name of the Native Authority by which the same is payable and the name of the person in whose favour the said amount shall be paid.

(2) On receipt of such certificate, the said amount shall be paid, upon the order of the Minister, to the said person out of the funds of the Native Authority named in such certificate.

(3) Where for convenience or otherwise the Native Authority named in such certificate shares a treasury with one or more other Native Authorities, and the funds of such Native Authorities are collectively held in common such funds shall be used for the purpose of satisfying such judgment.

(4) Where for convenience or otherwise Native Authorities collectively employ an individual for certain duties and judgment is entered up against a Native Authority in respect of the actions of such individual, such judgment shall be satisfied either—

    (a) if such Native Authority has separate funds, out of the funds of the Native Authority against which judgment has been entered; or

    (b) if such Native Authority has not separate funds, out of the funds held in common by that Native Authority and the other Native Authorities aforesaid.

(5) In this section—
"judgment" includes order or decree.
(*Adaptation by L.N. 131 of 1954; amended by N.N. No. 23 of 1961*)

PART VIII
NATIVE AUTHORITY POLICE FORCES

Definitions in Part VIII

114. In this Part—
"a force" means a police force established and constituted by a Native Authority under section 115 or deemed under section 123 to have been duly constituted;
"deputed police officer" means a superior police officer deputed as adviser to a Native Authority concerning a force under the provisions of section 124;
"superior police officer" has the same meaning as in the Police Ordinance.

Establishment of a Force

115. (1) A Native Authority with the approval of the Minister charged with responsibility for Native Authority Police may by order establish a force which shall consist of such number of fit and proper persons as the Native Authority may direct.

(2) A Native Authority shall furnish particulars and information concerning a force in such manner and to such persons as the Minister charged with responsibility for Native Authority Police may direct.

(*Adaptation by L.N. 131 of 1954 and N.R.L.N. 144 of 1960*)

Powers of the Minister in Relation to a Force

116. The Minister charged with responsibility for Native Authority Police may, when he considered it expedient so to do, limit the number of persons who may constitute a force or dismiss or suspend any or all of such persons, and a person so suspended may not exercise or perform the powers or duties of his office without the consent of the Minister charged with responsibility for Native Authority Police.

(*Adaptation by L.N. 131 of 1954 and N.R.L.N. 144 of 1960*)

Declaration

117. Every member of a force shall upon appointment make and sign a declaration in such form as the Governor may by Order in Council declare to be applicable to members of the particular force to which the member concerned belongs. (*Substituted by N.R. No. 3 of 1955*)

Powers of a Member of a Force

118. (1) A Native Authority may give a general authority to such members of a force as it may think proper either by name or according

to rank, title, or grade, to exercise on behalf of the Native Authority all or any of the powers conferred upon a Native Authority by section 30.

(2) A Native Authority shall send a copy of a general authority issued under this section to such persons as the Minister charged with responsibility for Native Authority Police may direct.

(*Adaptation by L.N.* 131 *of* 1954 *and N.R.L.N.* 144 *of* 1960)

Application of Term "Police Officer" to Members of a Force

119. Unless a contrary intention appear, the expression "police officer" or any other expression meaning a member of the Nigeria Police Force shall wherever it occurs in any law, whether enacted before or after the date on which this law comes into operation, include a member of a force.

Suspension and Dismissal

120. A Native Authority may suspend or dismiss any member of a force whom such Native Authority considers negligent in the discharge of his duty, or otherwise unfit for the same.

Effect of Suspension or Dismissal

121. Where a member of a force is dismissed or ceases to belong to the force, all powers vested in him as a member shall immediately cease.

Rules

122. (1) The Minister charged with responsibility for Native Authority Police and, subject to the provisions of any Ordinance or other Law for the time being in force, a Native Authority, with the concurrence of the Native Authority, if any, to which it is subordinate, and with the approval of the Minister charged with responsibility for Native Authority Police, may, in respect of a force established within its jurisdiction, make rules for all or any of the following purposes—

(*a*) the enlistment, engagement, discharge and service of members of a force;

(*b*) the ranks, titles or grades of which a force shall consist;

(*c*) the uniform or equipment of a force;

(*d*) the prevention of negligence or abuse on the part of members of a force and the maintenance of discipline;

(*e*) the efficient discharge of their duties by members of a force;

(*f*) for giving general effect to the provisions of this Part of this Law.

(2) Where a Native Authority has with the approval of the Minister charged with responsibility for Native Authority Police made rules in respect of any of the matters referred to in subsection (1), any rules made by the Minister charged with responsibility for Native Authority

Police in respect of the same matters shall cease to apply to any force to which the rules made by the Native Authority aforesaid apply.

(*Adaptation by L.N. 131 of 1954 and N.R.L.N. 144 of* 1960)

Existing Police Forces

123. (1) All Native Authority police forces existing at the commencement of this Law shall be deemed to have been duly constituted from the time when such force was first established and the provisions of this Law shall hereafter apply to every such force.

(2) Every member of such force shall be deemed to have been appointed under and in accordance with the provisions of this Law and to have made and signed the declaration in accordance with section 117 and to be subject to any rules made or to be made hereunder:

Provided that every member of such force shall remain subject to any rules to which he was subject before the commencement of this Law until such rules shall have been revoked or replaced by rules to be made hereunder. (*Amended by N.R. No. 37 of* 1960)

Deputing of Superior Police Officer to a Force

124. (1) The Commissioner of Police may, with the approval of the Minister charged with responsibility for Native Authority Police, depute a superior police officer to advice a Native Authority which has established a force.

(2) A deputed police officer shall advise the Native Authority on matters relating to the composition, strength, discipline, training, equipment and employment of a force and shall be entitled to examine all records kept by or relating to a force, and to inspect the force or any part or detachment of it.

(*Adaptation by L.N. 131 of 1954 and N.R.L.N. 144 of* 1960)

Reports on a Force

125. A deputed police officer shall submit to the Commissioner of Police an annual report containing such particulars as the Commissioner may require of the strength, discipline, training, efficiency and employment of any force concerning which the deputed police officer is adviser to a Native Authority and such other reports as the Commissioner may from time to time require.

Operational Control by Deputed Police Officers

126. A Native Authority may, with the approval of the Commissioner of Police and the Minister charged with responsibility for Native Authority Police, confer upon a deputed police officer such powers of operational control over a force, or any part of a force, as it may consider expedient and thereupon all members of the force, or of the part of the force over which the deputed police officer exercises operational control, shall obey any lawful orders given by him as if he were their superior officer in the force.

(*Adaptation by L.N. 131 of 1954 and N.R.L.N. 144 of 1960*)

PART IX

NATIVE AUTHORITY PRISONS

Definitions in Part IX

127. In this Part—

"a prison" unless the contrary intention appear means a prison established by a Native Authority under this Law;

"prison staff" includes the head warder, warders and wardresses.

Powers and Duties of Administrative Officers under this Part

128. The powers and duties conferred or imposed on an administrative officer by this Part shall only be exercised by such officer in the case of prisoners or of a prison within the administrative area of which he is in charge or in which he may be stationed.

Power of Native Authority to Constitute a Prison

129. A Native Authority with the approval of the Minister charged with responsibility for Prisons may by order declare any building within the area of its jurisdiction to be a prison under this Law and by the same or any subsequent order declare the district or place for which any such building shall be used for the purposes of a prison and may likewise order that any building declared a prison under this Law shall cease to be a prison.

(*Adaptation by L.N. 131 of 1954 and N.R.L.N. 144 of 1960*)

Extent of Prison

130. Every prison shall include the grounds and buildings within the prison enclosure.

Who may be Confined in a Prison

131. Any prisoner may be confined in a prison constituted under this Law who—

(a) is awaiting trial before any Native Court or who has been convicted by such court;

(b) has been committed to custody by the Supreme Court the High Court or any magistrate when the Governor-General in Council in exercise of the powers conferred upon him in section 26 of the Prisons Ordinance, has so ordered; or

(c) has been arrested without a warrant and is waiting to be brought before any magistrate's court or Native Court.

(*Adaptation by L.N. 131 of 1954 and L.N. 47 of 1955*)

Power of Native Authority to Constitute a Lock-up

132. A Native Authority with the approval of the Minister charged with responsibility for Prisons, may within the area of jurisdiction of the Native Authority declare any building, part of a building, or collection of buildings together with the enclosure, if any, relating thereto to be a lock-up and such declaration shall be made known within the area of the Native Authority in such manner as is customary.

(Adaptation by L.N. 131 of 1954 and N.R.L.N. 144 of 1960)

Period of Detention in a Lock-up

133. A prisoner who is awaiting trial or who has been convicted or who has been adjudged a debtor, may be detained in a lock-up for a period not exceeding fourteen days.

Prison and Lock-up Officers

134. The Native Authority shall appoint—

(*a*) for each prison a head warder, a prison clerk or scribe and such number of warders and wardresses as shall be necessary for the proper administration of the prison; and

(*b*) for each lock-up such officers as may be necessary.

Superintendence and Visitation of Prisons

135. (1) The Minister charged with responsibility for Prisons, shall appoint by name or office a person who shall have the general supervision of prisons established under this Law, shall advise the Native Authorities thereon, and shall submit to the Minister charged with responsibility for Prisons, for transmission to the Governor-General an annual report on the administration of the prisons and such other reports as the Governor-General or the Director of Prisons may consider necessary.

(2) The Chief Justice, Members of the Executive Council, Judges of the High Court, the Commissioner of Police, any Principal Medical Officer, the Senior Officer of the Queen's Own Nigeria Regiment in the Northern Region or a field officer nominated by him by name or office shall *ex-officio* be visitors of all prisons established under this part of this Law. (*Amended by N.R. No. 2 of 1958 and N.R. No. 37 of 1960*)

(3) In addition to the *ex-officio* visitors hereinbefore mentioned a magistrate shall be an *ex-officio* visitor in respect of each prison within the district in which he is officiating as a magistrate and there shall also be appointed by the Minister charged with responsibility for Prisons, not less than five other persons to be visitors in respect of any or all such prisons within the particular province.

(4) The Minister charged with responsibility for Prisons shall appoint one or more of such visitors to be a visiting committee for each prison, but the appointment of such committee shall not interfere with the general right of visitation on the part of the visitors.

(5) For the purposes of this section the expression "prison" includes a lock-up.

(Adaptation by L.N. 131 of 1954; L.N. 47 of 1955 and N.R.L.N. 144 of 1960)

Prisoners in Legal Custody of Head Warder

136. Subject to such regulations as may be made by the Governor under section 143 relating to prisoners under sentence of death, every prisoner shall be deemed to be in the custody of the head warder.

(Adaptation by L.N. 131 of 1954)

Provisions in the Case of Lunacy of Prisoners

137. (1) The head warder shall report to the Native Authority and also to a medical officer or to a district officer any prisoner who appears to be of unsound mind. If the prisoner shall be certified by a medical officer to be of unsound mind, the Minister charged with responsibility for Prisons, after consultation with the Native Authority constituted for the area within which the prison is situated, shall by order in writing under his hand authorise the removal of the prisoner to a lunatic asylum within the Northern Region to which the Lunacy Ordinance applies and which may have been appointed by the Governor for that purpose. *(Amended by N.R. No. 37 of 1960)*

(2) Any prisoner removed as aforesaid shall remain in such asylum until the term of imprisonment to which he is subject determines or until it shall be certified by a medical officer that he has become of sound mind in which latter case he shall by order of the Governor be re-delivered into the custody of the aforesaid head warder.

(3) Where a prisoner has been removed to a lunatic asylum in accordance with the provisions of subsection (1) and it has been certified by a medical officer that he is of unsound mind and his term of imprisonment is about to determine, it shall be the duty of the head warder to give information on oath to a magistrate as in the terms of Form B in the Schedule to the Lunacy Ordinance for the purpose of the adjudication of such person as a lunatic as from the date of the determination of his sentence.

(4) The provisions of this section shall not apply to persons of unsound mind to whom the provisions of Chapter XXVI of the Criminal Procedure Code apply.

(Adaptation by L.N. 131 of 1954; N.R.L.N. 120 of 1960 and N.R.L.N. 144 of 1960)

Prisoners to be Brought Before a Court

138. (1) The head warder, upon receiving the order of a court directing him to bring up a prisoner before the court at the time and place stated therein, shall obey such order and may, for the purpose of carrying out such order, cause the prisoner to be removed to another prison within the Northern Region established under this Law or under the Prisons Ordinance.

(2) If the prisoner shall be remanded, committed for trial, imprisoned, or detained by such court, he shall be so dealt with either in the prison whence he came, or in such other prison as such court may direct.

Removal of Prisoner in Other Cases

139. The Governor or the Minister charged with responsibility for Prisons or any officer who may have been authorised in that behalf by the Governor or the Minister charged with responsibility for Prisons may order any person imprisoned under the sentence of any court for an offence committed by him to be removed from the prison in which he is confined to any other prison within the meaning of this Law, and whenever any prisoner is removed to any other prison than that named in the warrant or order under which he may have been imprisoned, the said warrant or order, together with an order of removal, either endorsed on the warrant or order, or separate therefrom, shall be sufficient authority for the removal of such prisoner to the prison named in the order of removal, and his detention therein, and for carrying out the sentence described in the warrant or order of imprisonment, or any part thereof which may remain unexecuted:

Provided that a prisoner who has been committed to custody by the Supreme Court, the High Court, or a magistrate's court and is confined in a prison authorised in accordance with section 26 of the Prisons Ordinance as being a prison in which persons so committed to custody may be detained shall not be transferred to another prison except one so authorised.

(*Amended by N.R. No. 37 of 1960; adaptation by L.N. 131 of 1954; L.N. 47 of 1955 and N.R.L.N. 144 of 1960*)

Transfer of Prisoners to Other Prisons or Hospitals

140. The Governor or the Minister charged with responsibility for Prisons may order the transfer of any person from a prison to any other prison in the Northern Region established under any Ordinance or Law or, in the case of the illness or suspected illness of any person confined in a prison in which there is no suitable accommodation for such person, to a hospital or other place in the Northern Region outside the prison for treatment or observation.

(*Adaptation by L.N. 131 of 1954 and N.R.L.N. 144 of 1960*)

Rules

141. (1) The Governor and, subject to the provisions of any Ordinance or other Law for the time being in force, a Native Authority, with the concurrence of the Native Authority, if any, to which it is subordinate, and subject to the approval of the Minister charged with responsibility for Prisons, may, in respect of a prison established within its jurisdiction, make rules for all or any of the following purposes—

(a) relating to prison staff—
  (i) the engagement, discharge and service of members of a prison staff;
  (ii) the titles or grades of which a prison staff shall consist;
  (iii) the uniform or equipment of a prison staff;
  (iv) the prevention of negligence or abuse on the part of members of a prison staff, and the maintenance of discipline;
  (v) the efficient discharge of their duties by members of a prison staff;
  (vi) generally for ensuring the proper administration of and control over prison staff;

(b) relating to prisoners—
  (i) the return of a discharged prisoner to his ordinary place of abode and the necessary and proper precaution to ensure such return;
  (ii) the release of prisoners on the day preceding such holidays or other days as may be specified in the rules;
  (iii) the regulation of the work or labour of convicted persons;
  (iv) the remission of sentences for good conduct;
  (v) the discipline of the prisoners;
  (vi) for the removal of prisoners in case of infectious disease and the removal of sick prisoners to a hospital outside the prison and the custody of prisoners so removed;
  (vii) the health and diet of the prisoners;
  (viii) notwithstanding the particularity of the powers hereinbefore set forth, generally for regulating the management of prisons and matters affecting the health and treatment of prisoners therein;

(c) notwithstanding the particularity of the powers contained in paragraphs (a) and (b), generally for the regulation and government of a prison in so far as such rules do not conflict with regulations made by the Governor under section 143.

(2) Where a Native Authority has with the approval of the Minister charged with responsibility for Prisons made rules in respect of any of the matters referred to in subsection (1), any rules made by the Governor in respect of the same matters shall cease to have effect in respect of the prisons to which such Native Authority rules apply.

(3) The Northern Provinces Native Authority (Prison) Rules, 1951, shall be deemed to have been made under the provisions of this section and may be amended or revoked as if they had been so made.

(*Adaptation by L.N.* 131 *of* 1954 *and N.R.L.N.* 144 *of* 1960)

Existing Prisons Deemed to be Constituted under this Law

142. Any existing prison which at the commencement of this Law is under the control and management of a Native Authority shall be deemed to have been duly established under this Law and all members of the staff of any such prison shall be deemed to have been appointed

224

under and in accordance with the provisions of this Law and shall be liable to any rules made or to be made under this Part of this Law.

Regulations

143. (1) The Governor may make regulations in respect of prisons to which this Part applies for any or all of the following purposes—

(a) for regulating the legal custody of prisoners under sentence of death;

(b) the grant of licences to prisoners to be at large, the conditions of such licences and the penalties and procedure upon a breach of such conditions; and

(c) the conditions under which a person awaiting trial or a judgment debtor may be kept in custody in a lock-up.

(2) Regulations made under this section may be applied to prisons generally or to prisons in any specified area as may be provided therein.

(3) The Northern Region Native Authority (Prison) Regulations, 1952, and all other Regulations (if any) which are applicable to prisons in the Northern Region shall be deemed to have been made under the provisions of this section and may be amended or revoked as if they had been so made.

(Adaptation by L.N. 131 of 1954)

Saving of Powers of Governor under Part XLVI of Cap. 43

144. The provisions of this Part shall not be deemed to confer upon any person any of the powers vested in the Governor in relation to persons detained duting Her Majesty's pleasure.

(Adaptation by L.N. 131 of 1954 and N.R.L.N. 120 of 1960)

PART X

SIGNIFICATION AND PROMULGATION OF ORDERS AND RULES

Signification of Orders and Rules

145. (1) Where a Native Authority comprises more than one person and such Native Authority gives or makes any orders or rules which by virtue of and subject to the provisions of this or any other Law or any Ordinance it is empowered to give or make, such giving or making shall, subject to the provisions of subsection (2), be signified in accordance with the provisions of the Standing Orders of the Native Authority made in accordance with the provisions of and under the authority of section 52.

(2) Unless and until such Standing Orders have been made by such a Native Authority and countersigned by the Minister the giving or making of any order or rule by the said authority may be signified by such member or members of the Native Authority as may be authorised in that behalf by the Minister either generally or specifically.

(3) Any authorisation made by the Minister under the provisions of subsection (2) shall be kept and filed in the office of the divisional office concerned.

(*Adaptation by L.N.* 181 *of* 1954 *and N.R.L.N.* 144 *of* 1960)

Publication of Orders and Rules

146. (1) Subject to any specific or general directions given by the Governoror every order issued under section 43 or 44, other than an order issued to an individual, and all rules made under this Law shall be made known in such manner as is customary in the area of the Native Authority by which the order is issued or the rule made and thereupon the order or rule shall be in force and shall be binding upon and be obeyed by all persons by whom the order or rule, as the case may be, is to be obeyed or observed.

(2) Without prejudice to any other mode of proof, a certificate purporting to be signed by an administrative officer shall be sufficient evidence—

(*a*) of the terms of any such order or rule;

(*b*) that the concurrence of a superior Native Authority, if such was necessary, has been obtained;

(*c*) that the approval of the Governor, if necessary, has been given; and

(*d*) that the order or rule has been made known as required by this section.

(3) Where several orders are issued under section 63 or several sets of rules are made under this Law by several Native Authorities in similar terms and it is requisite or desirable that they shall be published in the Regional *Gazette* it shall be a sufficient publication therein of such orders or rules if the text of the orders or rules is published therein once only with a Schedule attached setting out the names of the Native Authorities by which the said orders or rules have been respectively issued or made and opposite to each of the said names the respective dates of issuing or making and, in the case of rules, the dates when the approval of the Governor or, in the case of rules made by a Native Authority under sections 41 or 141, of the Minister or the Minister charged with responsibility for Prisons respectively was given. (*Amended by N.R.L.N.* 44 *of* 1961)

(4) Any order or rules made by a Native Authority in similar terms to the text of an order or rules published in accordance with the procedure prescribed in subsection (3)—

(*a*) in the case of rules, shall not require the approval of the Governor but may be approved by the Minister responsible for the subject matter of the rules;

(*b*) in the case of both an order and rules, shall be sufficiently published by a notice in the *Northern Nigeria Gazette* stating that such order or rules has or have been made by such Native Authority in similar terms to the said text and specifying the date upon which such order or rules was or were made and, in the case of rules, the date of approval by the Minister responsible for the subject matter of the rules. (*Substituted by N.N. No. 23 of 1961*)

(5) Every order directed to an individual shall be binding upon him on his being notified thereof by or on behalf of the Native Authority.

(6) The provisions of this section shall also apply to rules made by Native Authorities under the authority of any other Law or of any Ordinance existing at the coming into force of this Law notwithstanding that such Law or Ordinance or any other Law or Ordinance requires such rules to be published in the *Gazette* or the Regional *Gazette* if the procedure in subsection (4) is followed notwithstanding that such Law or Ordinance requires such rules to be made with the approval of the Governor. (*Amended by N.R. No. 37 of 1960*)

(*Adaptation by L.N. 131 of 1954*)

Rules not requiring Approval of Governor

146A. The Governor in Council may by order published in the Regional *Gazette* provide that any rules made under section 37 or section 41 which are similar in form to any rules approved by the Governor and published in the Regional *Gazette* shall not require the approval of the Governor but shall be approved by the Minister responsible for the subject matter of the rules.

(*Inserted by N.R. No. 37 of 1960; amended by N.N. No. 23 of 1961*)

Custody of Copies of Orders and Rules

147. Where a Native Authority has issued an order under section 43, other than an order addressed to an individual, or has made rules under this Law, or the Governor has made an order under section 44 or has made rules under this Law the Native Authority or the Governor, as the case may be, shall deposit—

(a) one copy of the order or rule in the office of the Minister of Local Government;

(b) one copy in the provincial office;

(c) one copy in the divisional office;

(d) one copy in the main office of the Native Authority and

(e) one copy with the scribe of each Native Court having jurisdiction to enforce the order or rule.

(*Adaptation by L.N. 131 of 1954*)

PART XI

MISCELLANEOUS PROVISIONS

Procedure when Township taken over by Native Authority

148. When any area or place which was formerly a township under the provisions of the Townships Ordinance ceases to be a township

and is thenceforth to be administered by a Native Authority, all property movable and immovable, and all title to the use and occupation of land, which was formerly vested in the local authority shall vest in such Native Authority.

Procedure Regarding Township Subsidiary Legislation

149. Where property formerly vested in a local authority vests in a Native Authority under the provisions of section 148 all rules, bye-laws and notices made and issued by such local authority in respect of the particular area or place shall be enforced by the Native Authority as if it were the local authority which it has replaced, and any such rule, bye-law and notice shall remain in operation until it is replaced by a rule or order made under the provisions of this or any other, Law or any Ordinance and for this purpose the Native Authority shall have power to revoke any or all of the rules, bye-laws and notices so replaced.

Powers of Administrative Officers

150. In addition to the powers conferred upon them or any of them, by any other section of this Law, or by any other enactment, every Resident, and every district officer acting on the instructions of the Resident, shall have power at any time, within the Province to which he is appointed—

(a) to attend meetings and examine the records of Councils, and to take part in their discussions, but not to vote;

(b) to investigate and report to the appropriate authority on all allegations involving injustice, dishonesty or maladministration on the part of any member, officer or employee of a Native Authority or a Council;

(c) to tender advice to a Native Authority on any matter on which he may consider it expedient to do so;

(d) to inquire whether any instructions contained in Financial Memoranda issued under section 88 are being carried out and to make any recommendations which may be necessary in order to ensure that they are carried out; and

(e) to inspect the books of account and the cash and stores in the possession of a Native Authority;

151. (*Deleted by N.R.L.N.* 144 *of* 1960)

Delegation of Powers of Governor

152. (1) The Premier or the appropriate Minister as the case may be may, by notice published in the Regional *Gazette*, delegate to any person by name or office, subject to such conditions, exceptions and qualifications as may by specified in the said notice, any of the powers and duties conferred upon him by sections 7, 31, 41, and sections 52,

53, 54, 58, 64, 65, 66, 68, 74, 116, 126, 132, 135, 137, 139, 140 and 145 and thereupon or from the date specified in the notice the person to whom any of such powers and duties have been delegated shall have and exercise such powers and perform such duties subject as aforesaid. (*Amended by N.R. No. 3 of 1955 and N.R. No. 4 of 1957*)

(2) The Premier or the appropriate Minister as the case may be, may in like manner evoke any such notice and may exercise any powers or perform any duties conferred upon him by the said sections notwithstanding the delegation by him of such powers and duties.

(3) The appropriate Minister may delegate any of the powers conferred upon him by Part V to Residents in charge of Provinces in respect of the finances either of Native Authorities generally or of specified Native Authorities or to specified Native Authorities in respect of their own finances.

(4) Any delegation made under subsection (3) shall be subject to such conditions, exceptions and qualifications as the appropriate Minister may prescribe, and shall be revocable at will and the appropriate Minister may exercise any powers conferred upon him by Part V notwithstanding the delegation by him of such powers.

(*Adaptation by L.N. 131 of 1954; L.N. 120 of 1957 and N.R.L.N. 144 of 1960*)

Repeal and Saving

153. (1) The Ordinances set out in the first column of the Third Schedule shall, to the extent mentioned in the third column of the said Schedule, cease to apply to any part of the Northern Region for which an office of Native Authority is constituted or deemed to be constituted under the provisions of this Law, and the Laws set out therein are hereby repealed.

(2) Nothing in subsection (1) shall affect—

(a) (*Deleted by N.R. No. 3 of 1955*)

(b) any rule or order heretofore made or issued and existing at the coming into operation of this Law and such rule or order shall be deemed to have been made and issued under and in accordance with the provisions of this Law;

(c) any suit which may have been instituted by or against any Native Authority under and in accordance with the provisions of the Native Authority Ordinance, and any such suit pending at the coming into operation of this Law shall be deemed to have been instituted under and in accordance with the provisions of this Law.

Appendices

First Schedule

(Section 49)

Authority under which rules made	Provision of this Law under which rules to be deemed to have been made
The Births, Deaths and Burials Ordinance (chapter 20) section 46.	Section 37
The Markets Ordinance (chapter 127) section 5.	Section 41
The Public Health Ordinance (chapter 183) sections 41 and 42.	Section 37

Second Schedule

(Section 64)

Chapter 24 The Building Lines Regulation Ordinance.

„ 31 The Children and Young Persons Law, 1958.

„ 52 The Destruction of Mosquitoes Ordinance.

„ 55 The Diseases of Animals Ordinance.

„ 56 The Dogs Ordinance.

„ 75 The Forestry Ordinance.

„ 105 The Land Tenure Law, 1962.

„ 112 The Leprosy Ordinance.

„ 114 The Liquor Ordinance.

„ 155 The Nigeria Town and Country Planning Ordinance.

„ 177 The Prisons Ordinance.

„ 178 The Private Hospitals Ordinance.

„ 181 The Provident Funds Ordinance.

„ 183 The Public Health Ordinance.

„ 208 The Sleeping Sickness Ordinance.

„ 224 The Vaccination Ordinance.

„ 227 The Waterworks Ordinance.

No. 43 of 1947 The Road Traffic Ordinance.

No. 37 of 1950 The Agriculture Ordinance.

No. 29 of 1952 The Survey Ordinance.

THIRD SCHEDULE

(SECTION 153)

Ordinance or Law	Chapter or Number	Extent
ORDINANCES		
1. The Births, Deaths and Burials Ordinance	Chapter 20	Section 46
2. The Native Authority Ordinance	„ 140	The whole Ordinance
3. The Native Courts Ordinance	„ 142	Section 18
4. The Public Health Ordinance	„ 183	Paragraph (c) of section 41 and of section 42
NORTHERN REGIONAL LAWS		
5. The Native Authority (Borrowing Powers) Law, 1952	No. 2 of 1952	The whole Law
6. The Native Authority (Definition of Functions) Law, 1952	No. 3 of 1952	The whole Law

(*Amended by N.R. No. 3 of 1955*)

INDEX

Page

Page

Page

R

S

Page

T

V

W

Z